Mayne Reid

The Rifle-Rangers

Or, Adventures in Southern Mexico

Mayne Reid

The Rifle-Rangers
Or, Adventures in Southern Mexico

ISBN/EAN: 9783337179052

Printed in Europe, USA, Canada, Australia, Japan

Cover: Foto ©ninafisch / pixelio.de

More available books at **www.hansebooks.com**

POPULAR WORKS
BY
CAPTAIN MAYNE REID.

A NEW EDITION IN TEN VOLS.

1.—THE SCALP HUNTERS.
2.—THE WHITE CHIEF.
3.—THE RIFLE RANGERS.
4.—THE TIGER HUNTER.
5.—THE WAR TRAIL.
6.—THE HUNTER'S FEAST.
7.—THE WOOD RANGERS.
8.—WILD LIFE.
9.—THE WILD HUNTRESS.
10.—OSCEOLA, THE SEMINOLE.

Captain Mayne Reid's works are of an intensely interesting and fascinating character. Nearly all of them being founded upon some historical event, they possess a permanent value, while presenting a thrilling, earnest, dashing fiction surpassed by no novel of the day.

All published uniform with this volume, at $1.50 each, and sent by mail, *postage free*, on receipt of price, by

G. W. CARLETON & CO., Publishers,
New York.

THE RIFLE-RANGERS;

OR,

Adventures in Southern Mexico.

By CAPTAIN MAYNE REID.

AUTHOR OF "THE SCALP HUNTERS,"—"THE WOOD-RANGERS,"—"THE TIGER HUNTER,"—"THE WAR TRAIL,"—"THE HUNTER'S FEAST,"—"THE WHITE CHIEF,"—"THE QUADROON,"—"THE WILD HUNTRESS,"—"WILD LIFE,—"THE MAROON,"—"THE HEADLESS HORSEMAN,"—"THE WHITE GAUNTLET,"
ETC., ETC., ETC.

NEW YORK:
Carleton, Publisher, Madison Square.
LONDON: S. LOW, SON & CO.
M DCCC LXXV.

PREFACE.

THE following interesting volume is based upon the various incidents and personal adventures which befel the author in his travels in the flowery lands of Mexico, whither he had betaken himself on the first demand of his country for volunteers to sustain the supremacy of the stars and stripes—which supremacy was most nobly vindicated in many a bloody field, in all of which the author nobly acquitted himself.

The war being ended, our gallant Captain betook himself to the contemplation of the country and its fair dames, among whom he seems to have been an especial favorite. His attentions to the fair Mexicanas, though generally received with a sparkling eye and graceful smile, in many instances gave umbrage to some proud noble, who scrupled not at any means to remove a formidable rival from his path. To the narration of the bitter and unceasing vengeance of one of these baffled lovers—Dubrosc—and the recital of the hair-breadth escapes of our author from the many deep laid plans for his capture, are we indebted for the volume which we present to the American reader, who we have little doubt will be willing to accord to Captain Reid the same meed of praise as has been vouchsafed to him in England, where the work was first published under auspices as flattering as the results were gratifying—the book having achieved an immense success.

CONTENTS

CHAPTER I.
An Adventure among the Creoles of New Orleans

CHAPTER II.
A Volunteer Rendezvous

CHAPTER III.
Life on the Island of Lobos

CHAPTER IV.
Lieutenant Sibleys' Story of a Georgia Hotel

CHAPTER V.
Old Blowhard's Story of the Guyas-Cutis

CHAPTER VI.
Moonlight Scene—A Spy in Camp—A Skeleton Adventure

CHAPTER VII.
The Landing at Sacrificios

CHAPTER VIII.
The Investment of Vera Cruz

CHAPTER IX.
Major Blossom

CHAPTER X.
Going on the Scout

CHAPTER XI.
Adventure with a Cayman

CHAPTER XII.
Don Cosme Rosales

CHAPTER XIII.
A Mexican Dinner

CHAPTER XIV.
A Subterranean Drawing-room

CHAPTER XV.
The Norther

CHAPTER XVI.
A little Fair Weather again

CHAPTER XVII.
The Scout continued, with a variety of Reflections

CHAPTER XVIII.
One way of Taming a Bull

CHAPTER XIX.
A Brush with the Guerilleros

CHAPTER XX.
A Herculean Feat

CHAPTER XXI.
Running the Gauntlet

CHAPTER XXII.
A Shor Fight at "Long Shot"

CHAPTER XXIII.
The Rescue 125

CHAPTER XXIV.
he Cocuyo 12

CHAPTER XXV.
.upe and Luz 134

CHAPTER XXVI.
A Tough Night of It after all 138

CHAPTER XXVII.
The Light after the Shade 141

CHAPTER XXVIII.
A Disappointment and a new Plan 147

CHAPTER XXIX.
A Fool-hardy Adventure 151

CHAPTER XXX.
Help from Heaven 154

CHAPTER XXXI.
A Shot in the Dark 161

CHAPTER XXXII.
Captured by Gueriileros 169

CHAPTER XXXIII.
Blind Ride 17

CHAPTER XXXIV.
A Stampede 174

CHAPTER XXXV.
A Drink à la Cheval 177

CONTENTS.

CHAPTER XXXVI.
An Odd way of Opening a Letter 160

CHAPTER XXXVII.
The Cobra di Capello 164

CHAPTER XXXVIII.
The Hacienda 18

CHAPTER XXXIX.
The Head-quarters of the Guerrilla 193

CHAPTER XL.
Chane's Courtship 197

CHAPTER XLI.
The Dance of the Tagaroto 202

CHAPTER XLII.
A Kiss in the Dark 205

CHAPTER XLIII.
Maria de Merced 210

CHAPTER XLIV.
The Pursuit 214

CHAPTER XLV.
A new and terrible Enemy 217

CHAPTER XLVI.
A Battle with Bloodhounds 220

CHAPTER XLVII
An Indian Ruse 22

CHAPTER XLVIII.
A Coup d'Eclair 225

CHAPTER XLIX.
A Bridge of Monkeys 228

CHAPTER L.
The Jarochos 232

CHAPTER LI.
Padre Jarauta 237

CHAPTER LII.
A Hung by the Heels 243

CHAPTER LIII.
A very short Trial 249

CHAPTER LIV.
A Bird's Eye View of a Battle 253

CHAPTER LV.
An odd way of Escaping from a Battle Field 257

CHAPTER XVI.
A Wholesale Capture 261

CHAPTER LVII.
A Duel, with an odd Ending 268

CHAPTER LVIII.
An Adios 271

THE

RIFLE RANGERS.

CHAPTER I.

AN ADVENTURE AMONG THE CREOLES OF NEW ORLEANS.

In the "fall" of 1846, I found myself in the city of New Orleans, filling up one of those pauses that occur between the chapters of an eventful life—doing nothing. I have said an eventful life. In the retrospect of ten years, I could not remember as many weeks spent in one place. I had traversed the continent from north to south, and crossed it from sea to sea. My foot had pressed the summits of the Andes, and climbed the Cordilleras of the Sierra Madre. I had steamed it down the Mississippi, and sculled it up the Orinoco. I had hunted buffaloes with the Pawnees of the Platte, and ostriches upon the Pampas of the Plata: to-day shivering in the hut of an Esquimaux—a month after, taking my siesta in an aëry couch under the gossamer frondage of the Corozo palm. I had eaten raw meat with the trappers of the Rocky Mountains, and roast monkey among the Mosquito Indians; and much more, which might weary the reader, and which ought to have made the writer a wiser man. But, I fear, the spirit of adventure—its thirst—is within me slakeless. I had just returned from a "scurry" among the Comanches of Western Texas, and the idea of "settling down" was as far from my mind as ever.

'What next? what next?" thought I. "Ha! the war with Mexico."

The war between the United States and that country had now fairly com menced. My sword, a fine Toledo, taken from a Spanish officer at San Jacinto, hung over the mantel, rusting ingloriously. Near it were my pistols, a pair of Colt's revolvers, pointing at each other in sullen muteness. A warlike ardor seized upon me; and clutching, not the sword, but my pen, I wrote to the War-department for a commission, and, summoning all my patience, awaited the answer.

But I waited in vain. Every bulletin from Washington exhibited its list; but my name appeared not among them. Epaulettes gleamed upon every shoulder, while I, with the anguish of a Tantalus, was compelled to look idly on. Dispatches came in daily from the seat of war, filled with newly-glorious names; and steamers, from the same quarter, brought fresh batches of heroes some legless, some armless, and others with a bullet-hole through the cheek, and, perhaps, the loss of a dozen teeth or so; but all thickly covered with laurels.

November came, but no commission. Impatience and ennui had fairly mastered me. The time hung heavily upon my hands. "How can I best kill it? I will go to the French theatre, and hear Calvé."*

Such were my reflections, as I sat one evening in my solitary chamber. In obedience to this impulse, I repaired to the theatre; but instead of soothing, the bellicose strains of the opera only heightened my warlike enthusiasm; and I walked homeward, abusing, as I went, the President and the Secretary of War, and the whole department. "I have 'surely put in strong enough,' for it," thought I to myself; "my political connection—besides, the government owes me—".

"Clar out, ye niggers! what de yer want?"

This was a voice that reached me, as I passed the dark corner of the Faubourg Tremé.† Then followed some exclamation in French, a scuffle ensued, a pistol went off, and I heard the same voice again, calling out·

"Four till one! Injuns!—murder!—help, hyeer!"

I ran up. It was very dark, but the glimmer of a distant lamp enabled me to perceive a man, out in the middle of the street, defending himself against four others. He was a man of giant size, and flourished a bright weapon which I took to be a bowie knife, while his assailants struck at him on al

---

* The *prima donna* of a French operatic *troupe*, then highly popular among the Creoles. Half a score of duels were fought on her account by this fiery race

† A quarter of New Orleans noted as the scene of frequent assassinations and midnight quarrel. The neighborhood of the Quadroon and masked balls.

sides with sticks and stilettoes. A small boy ran back and forth upon the banquette, calling for help.

Supposing it to be some street quarrel, I endeavored to separate the parties by remonstrance. I rushed between them, holding out my cane; but a sharp cut across the nuckles, which I received from one of the small men, together with his evident intention to follow it up, robbed me of all zest for pacific mediation, and, keeping my eye upon the one who had cut me, I drew a pistol (I could not otherwise defend myself) and fired. He fell dead in his tracks, without a groan. His comrades hearing me re-cock, took to their heels, and disappeared up a neighboring alley.

The whole scene did not occupy the time you have spent in reading this relation of it. One minute I was plodding quietly homeward; the next I stood in the middle of the street; beside me a stranger of gigantic proportions; at my feet a black mass of dead humanity, half doubled up in the mud as it had fallen; on the banquette the slight, shivering form of a boy; while above and around were silence and darkness!

I was beginning to fancy the whole thing a dream, when the voice of the man at my side dispelled this delusion.

"Mister," said he, placing his arms akimbo, and facing me; "if ye'll tell me yer name, I aint a gwine to forgit it. No, Bob Linkin aint that sorter."

"What! Bob Lincoln? Bob Lincoln of the Peaks?"* In the voice I had recognised a celebrated mountain trapper, and an old acquaintance, whom I had not met for several years.

"Why, Lord save us from Injuns! it aint you, Cap'n Haller? May I be dog-goned if it aint! Whooray—whoop! I knowed it warnt no store-keeper fired that shot. Haroo! whar air yer, Jack?"

"Here I am!" answered the boy, from the pavement.

"Kum yeer, then. Ye aint badly skeert, air yer?"

"No," firmly responded the boy, crossing over.

"I tuk him from a scoundrelly Crow,† thet I overhauled on a fork of the Yellerstone. He gin me a long pedigree; that is, afore I kilt the skunk. He made out as how his people hed tuk the boy from the Kimanches, who hed brought him from somewhar down the Grand. I knowd it wur all bamboozle. The boy s white, American white. Who ever seed a yeller-hided

---

* The Spanish Peaks—a range of the Rocky Mountains, where I had first met Lincoln.

† Lincoln refers to an Indian of the Crow tribe.

Mexikin with them eyes and har? Jack! this yeer's Cap'n Haller. If yer kin iver save his life by giving yer own, yer must do it, de yer hear?"

"I will," said the boy, resolutely.

"Come, Lincoln," I interposed, "these conditions are not necessary. You remember I was in your debt."‡

"Aint worth mentionin', Cap; let byegones be byegones!"

"But what brought you to New Orleans? or, more particularly, how came you into this scrape?"

"Wal, Cap'n, bein as the last question is the most partickler, I'll gin yer the answer to it fust. I hed jest twelve dollars in my pouch; an I tuk a idee inter my head thet I mout as well double it. So I stepped into a shanty whar they wur a playin craps.§ After bettin a good spell, I wun somewhar about a hundred dollars. Not likin the sign ‖ I seed about, I tuk Jack and put out. Wal, jest as I was kummin roun this yeer corner, four fellers—them ye seed—run out and jumped me, like so many painters. I tuk them .r the same chaps I hed seed parleyvooing at the craps table, an tho't they wur only jokin, till one of them gin me a a sockdolloger over the head, an fired a pistol. I then drewed my bowie, an the skrimmage begun; an thet's .l I know about it, Cap'n, more'n yerself."

"Let's see if it's all up with this'n," continued the hunter, stooping. I'deed, yes," he drawled out; "dead as a buck. Thunder! ye've gin it im atween the eyes, plum! He *is* one of the fellers, es my name's Bob inkin. I kud swar to them mowstaches among a million."

At this moment, a patrol of night gens-d'armes came up; and Lincoln, and ack, and myself were carried off to the Calaboose, where we spent the remainder of the night. In the morning, we were brought before the Recorder; ut I had taken the precaution to send for some friends, who introduced me o his worship in a proper manner. As my story corroborated Lincoln's, and is mine, and Jack's substantiated both—and as the comrades of the dead reole did not appear, and he himself was identified by the police as a notoious robber, the Recorder dismissed the case, as one of "justifiable homicide self-defence," and the hunter and I were permitted to go our way with irther interruption.

‡ I alluded to an adventure in the Rocky Mountains several years before, in which at for Lincon, I should have lost my life.

§ Craps. A popular game among the Creoles of New Orleans.

‖ "Sign," a word professional with Lincoln, referring to the tracks or other indications of the bearer.

CHAPTER II.

A VOLUNTEER RENDEZVOUS.

"Now, Cap," said Lincoln, as we seated ourselves at the table of a *café*, "I'll answer tother question yer put last night. I wur up on the head of Arkansaw an hearin they wur raisin volunteers down yeer, I kim down ter jine. It aint often I trouble the Settlements; but I've a mighty puncheon as the Frenchman says, to hev a crack at them yeller-bellies.* I haint forgot a mean trick they sarved me two yeern ago, up thar by the Peaks."

"And so you have joined the volunteers?"

"That's sartin. But why aint you a gwine to Mexiko? That ere's wonder to me, Cap."

"So I purposed long since, and wrote on for a commission; but the Government seems to have forgotten me."

"Dod rot the Government! git a commission for yerself."

"How?" I asked.

"Jine us, an be illected—thet's how."

This had crossed my mind before, but, believing myself a stranger amor these volunteers, I had given up the idea. Once joined, he who failed in bei elected an officer, was fated to shoulder a firelock. It was neck or nothin then. Lincoln set things in a new light. They were strangers to each other he affirmed, and my chances would therefore be as good as any man's.

"I'll tell yer what it is," said he, "yer kin kum with me ter the rendevóor

---

* Yellow bellies—a name given by Western hunters and soldiers of the U. S A. to the Mexicans.

an see for yerself; but if ye'll only jine, and licker freely, I'll lay a pack of beaver agin the skin of a mink, that they'll illect yer captain of the company."

"Even a lieutenancy?" I interposed.

"Neer a bit of it, Cap. Go the big figger. 'Taint more ner yer entitled to. I kin git yer a good heist among some hunters thet's thar; but thar's a buffalo drove of them parleyvoos, an a feller among 'em, one of these yeer Creeholes, thet's been a showin off and fencin with a pair of skewers from mornin till night. I'd be dog-gone glad to see the starch taken out of that feller."

I took my resolution. In half an hour after, I was standing in a large hall or armory. It was the rendezvous of the volunteers, nearly all of whom were present; and perhaps a more variegated assemblage was never grouped together. Every nationality seemed to have its representative; and for variety of language, the company might have rivalled the masons of Babel.

Near the head of the room was a table, upon which lay a large parchment, covered with signatures. I added mine to the list. In the act I had staked my liberty. It was an oath.

"These are my rivals; the candidates for office," thought I, looking at a group who stood near the table. They were men of better appearance than the οἱ πολλοί. Some of them already affected a half-undress uniform; and most wore forage caps with glazed covers, and army buttons over the ears.

"Ha! Clayley!" said I, recognising an old acquaintance. This was a young cotton planter—a free dashing spirit—who had sacrificed a fortune at the shrines of Momus and Bacchus.

"Why, Haller, old fellow! glad to see you. How have you been? Think of going with us?"

"Yes, I have signed. Who is that man?"

"He's a Creole; his name is Dubrosc."

It was a face purely Norman, and one that would halt the wandering eye in any collection. Of oval outline, framed by a profusion of black hair, wavy and perfumed. A round black eye spanned by brows arching and glossy. Whiskers, that belonged rather to the chin, leaving bare the broad jaw-bone, expressive of firmness and resolve. Firm thin lips, handsomely moustached; when parted, displaying teeth well set and of dazzling whiteness. A face that might be called beautiful—and yet its beauty was of that negative order, which we admire in the serpent and the pard. The smile was cynical. The eye cold, yet bright; but the brightness was altogether *animal*—more the light of instinct than intellect. A face that presented in its expression a strange admixture of the lovely and the hideous—physically fair, morally dark—beautiful, yet brutal.

From some undefinable cause, I at once conceived for this man a strange feeling of dislike. It was he of whom Lincoln had spoken; and who was likely to be my rival for the captaincy. Was it this that rendered him repulsive? No. There was a cause beyond. In him I recognised one of those abandoned natures, who shrink from all honest labor, and live upon the sacrificial fondness of some weak being who has been enslaved by their personal attractions. There are many such. I have met them in the *salons* of Paris; in the dance-rooms of London; in the *cafés* of Havanna and New Orleans—everywhere, in the crowded haunts of the world. I have met them with an instinct of loathing—an instinct of antagonism.

"The fellow is likely to be our captain," whispered Clayley, noticing that I observed the man with more than ordinary attention. "By the way," continued he "I don't half like it. I believe he's an infernal scoundrel."

" I quite agree with you. But if so, how can he be elected?"

"Oh! no one here knows another; and this fellow is a splendid swordsman, like all the Creoles you know. He has used the trick to advantage, and has created an impression. By the bye, now I recollect, you are no slouch at that yourself. What are you up for?"

"Captain." I replied.

"Good! then we must go the whole hog in your favor. I have put in for the first-lieutenancy, so we won't run foul of each other. Let us 'hitch teams!'"

"With all my heart." Said I.

"You came in with that long-bearded hunter. Is he your friend?"

"He is."

"Then I can tell you, that among these fellows he's a 'whole team and a cross dog under the wagon' to boot. See him! he's at it already."

I had noticed Lincoln in conversation with several leather-legging gentry like himself, whom I knew from their costume and appearance to be back-woodsmen. All at once, these saturnine characters commenced moving about the room, and entering into conversation with men whom they had not hitherto deigned to notice.

"They are canvassing." Said Clayley.

Lincoln, brushing past, whispered in my ear: "Cap'n, I understan these yeer critters better 'n your kin. Yer must mix among 'em—mix and licker, thet's the idee."

"Good advice," said Clayley; "but if you could only take the shine out of that fellow at fencing, the thing's done at once. By Jove! I think you might do it, Haller!"

"I have made up my mind to try, at all events."

"Not until the last day; a few hours before the election."

"You are right; that will be better: very well," and Clayley walked away.

During the next three days, the enrolment continued, and the canvass was kept up with energy. The election was to take place on the evening of the fourth. My dislike for my rival had been strengthened by observation; and, as is always so in such cases, the feeling was reciprocal. On the afternoon of the day in question, we stood before each other, foil in hand, both of us nerved by an intense, though as yet unspoken, enmity. This had been observed by most of the spectators, who approached, forming a circle around us; all of them highly interested in the result, which, they knew, would be an index to the election.

The room was an armory, and all kinds of weapons for military practice were kept in it. Each had helped himself to his foil. One of the weapons was without a button, and sharp enough to be dangerous in the hands of an angry man. I noticed that my antagonist had chosen this one.

"Your foil is not in order; it has lost the button—has it not?"

"Ah! Monsieur, pardon. I did not perceive that."

"A strange oversight," muttered Clayley, with a significant glance.

The Frenchman returned the imperfect foil, and took another.

"Have you a choice, Monsieur?" I inquired.

"No thank you; I am satisfied."

By this time every person in the rendezvous had come up, and waited with breathless anxiety. We stood face to face, more like two men about to engage in a deadly duel, than a pair of amateurs with blunt foils. My antagonist was evidently a practised swordsman. I could see that as he came to guard. This exercise had been a foible of my college days, and for years I had not met my match; but I was out of practise.

We commenced unsteadily. Both were excited by unusual emotions, and our first thrusts were neither skilfully aimed nor guarded. We fenced with the energy of anger; and the sparks crackled from the friction of the grazing steel. For several minutes it was a doubtful contest, but I grew cooler every instant, while a slight advantage I had gained irritated my adversary. At length, by a lucky hit, I succeded in planting the button of my foil upon his cheek. A cheer greeted this, and I could hear the voice of Lincoln shouting ut:

"Wal done, Cap'n! whooray!"

This added to the exasperation of the Frenchman, causing him to strike wilder than before; and I found no difficulty in repeating my former thrust. It was now a sure blow; and, after a few passes, I thrust my adversary for the third time, drawing blood. The cheer rang out louder than before. The Frenchman could no longer conceal his mortification; and, grasping his foil in both hands, he snapped it over his knee, with an oath. Then muttering some words about better weapons and another opportunity, he strode off among the spectators. Two hours after the combat I was his captain. Clayley was elected first-lieutenant; and in a week from that time the company was mustered into the service of the United States' Government, and armed and equipped as an independent corps of "RIFLE RANGERS." On the 20th of January, 1847, a noble ship was bearing us over the broad blue water, toward the shores of a hostile land.

CHAPTER III.

LIFE ON THE ISLAND OF LOBOS.

AFTER calling at Brazos Santiago, we were ordered to land upon the island of Lobos, fifty miles north of Vera Cruz. This was to be our "drill rendezvous." We soon reached this point. Detachments from several regiments debarked together; the jungle was attacked; and, in a few hours, the green grove had disappeared, and in its place stood the white pyramids of canvass with their floating flags. It was the work of a day. When the moon looked down upon Lobos, it seemed as if a warlike city had sprung suddenly out of the sea, with a navy at anchor in front of its bannered walls!

In a few days, six full regiments had encamped upon this hitherto uninhabited island; and nothing was heard but the voice of war.

These regiments were all "raw," and my duty, with others, consisted in licking them into shape." It was drill, drill, from morning till night; and by early tatoo I was always glad to crawl into my tent, and go to sleep—such sleep as a man can get among scorpions, centipedes, and soldier-crabs; for the little islet seemed to have within its boundaries a specimen of every reptile that came safe out of the ark.

The 22d being Washington's birthday, I could not get to bed as usual. I was compelled to accept an invitation, obtained by Clayley, to the tent of Major Twing; where they were—using Clayley's own words—"to have a night of it."

After tatoo, we set out for the Major's marquee, which lay near the centre of the islet, in a coppice of caoutchouc trees. We had no difficulty in finding it—guided by the jingling of glasses, and the mingling of many voices in loud laughter.

As we came near, we could perceive that the marquee had been enlarged, by tucking up the flaps in front, with the addition of a fly stretched over an extra ridge-pole. Several pieces of rough plank, spirited away from the ships, resting upon empty bread barrels, formed the table. Upon this might be recognised every variety of bottles, glasses and cups. Open boxes of sardines, piles of ship-biscuits, and segments of cheese, filled the intervening spaces. Freshly drawn corks and glistening fragments of lead were strewed around, while a number of dark, conical objects under the table told that not a few champagne bottles were already "down among the dead men."

On each side of the table was a row of colonels, captains, subalterns, and doctors; seated without regard to rank or age, according to the order in which they had "dropped in." There was also a sprinkling of strange, half-sailor-looking men, the skippers of brigs, steamboats, &c.; for Twing was a thorough republican in his entertainments; besides, the day levelled all distinctions.

At the head of the table was the Major himself—one of those wiry, hard-headed, hard-drinking devils—who always carried a flask suspended from his shoulders by a green string; and without this flask, no one ever saw Major Twing. He could not have stuck to it more closely had it been his badge of rank. It was not unusual, on the route, to hear some wearied officer exclaim: "If I only had a pull at old Twing's pewter!" and "equal to Twing's flask," was an expression which stamped the quality of any liquor as superfine. Such was one of the Major's peculiarities, though by no means the only one.

As my friend and I made our appearance under the fly, the company was in high glee; every one enjoying himself with that freedom from restraint of rank peculiar to the American army-service. Clayley was a great favorite with the Major, and at once caught his eye.

"Ha, Clayley! that you? Walk in with your friend. Find seats there, gentlemen."

"Captain Haller—Major Twing," said Clayley, introducing me.

"Happy to know you, Captain. Can you find seats there? No. Come up this way. Cudjo! boy! run over to Colonel Marshall's tent, and steal a couple of stools. Adge, twist the neck off that bottle. Where's the screw? Hang that screw! Where is it, any how?"

"Never mind the screw, Mage," cried the Adjutant; "I've got a paten universal here." So saying, the gentleman held out a champagne bottle in his left hand, and with a down stroke of his right, cut the neck off as if it had been filed!

"Nate!" ejaculated Hennessy an Irish officer, who sat near the head of the table.

"What we call a Kentucky corkscrew," said the Adjutant, coolly. "It offers a double advantage. It saves time, and you get the wine clear of—"

"My respects, gentlemen! Captain Haller—Mr. Clayley."

"Thank you, Major Twing. To you, Sir!"

"Ha! the stools at last! Only one! What the devil, Cudjo? Come, gentlemen—squeeze yourselves up this way. Here, Clayley, old boy, here's a cartridge-box. Adge! up-end that box. So—give us your fist, old fellow; how are you? Sit down, Captain; sit down. Cigars, there!"

As soon as we had got seated, several voices were heard vociferating "the song! the song! round with the song!" and I learnt that the order of the night was "a song, a story, or half-a-dozen bottles of champagne."

"Sibley's turn next!" shouted one.

"Sibley! Sibley!" cried several voices.

"Well, gentlemen," said the officer called upon, a young South Carolinian, "as I make no pretensions to singing, I will endeavor to clear the forfeit by a story."

"Good! a story, by all means—nothing like variety."

"Liftinant, take a trifle of the squeezed lemon before ye begin."

"Thank you, Captain Hennessy. Your health, Sir!"

CHAPTER IV.

LIEUTENANT SIBLEY'S STORY OF A GEORGIA HOTEL.

"Well, gentlemen, about six months ago, I had occasion to make a journey to Pensacola on horseback. My road of course lay through the State of Georgia.

"It is well known, gentlemen, that there are large tracts in the territory of our Southern neighbor, that have proved very ungrateful to the labors of the husbandman. These districts are, in consequence, but sparsely settled and ill-provided with the necessaries of life."

Here the Lieutenant looked significantly towards some Georgians who were present.

"On the third day of my journey, I had ridden about twenty miles through one of these tracts—a dry pine barren—without having caught the first glimpse of a human habitation. I was faint with hunger and thirst; so was my horse, who stretched out his neck and moaned piteously, as each new and apparently illimitable prospect of the hot, sandy road opened before us. There no help for it, however; so we jogged on painfully, both of us keeping a sharp look a-head. You cannot fancy my delight, when, on turning a corner I saw before me a large and substantial log-house, with a pine mast stuck up before the door, and a broad swinging sign, upon which was legible, in bold characters, the word 'Hotel.'

"I rubbed my eyes, and then shaded them with my hand, to make sure it was not the *mirage*, which frequently makes its appearance upon these sandy plains. But no; it was a house, and, better still, a hotel.

"I straightened myself in the saddle. My horse whighered and stepped out cheerily. 'Come,' said I, patting him on the neck, 'we're through it at last, ol· fellow; you'll soon be up to your ears in the best of Georgia corn, and I—.' Here the anticipated enjoyment of ham and eggs, fried chicken, strong coffee, hot biscuit and waffles deprived me of the power of speech, and I rode up to the 'hotel' in silence.

"As I got nearer the house, it began to look weather-beaten and desolate-like; and I was growing fearful that it might be uninhabited; but no, there sat the landlord in the porch, and his two sons. 'It's all right,' thought I; so I rode up, and drew bridle in front of the door.

"So far, the three individuals whom I had observed in the porch—three sallow, dry-looking chaps, in their shirt-sleeves—had not moved an inch! I am not certain that they even changed the direction of their eyes! A couple of gaunt, yellow dogs, that lay on the stoop, remained equally motionless!

"'Come,' thought I, 'this is cool for people who keep a house of entertainment. They ought to know, from the direction in which I have come, that I am likely to put up for the night. They might offer to take one's horse. I should think!' But no one stirred. I began to suspect that the house might not be a tavern, as I had at first supposed; and I looked up at the sign. Enough—the word 'hotel' was there in large letters.

"'Can I stop here for the night?' I inquired at length.

"I waited for an answer, but none came. I repeated the question in a louder and more imperious tone.

"'You kin if yer like, stranger,' replied the oldest of the three, but without moving a muscle, except those of his mouth.

"'Have you got any corn?' I inquired, intending to make sure before alighting; as the house, on a nearer inspection, looked naked and empty.

"'Got any corn?' echoed the same speaker as before.

"'Yes,' said I, 'corn.'

"'No, we haint got any,' was the reply.

"'Well, have you got any fodder, then?'

"'Got any fodder?'

"'Yes—fodder.'

"'No, we haint got any.'

"'This is bad,' thought I, 'my poor horse—I will have to turn him loose and I might as well tie him up for that matter,' as, on looking around, I could not see a blade of grass within the circuit of a mile! 'I had best hitch him to the post—take a hurried snack myself, and then ride on to the next house—but first let me see what they can give me to eat.'

"All the time I was occupied with these reflections, the three men remained silent and motionless, except when one or the other of them would bring his hand down with a smart slap over his cheek, or along his thigh, or behind his ear, as though one and all of them were afflicted with the malady of St. Vitus!

"I was at first startled with these demonstrations; but, upon further observation, I perceived that my saturnine friends were only killing musquitoes

"'Have you got any ham and eggs?' I asked.

"'Got any ham and eggs?' echoed the original speaker, with an emphasis that clearly betokened surprise.

"'Yes—ham and eggs,' repeated I.

"'No, we haint got any.'

"'A pity; I am fond of ham and eggs. Have you any chickens, then?'

"'Chickens?'

"'Yes,' said I, 'chickens.'

"'No, we haint got any chickens—nery chicken.'

"'Well, have you got any meat?'

"'Got any meat?'

"'Yes—any sort of meat—beef, pork, mutton or veal. I'm not particular—I'm hungry.'

"'No, we haint got any.'

"'Have you any bread, then?'

"'Any bread?'

"'Yes—bread—a piece of bread and a glass of water. That to a hungry man is a banquet.'

"'No; we haint got no bread.'

"'Well, my friend, have you got anything to eat of any kind?'

" 'Anything to eat of any kind?'

"'Yes, anything. I'm as hungry as a wolf.'

"'No, we haint got nothing to eat of nery kind.'

"'Can you give my horse some water? and I'll ride on.'

"'We haint none drawed, strenger; but the crick aint more'n a kupple o miles ahead—yer kin git water thar.'

"'Good God!' I ejaculated, involuntarily; 'no meat, no bread, no corn, no water, no nothing! Look here, old fellow! will you tell me how the devil you do here, anyhow?'

"Not at all put out by the question, the old chap looked up sideways, and replied:

"'*Very well, I thank ye, strenger, how de yer deo yerself?*'"

"I gave a violent wrench at the bridle, which brought my horse round like a pivot, and, digging the spurs into his sides, I headed him at the road. But the poor beast did not need any driving; for, whether he had been satisfied by his own inspection of the place, or whether he had understood the conversation, he broke into a sort of despairing gallop, and did not stop until we had reached the top of a long hill! Here I had the curiosity to turn round in the saddle, and look back; and, to my astonishment, the three men were still seated just as I had left them; and I really believe that they are sitting there to this day! Captain Hennessy, I'll trouble you again."

"With all the pleasure of life—here's at you, Liftinant!"

"Fill up, gentlemen! fill up!" shouted the sharp, hard voice of the Major as soon as the laughter had subsided; "fill up—there's a basket left."

"Ay, and when that's through, Old Blowhard here has another stowed away in the lockers of his steamer."

"Ay, a dozen of 'em for such a day as this," said the transport master who was known among the officers at Lobos as "Old Blowhard."

"Speaking of the day, allow me, gentlemen, to propose a sentiment, which, until now, we have by some accident, overlooked."

This came from a tall, grey-haired officer of a venerable aspect.

"Sentiment from Colonel Harding!"

"Colonel Harding's sentiment!"

"Fill up for the Colonel's toast; pass that champagne."

"*The memory of the immortal man, whose birth-day we célebrate.*"

This toast was drunk standing—all heads uncovered—and in perfect silence The riot that rung but a moment ago through the crowded canvass was hushed, out of respect for the memory of the illustrious dead. The silence was only momentary. Like waves for a while baffled, and back returning, the sounds of revelry again broke forth. Above the din of conversation, several voices were heard, vociferating:

"A story from Old Blowhard!—A back hit from Georgia!"

"Well, gentlemen," responded the old transport-master, a thorough-bred Georgian; "I'm ready as soon as you have all filled; I don't like to be interrupted."

"Fill up, gentlemen!" shouted the Major, "Adge out with some corks Cudjo, where's the screw? Hang that screw! I believe it's sunk into the sand; look out for your purses, gentlemen, if you drop them there, they're gone I've lost several valuable articles in this cursed sand-hole."

"Mine is as low, as it can possibly get," cried a voice.

"Never mind the screw, Adge," said Hillis, the Adjutant, who by this time had broken—Kentucky fashion—the necks of several bottles, and was puring out their foaming contents.

"Now, gentlemen," cried the Georgian, after swallowing a cup of champagne, "I'm at your service."

CHAPTER V.

OLD BLOWHARD'S STORY OF THE GUYAS-CUTIS.

"MINE, gentlemen, is also a travelling story," Here the Georgian looked significantly towards Sibley.

" I was journeying to the City of Washington, in company with a friend—a Georgian boy, like myself. We went, as thousands have gone before an since, to try our luck at office-hunting. You are all well aware, gentlemen that the road from Georgia to Washington passes through the Palmetto State; a State distinguished for the fertility of its soil, as well as for the wealth, chivalry, and intelligence of her sons." Here "Old Blowhard winked knowingly at the company with one eye while he kept the other fixed upon the South Carolinian.

" I thought myself a smart traveller, gentlemen; but compared with my companion, I was as green as a blade of spring grass. He was naturally sharp, but experience had polished his wits to the keenness of a cambric needle His name was Cobb—Wiley Cobb.

" We started from home on a capital of three hundred dollars. It was all we could rake together. But we had a couple of stout Georgia ponies; and this, we concluded, would be enough to put us through to Washington and back.

"'If we're stumped,' said Cobb, 'we can sell the cattle.'

" Unfortunately, before entering the Palmetto State, it was our luck to pas through the town of Augusta, on the Georgia side, where we halted to feed. Augusta had always been considered a "brisk little place." We found it so. N it being in a great hurry, we remained over night and the next day. We had fallen in with some very agreeable acquaintances. We got to playing at ninepenny *poker;* then quarter a dollar *loc;* then *brag;* and finally, our Augusta friends introduced us to the interesting game of *faro.* We played all night, and by daybreak on the morning of the second day, had deposited our three hundred dollars in the "bank" where it stayed.

"'What's to be done?' said I.

"'I'm thinking,' answered Cobb.

"'Sell the ponies and start back?' suggested I.

"'No such thing!' sharply responded Cobb.

"'What better can we do?' I asked.

"'What have you got in your saddle-bags?' inquired my friend, without heeding my last interrogatory.

"'A shirt, a pair of pistols, a plug of tobacco, and a bowie,' was my reply.

"'We must sell the bowie first,' said Cobb; 'it will pay our tavern bill, and get us out of this infernal hole.'

"'And what next? On to Washington?' I inquired.

"'Of course,' said Cobb, 'we would look wise turning back: we would be the standing joke of the county,' added he.

"'But how can we travel without funds?' I asked.

"'That we will have to find out,' said Cobb, with a look as cheerful and happy as if he had had relays of horses all along to Washington, and his bill paid at every tavern upon the road.

"'I have an acquaintance,' continued he, 'at the end of the first stage from here; we can stop all night with him, that won't cost anything; beyond that, we must trust to the hospitality of the farmers. I think we can get through South Carolina handsomely; good, generous fellows, the South Carolinians. Here Blowhard again looked significantly across the table. 'The danger is, we may stick in the Turpentine State. We must travel through it on the proceeds of your pistols. But come, let us first dispose of the bowie, and get out of this sharper's nest.'

"As Cobb was my senior, and in my estimation a great genius, I of course acquiesced. He sold the bowie-knife to one of our gambling friends, for six dollars; the tavern bill was liquidated, leaving a few shillings in our joint purse; and with this we took the road through South Carolina.

"At the end of the first day, we stopped with Cobb's friend and were hospitably entertained. Cobb felt a strong inclination to borrow from him, but could not bring himself to confess the cause of our necessity.

"We left his friend's house, therefore, after an excellent breakfast, our horses well fed and curried, but without any increase to our finances. On the contrary, we had given a shilling to the 'darkie' who had saddled our ponies.

"We were now fairly *en route*, travelling through, to both of us, a *terra incognita*.

"That night we stopped at a planter's house. I do not know what Cobb told the owner, as we were preparing to leave in the morning; but I heard the latter remark somewhat sneeringly, as we got into our saddles, 'It aint usual for folks to travel through these parts without money,' and then there was half-stifled, angry-like ejaculation, followed by a hissing through his teeth of words, which would have sounded badly in polite ears.

"'Rather an inhospitable sort of a chap,' whispered I, as we rode off.

"'Cursed inhospitable!' said Cobb, 'especially for a South Carolinian But he's an exception, I guess.'

"And he *was* an exception; for the next place we stopped at, they turned to, and blackguarded us outright, calling us 'impostors,' and 'Georgia Yankees;' and the next after that, the landlord of the house, which was a tavern threatened to levy upon our saddle-bags. This he certainly would have done but Cobb told him very significantly, that they contained only a pair of pistols and that these were loaded, and might go off. Saying this, Cobb took out the pistols, and handed one of them to me; then, cocking his own, he told the landlord he 'might have the saddle-bags now, as they were empty.'

"But Cobb was six feet two, with a pair of fierce whiskers, and an eye as black as a coal; and the landlord concluded to let the bags hang where they were: so we leaped into our saddles, and rode off.

"'This will never do, Harry,' said Cobb, as we jogged leisurely along.

"'Never,' said I.

"'We must hit upon some plan to raise the wind,' continued he.

"'I wish we could,' said I.

"'Think,' said he.

"'I'll try,' said I; and I commenced turning over in my mind every plan I could think of, that would be likely to relieve us from our difficulty.

"But 'raising the wind' by the mere process of thought, is an achievement which has puzzled sharper intellects than mine; and I was about abandoning he twentieth project, when Cobb, who was riding some distance in advance suddenly checked his horse, and, wheeling round in the saddle, with a triumphant gesture, shouted out:

"'Harry, I have it!'

"'Good!' cried I.

"'I've tree'd the varmint!' continued he.

"'Like a knife!' said he.

"'I'm glad of it,' said I; 'but how?'

"'Never mind, I'll tell you at night. I haven't got the thing straightened out yet. How far do you suppose we are from Columbia?' inquired he.

"'About twenty miles! I should think. We have come five, and they said it was twenty-five from the tavern.'

"'Well, then, ride slowly,' said Cobb. 'We must not reach Columbia before dark. What sized place is it?'

"'I haven't an idea,' replied I. 'It ought to be a good chunk of a place though—it's the State capital.'

"'So it is—you're right—it'll do,' said he; and we rode on in silence, Cobb buried in profound meditation, maturing his plans, and I dying with curiosity to know them.

"About half an hour after dark, we entered the town, and rode up the streets, Cobb looking inquiringly into the different stores, as we passed.

"'Here's the thing!' ejaculated he, pulling up in front of a shoe-shop, and getting off his horse.

"He entered the shop. I could see, by his gesticulations to the owner of the establishment, that he was in treaty for a large empty box, which stood in the middle of the store. All that I could hear was the following:

"After you have made the hole, you may nail down the lid, and paint the letters upon it. Here they are.'

"Saying this, he took up a scrap of paper, and writing some words upon it, handed it to the storekeeper.

"'I'll send a dray for it in half-an-hour,' continued he. He then paid for the box; and, bidding the man good night, we continued our way to the principal hotel, where we drew up and dismounted.

"'I'll be back in an hour, Harry,' said Cobb, throwing me his bridle; 'in the meantime, take your supper, engage a snug room, and wait for me. Don't register till I come—I'll attend to that.' So saying, he disappeared down the street.

"Agreeably to his instructions, I ate supper—and heartily too, for we had not tasted victuals since morning. I was then shown to my room, where I waited patiently for about two hours. I was still ignorant how the supper was to be paid for, when the door opened, and Cobb entered. A couple of darkies' followed at his heels, carrying the box that I had seen him purchase, upon the lid of which was painted in large bold letters:

"'THE WONDERFUL GUYAS-CUTIS!'

Underneath was an oblong hole, or slit, newly chiselled in the wood!

"Cobb held in his hand a broad sheet of paper. This, as soon as the darkies had gone out of the room, he spread upon the table, and, pointing to it, triumphantly exclaimed:

"'There, now, Harry, that's it!'

"'What the devil is *it*?' asked I.

"'Read for yourself old fellow!' cried he.

"I commenced reading:

"'THE WONDERFUL GUYAS-CUTIS!

"'*Caught in the Wilds of Oregon! near the Boundary of* 54° 40'!!'

"This was in large capitals. Then followed the description in smaller letters:

"'This remarkable animal, hitherto unknown to the naturalists, possesses all the intelligence of the human, combined with the ferocity of the tiger, and the agility of the ourang-outang! He is of a bright sky-blue color, with eleven stripes upon his body, and one more round his nose, which makes the even dozen; and ne'er a one of them alike!!

"'In his rage, he has been known to carry Indians up to the tops of the highest trees, and there leave them to perish with hunger, thirst, and cold; which accounts satisfactorily for the uncivilized nature of the red man!!

"'The highly-intelligent citizens of Columbia are respectfully informed that this wonderful quadruped has arrived among them, and will be exhibited this evening, Tuesday, at the Minerva Rooms, at the hour of eight o'clock. Admittance 25 cents!'

"'But,' said I, 'my dear Wiley,' now, for the first time, catching the idea of Cobb's project, 'you don't intend—'

"'But I *do*, though,' interrupted he; 'and I will—that's as certain as my name's Wiley Cobb of the state of Georgia.'

"'But you do not really think you can gull the intelligent people—?'

"'Bah! intelligent people! it's plain, Harry, you don't know the world,' said Cobb, contemptuously.

"'And what do you expect *me* to do?' I asked.

"'Nothing but stay in this room to-morrow, and see that nobody peeps in to that box.'

"'But, at night?'

"'At night you will stand at the door, take the money, and when you hear me groan and shake the chain, run in behind the screen—that's all.'

' Beginning to look upon the thing as a good joke, I promised faithfully to follow Cobb's instructions; not without some disagreeable anticipations, that both he and I would spend the following night in the Columbia jail.

"Next morning, Cobb was up at an early hour; and, after moaning piteously, and groaning in the most hideous and frightful manner, and talking at intervals into the box, as—'be still Guy!' 'down Guy, down!' he left the room, bidding me keep a sharp look out.

"As soon as he had gone, I heard a considerable shuffling and whispering outside the door, and presently a darkie looked in, and asked me if I wanted anything.

"'Not anything,' said I; don't come in!'

"The darkie drew back his head, with a look of terror, and pulled to the door.

"Shortly after, the whispering re-commenced, and the door again opened. This time it was the landlord of the hotel, whose curiosity had brought him up to see the elephant.'

"'It's a fierce critter, that;' said he, putting his head inside the door, but still holding on to the handle.

"'Dreadful!' said I.

"'Could I not have a peep?' inquired he.

"'It's against the rules,' answered I, 'besides a stranger makes him savage!'

"'Oh, it does?' said he, apologizingly.

"'Terrible!' said I.

"'You'll have a good house, I think,' said he, after a short pause.

"'I hope so,' said I.

"'The bills is out. Mr. Van Amburgh was about putty early this mornin''

"'Mr. Van Amburgh!' ejaculated I.

"'Yes; Mr. Van Amburgh—your partner.'

"'Oh!—yes; Mr. Van Amburgh, my partner,' I chimed in, as I saw that this must be the new title of my friend, Cobb. 'But Mr. Van Amburgh did not put out the bills himself?'

"I said this to cover the mistake I had made.

"'Oh—no; of coorse not,' replied the landlord: 'he hired a boy.'

"'Certainly—that was right,' I added.

"'Breakfast 'll be ready in a minute; ye'll come down?'

"Oh! of course.'

"At this, Boniface took himself off, to my great satisfaction.

"Cobb now returned, bringing with him about six feet of a log-chain, done up in paper.

"After repeating his groaning and growling, we descended to breakfast—Cobb first carefully locking the door, and putting the key in his pocket.

"We were evidently objects of great interest at the breakfast-table—Cobb calling me 'Mr. Wolfe,' and I addressing him as 'Mr. Van Amburgh.' The servants waited upon us with delighted attention.

"After breakfast, we returned to the room, when Cobb again went through the groaning rehearsal, and shortly after left me.

"This he repeated at intervals during the day; upon each succeeding occasion, louder and more terrific than before!

"Night came at length, and with our box, covered up in one of the landlord's quilts, we started for the Minerva rooms, which I found fitted up with a running screen, and brilliantly lighted with candles. Cobb had the box and chain carried behind the screen, while I remained at the door to look after the treasury. We had no tickets, each one paying his or her "quarter," and passing in.

"In a short time, the room was full of ladies, gentlemen, and children—tradesmen and their wives; merchants and their families; young bucks and their sweethearts, and even a number of the intelligent members of the State Assembly! Expectation was on tip-toe to see the 'Wonderful Guyas-Cutis.'

"At length, a low moaning was heard behind the screen

"'Down Guy, down! Still dog, still!' cried a voice in hoarse commanding accents.

"The people had now all arrived, and began to stamp and clap their hands, and exhibit the usual symptoms of impatience, crying out at intervals The Guyas-Cutis! the Guyas-Cutis!'

"'Bring him out, Mr. Showman; trot him out!'

"'Let us see the savage varmint!'

"The Guyas-Cutis growled fearfully.

"'Give him a bone!' cried one.

"'Go it, old fifty-four forty!' exclaimed another

"'The whole, or none!' shouted a third.

"'Fifty-four forty, or fight!' cried a fourth.

"'Go it old K. Polk!' from a distant part of the room.

"At this, the audience became convulsed with laughter. The groaning grew louder and more terrible; and Cobb's voice was heard in hoarse accents, apostrophizing the Guyas-Cutis. Then was heard a struggle behind the screen, followed by the rattling of a chain.

"This was my cue. Putting on a look of terror—as I had been instructed by Cobb—I rushed up the open space between the spectators, and pushed in behind the curtain. I stole a glance backward, as I entered, and saw that the audience had already caught the alarm. Some of the people had risen to their feet, and stood pale and trembling! Behind the screen, Cobb was running to and fro, scraping the sanded floor, rattling the chain, and chiding an imaginary object in the most threatening accents! He was in his shirt sleeves, and streams of what appeared to be blood were running over his face, neck and bosom!

"'Down, savage; down!' cried Cobb.

"'Boo-boo, oow-wow!' growled the Guyas-Cutis

"'Oh, Mr. Wolfe,' cried Cobb, 'come here—help! help, or he'll be off!'

"'Hold on to him!' shouted I, in a loud voice, 'hold on!'

"'Bow-oow, wow-awow!' roared the Guyas-Cutis.

"'Help, help!' cried Cobb.

"'Hold on!' shouted I.

"Cobb seized the chain in both hands, and, after giving it a fierce rattle rushed in front of the screen, shouting in a voice of thunder:

"'*Save yourselves, gentlemen! Save your wives and children! The Guyas-Cutis is loose!*'

"Gentlemen," said Blowhard, drawing a long breath, "it's more than I can do to describe the scene that followed. In less than two minutes the room was empty; and when Cobb and myself reached the street, there was not a soul—man, woman, or child—to be seen! We hurried to the hotel, and ordered our horses to be saddled with all dispatch, Cobb telling the landlord that the Guyas-Cutis had taken to the fields, and we must pursue him on horseback! While our horses were being saddled, we settled the landlord's bill out of our newly-acquired funds. Starting at a brisk gallop, we did not draw bridle until we had put twenty miles between us and the good city of Columbia. Then we halted, and counted our receipts which amounted to—how much, Mr. Cobb?"

"Sixty-six dollars seventy-five cents, to a figger," said a tall swarthy personage, who sate someway down the table, and whose dark, saturnine countenance would never have betrayed him as the hero of the story; but it was he, indeed; and peals of laughter followed the discovery.

* * * * * * * *

"Now the Major! the Major!" shouted several voices.

At that moment, the report of a musket was heard without the tent, and simultaneously a bullet whistled through the canvass. It knocked the fore ging cap from the head of Captain Hennessy, and, striking a decanter shivered the glass into a thousand pieces!

"A divilish nate shot that, I don't care who fired it," said Hennessy, coolly picking up his cap. "An inch of a miss—good as a mile," added he, thrusting his thumb into the bullet-hole.

By this time every officer present was upon his feet, most of them rushing towards the rear of the marquee. A dozen voices called out together:

"Who fired that gun?"

There was no answer, and several plunged into the thicket in pursuit. The chapparal was dark and silent, and these returned after a fruitless search.

"Some soldier, whose musket has gone off by accident," suggested Colonel Harding. "The fellow has run away, to avoid being put under arrest."

"Come, gentlemen, take your sates again," said Hennessy; let the poor divil slide—yez may be thankful it wasn't a shell."

"You, Captain, have most cause to be grateful for the character of the missile."

"By my sowl, I don't know about that—a shell or a twenty-four would have grazed me all the same; but a big shot would have been mighty inconvanient to the head of my friend Haller, here."

This was true. My head was nearly in range; and, had the shot been a large one, it would have struck me upon the left temple. As it was, I felt the "wind" of the bullet, and I already began to suffer a painful sensation over the eye.

"I'm mighty curious to know which of us the fellow has missed, Captain," said Hennessy, turning to me as he spoke.

"If it were not a 'bull,' I should say I hope neither of us. I'm inclined to think with Colonel Harding, that it was altogether an accident."

"By the powers! an ugly accident, too, that has spoiled five dollars' worth of an illigant cap, and a pint of as good brandy as ever was mixed with a lemon."

"Plenty left, Captain," cried the Major. "Come, gentlemen, don't let this lamp us:—fill up! fill up! Adge, out with the corks! Cudjo, where's the crew?—curse that screw!"

"Never mind the screw, Mage," cried the Adjutant, repeating his old trick pon the neck of a fresh bottle, which, nipped off under the wire, fell upon a cap of others that had preceded it.

And the wine again foamed and sparkled; and glasses circled round and the noisy revelry waxed as loud as ever. The incident of the shot was soon forgotten. Songs were sung, and stories told, and toasts drank; and with song and sentiment, and toast and story, and the wild excitement of wit and wine, the night waned away. With many of those young hearts, bold with hope, and burning with ambition, it was the last "Twenty Second" they would ever celebrate. Half of them never hailed anoth

CHAPTER VI.

MOONLIGHT SCENE—A SPY IN CAMP—A SKELETON ADVENTURE.

It was past midnight when I withdrew from the scene of wassail. Clayley was one of those tireless spirits, who could "drink all night till broad daylight;" and, as he preferred remaining for some time longer, I walked out alone. My blood was flushed, and I strolled down upon the beach, to enjoy the cool, fresh breeze that was blowing in from the ocean.

The scene before me was one of picturesque grandeur, and I paused a moment to gaze upon it. The wine even heightened its loveliness to an illusion.

The full, round moon of the tropics was sweeping over a sky of cloudless blue. The stars were eclipsed, and scarcely visible—except a few of the larger ones, as the belt of Orion, the planet Venus, and the luminous radii of the Southern Cross.

From my feet, a broad band of silver stretched away to the horizon, marking the meridian of the moon. This was broken by the line of coral reef, over which the surf curled and sparkled with a phosphoric brightness. The reef itself, running all around, seemed to gird the islet in a circle of fire! Here only were the waves in motion, as if pressed by some subaqueous and invisible power; for beyond, scarcely a breath stirred the sleeping sea! It lay smooth and silent, while a satellite sky seemed caved out in its azure depths!

On the south, a hundred ships were in the deep roadstead, a cable's length from each other—their hulls, spars and rigging magnified to gigantic proportions, under the deceptive and tremulous moonbeam. They were motionless as if the sea had been frozen around them into a solid crystal

Their flags drooped listlessly down, trailing along the masts, or warped and twined around the haulyards.

Up against the easy ascent extended the long rows of white tents, shining under the silvery moonbeam, like pyramids of snow. In one a light was still gleaming through the canvass, where, perchance, some soldier sate up wearily wiping his gun, or burnishing the brasses upon his belts.

Now and then dark forms—human and uniformed—passed to and fro from tent to tent, returning from the visit to some regimental comrade. At equal distances round the camp, others stood upright and motionless, the gleam of the musket showing the sentry on his silent post.

The plunge of an oar—as some boat was rowed out among the anchored ships—the ripple of the light breaker—at intervals the hail of a sentinel: "Who goes there?"—the low parley that followed—the chirp of the cicada in the dark jungle—or the scream of the sea-bird, scared, by some submarine enemy, from its watery rest—were the only sounds that disturbed the deep stillness of the night.

I continued my walk along the beach, until I had reached that point of the island directly opposite to the mainland of Mexico. Here the chapparal grew thick and tangled, running down to the water's edge, where it ended in a clump of mangroves. As no troops were encamped here, the islet had not been cleared at this point, and the jungle was dark and solitary.

The moon was now going down, and straggling shadows began to fall upon the water.

"Certainly some one skulked into the bushes!—a rustling in the leaves—yes! some fellow who has strayed beyond the line of sentries, and afraid to return to camp? Ha! a boat! a skiff it is—a net and buoys! As I live, 'tis a Mexican craft! who can have brought it here? Some fisherman from the coast of Tuspan.* No—he would not venture—it must be—" A strange suspicion flashed across my mind, and I rushed through the mangrove thicket, where I had observed the object a moment before. I had not proceeded fifty yards, when I saw the folly of this movement. I found myself in the midst of a labyrinth, dark and dismal, surrounded by a wall of leaves and brambles. Vines and lianas barred up the path, and laced the limbs together.

"If they be spies, I have taken the worst plan to catch them. I may as well go through now. I cannot be distant from the rear of the camp. Ugh! how dismal!"

* The village of Tuspan is nearly opposite Lobos, on the mainland.

I pushed on, climbing over fallen trunks, and twining myself through the viny cordage. The creepers clung to my neck—thorns penetrated my skin—the *mezquite* slapped me in the face, drawing blood! I laid my hand upon a pendant limb; a clammy object struggled under my touch, with a terrified yet spiteful violence, and freeing itself, sprang over my shoulder, and scampered off among the fallen leaves. I felt its fetid breath, as the cold scales brushed against my cheek. It was the hideous Iguana!

A huge bat flapped its sail-like wing in my face, and returned again and again, breathing a mephitic odor that caused me to gasp! Twice I struck at it with my sword, cutting only the empty air. A third time my blade was caught in the trellis of parasites. It was horrible; I felt terrified with such strange enemies.

At length, after a continued struggle, an opening appeared before me—a glade! I rushed to the welcome spot.

"What a relief!" I ejaculated, emerging from the leafy darkness. Suddenly, I started back with a cry of horror; my limbs refused to act; the sword fell from my grasp; and I stood palsied and transfixed, as if by a bolt from heaven!

Before me, and not over three paces distant, the image of death itself rose out of the earth, and stretched forth his skeleton arms to clutch me! It was no phantom. There was the white naked skull, with its eyeless sockets; the long fleshless limbs; the open, serrated ribs; the long jointed fingers of death itself!

As my bewildered brain took in these objects, I heard a noise in the bushes, as of persons engaged in an angry struggle.

"Emile! Emile!" cried a female voice, "you shall not murder him—you shall not!"

"Off! off! Marie, let me go!" was shouted in the rough accents of a man.

"Oh, no!" continued the female, "you shall not—no—no—no!"

"Curses on the woman! there! let me go now!"

There was a sound as of some one struck with violence—a scream; and, at the same moment, a human figure rushed out of the bushes, and, confronting me, exclaimed:

"Ha! Monsieur le Capitaine! coup pour coup!"

I heard no more; a heavy blow descending upon my temples, deprived me of all power and I fell senseless to the earth.   .   .   .   .   .

When I returned to consciousness, the first objects I saw were the huge brown whiskers of Lincoln; then Lincoln himself—then the pale face of the boy Jack; and finally, the forms of several soldiers of my company. I saw that I was in my own tent, and stretched upon my camp-bed.

"What? how? what's the matter?—what's this?" I said, raising my hands to the bandage of wet linen that bound my temples.

"Keep still, Cap'n!" said Bob, taking my hand from the fillet, and placing it by my side.

"Och! by my sowl, he's over it; thank the Lord for his goodness!" said Chane, an Irish soldier.

"Over what? what has happened to me?" I inquired.

"Och, Captin, yer honnor, you've been nearly murthered, and all by thim Frinch schoundrels; bad luck to their dirty frog-atin piethers!"

"Murdered! French scoundrels! Bob, what is it?"

"Why, yer see, Cap'n, ye've had a cut yeer over the head; and we think it's them Frenchmen."

"Oh! I remember now; a blow—but the death?—the death?"

I started up from the bed, as the phantom of my night adventure returned to my imagination.

"The death, Cap'n?—what do yer mean?" inquired Lincoln, holding me in his strong arms.

"Oh! the Cap'n manes the skilleton, may be," said Chane.

"What skeleton?" I demanded.

"Why, an owld skilleton'* the boys found in the chapparil, yer honner. They hung it to a three; and we found yer honner there, with the skilleton swinging over yez like a sign. Och! the Frinch bastes!"

I made no further inquiries about the "death."

"But where are the Frenchmen?" asked I, after a moment.

"Clane gone, yer honner," replied Chane.

"Gone?"

"Yes, Cap'n; thet's so as he sez it," answered Lincoln.

"Gone!—what do you mean?" I inquired.

"Desarted, Cap'n."

"How do you know that?"

"Because the yaint here."

"On the island?"

"Sarched it all, every bush."

'But who? which of the French?"

---

* Lobos was a noted resort of the West Indian pirates. Many *souvenirs* of these gentry were found upon the island: a human skeleton, also; but whether some victim of the freebooters, or not, is left to the speculations of the curious

' Dubrosc and that ere boy that was always with him ; both desarted."

' Ay, and the devil go wid them! He'll niver hive his own till he gets a hoult ov Misther Dubrosc ; bad 'cess to him!"

"You are sure they are missing ?"

"Looked high and low, Cap'n. Gravenitz seed Dubrosc steal into the chapparil with his musket. Shortly afterwards we heern a shot ; but thought nothin' of it till this mornin', when one of the sodgers foun' a Spanish sombrary out thar ; and Nath heern some'dy say the shot passed through Major Twing's markey. Besides, we foun' this yeer butcher-knife where yer was layin'."

Lincoln here held up a species of Mexican sword called a *machete*.*

"Ha!—well ?"

"That's all, Cap'n ; only it's my belief, there was Mexikins on this island, and them Frenchmen's gone with them."

After Lincoln left me, I lay musing on this still somewhat mysterious affair. My memory, however, gradually grew clearer; and the events of the preceding night. soon became linked together, and formed a complete chain. The shot that passed so near my head in Twing's tent—the boat—the French words I had heard before I received the blow—and the exclamation, " coup pour coup !" all convinced me, that Lincoln's conjectures were right.

Dubrosc had fired the shot, and struck the blow that had left me senseless.

But who could the woman be, whose voice I had heard pleading in my behalf ?

My thoughts reverted to the boy, who had gone off with Dubrosc; and whom I had observed often in the company of the latter. A strange attachment appeared to exist between them ; in which the boy seemed to be the devoted slave of the strong fierce Frenchman—Could this be a woman ?

I recollected having been struck with his delicate features, the softness of his voice and the smallness of his hands. There were other points besides, in the *tournure* of the boy's figure, that had appeared singular to me. I had frequently observed the eyes of this lad bent upon me, when Dubrosc was not present, with a strange and unaccountable expression !

Many other peculiarities connected with the boy and Dubrosc, which at the time had passed unnoticed and unheeded, now presented themselves to my recollection, all tending to prove the identity of the boy with the woman whose voice I had heard in the thicket.

* The *Machete* is a half-sword—half-knife.

I could not help smiling at the night's adventures; determined, however, to conceal that part which related to the skeleton.

In a few days, my strength was restored. The cut I had received was not deep, thanks to my forage cap, and the dullness of the Frenchman's weapon.

CHAPTER VII.

THE LANDING AT SACRIFICIOS.

EARLY in the month of March, the troops at Lobos were re-embarked, and dropped down to the roadstead of Anton Lizardo.* The American fleet was already at anchor there, and in a few days above a hundred sail had joined it. There is no city, no village, hardly a habitation upon this half-desert coast. The aspect is a series of hirsute hills, rendered picturesque by the plumed frondage of the palm tree.

We dared not go ashore, although the smooth, white beach, tempted us strongly. A large body of the enemy was encamped behind the adjacent hills; and patrols could be seen, at intervals, gallopping along the shore.

I could not help fancying what must have been the feeling of the inhabitants in regard to our ships—a strange sight upon this desert coast, and not a pleasing one to them, knowing that within those dark hulls were concealed the hosts of their armed invaders. Laocoon looked not with more dread upon the huge ribs of the Danaic horse, than did the simple peasant of Anahuac upon this fleet of "oak Leviathans," that lay within so short a distance of his shores.

To us the scene possessed an interest of a far different character. We looked proudly upon these magnificent models of naval architecture—upon their size, their number and their admirable adaptation. We viewed with a changing cheek, and a kindling eye this noble exhibition of a free people's strength; and as the broad banner of our country swung out upon the breeze of the

---

* An anchorage thirteen miles from Vera Cruz, down the coast.

tropics, we could not help exulting in the glory of that great nation whose uniform we wore around our bodies.

It was no dream. We saw the burnished gun and the bright epaulette—the gleaming button, and the glancing bayonet. We heard the startling trumpet, the stirring drum, and the shrill and thrilling fife; and our souls drank in all those glorious sights and sounds that form at once the spirit and the witchery of war!

The landing was to take place on the 9th; and the point of debarkation fixed upon was the beach opposite the island of Sacrificios, just out of range of the guns of Vera Cruz.

The 9th of March rose like a dream, bright, balmy, and beautiful. The sea was scarce stirred by the gentlest breeze of the tropics; but this breeze, light as it was, blew directly in our favor.

At an early hour, I observed a strange movement among the ships composing the fleet. Signals were changing in quick succession; and boats gliding rapidly to and fro.

Before daybreak the huge surf-boats had been drawn down from their moorings; and with long hempen hawsers attached to the ships and steamers.

The descent was about to be made. The ominous cloud which had hung dark and threatening over the shores of Mexico was about to burst upon that devoted land! But where? The enemy could not tell, and were preparing to receive us on the adjacent shore!

The black cylinder began to smoke, and the murky cloud rolled down upon the water, half obscuring the fleet. Here and there a broad sail, freshly unfurled, hung stiffly from the yard; the canvass escaping from its gasket fastenings, had not yet been braced round to the breeze.

Soldiers were seen standing along the decks; some in full equipments, clutching the bright barrels of their muskets—while others were buckling on their white belts, or cramming their cartouche boxes.

Officers, in sash and sword, paced the polished quarter-decks, or talked earnestly in groups, or watched, with eager eyes, the motions of the various ships.

Unusual sounds were heard on all sides. The deep-toned chorus of the sailor—the creaking of the capstan, and the clanking of the iron cogs—the "heave-ho," at the windlass, and the grating of the huge anchor-chain, as link after link rasped through the rusty ring—sounds that warned us to make ready for a change.

In the midst of these came the brisk rolling of a drum. It was answered by another, and another, and still another, until all voices were drowned by the deafening noise. Then followed the mingling shouts of command—a rushing over the decks—and streams of blue-clad men poured down the dark sides, and seated themselves in the surf-boats. These were filled in a twinkling, and all was silent as before. Every voice was hushed in expectation, and every eye bent upon the little black steamer, which carried the commander-in-chief.

Suddenly a cloud of smoke rose up from her quarter; a sheet of flame shot out horizontally; and the report of a heavy gun shook the atmosphere like an earthquake. Before its echoes had subsided, a deafening cheer ran simultaneously through the fleet; and the ships, all together, as if impelled by some hidden and supernatural power, broke from their moorings, and dashed through the water with the velocity of the wind! Away to the north-west, in an exciting race; away for the isle of Sacrificios!

On struggled the ships, bending to the breeze, and cleaving the crystal waves with their bold bows; on the steamers, beating the blue water into a milky-way, and dragging laden boats in their foamy track! On followed the boats through the hissing and frothy cauldron! Loud rolled the drum, loud brayed the bugle, and loud huzzas echoed from the adjacent shores!

Already the foe was alarmed and alert. Light horsemen with streaming haste gallopped up the coast. Lancers, with gay trappings and long pennons, appeared through the openings of the hills. Foaming, prancing steeds flew, with light artillery over the naked ridges, dashing madly down deep defiles and crushing the cactus with their whirling wheels. "Andela! Andela!"* was their cry. In vain, they urged their horses—in vain, they drove the spur deep and bloody in their smoking sides. The elements were against them, and in favor of their foes.

The earth and the water were their impediments, while the air and the water were the allies of their enemies. *They* clung and sweltered through the hot and yielding sand, or sank in the marshy borders of the Mandinga and the Medellin, while steam and the wind drove the ships of their adversaries like arrows through the water!

The alarm spread up the coast. Bugles were sounding, and horsemen gallopped through the streets of Vera Cruz. The alarm-drum beat in the plazza, and the long roll echoed in every *cuartel!*

Signal rockets shot up from San Juan, and were answered by others from Santiago and Concepcion!

Thousands of dark forms clustered upon the roofs of the city and the ram

---

* A charging shout, synonymous with our "Forward!"

parts of the castle; and thousands of pale lips whispered in accents of terror. "They come! they come!"

As yet they knew not how the attack was to be made, or where to look for the descent.

They imagined that we we were about to bombard their proud fortress of San Juan; and expected soon to see the ships of these rash invaders shattered and sunk before its walls.

The fleet was almost within long range—the black buoyant hulls bounding fearlessly over the water. The eager crowd thickened upon the walls. The artillerists of Santiago had gathered around their guns, silent and waiting orders. Already the burning fuse was sending forth its sulphurous smell, and the dry powder lay tempting on the touch, when a quick, sharp cry was heard along the walls and battlements—a cry of mingled rage, disappointment, and dismay!

The foremost ship had swerved suddenly from the track; and bearing sharply to the left, under the *manège* of a skilful helmsman, was running down under the shelter of Sacrificios!

The next ship followed her guide, and the next, and the next; and, before the astonished multitude recovered from their surprise, the whole fleet had come to, within pistol-shot of the island!

The enemy now, for the first time, perceived the *ruse*, and began to calculate its results. Those giant ships, that but a moment ago seemed rushing to destruction, had rounded to at a safe distance, and were preparing, with the speed and skilfulness of a perfect discipline, to pour a hostile host upon the defenceless shores. In vain the cavalry-bugle called their horseman to the saddle; in vain the artillery-car rattled along the streets; both would be too late!

Meanwhile, the ships let fall their anchors with a plunge, and a rasping, and a rattle. The sails came down upon the yards; and sailors swung themselves into the great boats, and mixed with the soldiers, and seized the oars.

Then the blades were suddenly and simultaneously dropped on the surface of the wave—a naval officer in each boat, directing the movements of the oarsmen.

And the boats pulled out nearer the shore; and, by an *échellon* movement took their places in line.

Light ships of war were thrown upon our flanks, to cover the descent by a cross fire. No enemy had yet appeared, and all eyes were turned landward with fiery expectation. Bounding hearts waited impatiently for the signal.

The report of a single gun was at length heard from the ship of the commander-in-chief; and, as if by one impulse, a thousand oars struck the water and flung up the spray upon their broad blades. A hundred boats leaped forward simultaneously, The powerful stroke was repeated, and propelled them with lightning speed. Now was the exciting race—the regatta of war! The Dardan rowers would have been distanced here.

On. on! with the velocity of the wind, over the blue waves, through the snowy surf—on!

And now we neared the shore, and officers sprang to their feet, and stood with their swords drawn; and soldiers half state, half crouched, clutching their muskets. And the keels gritted upon the gravelly bed; and, at the signal, a thousand men, in one plunge, flung themselves into the water, and dashed wildly through the surf! Thousands followed, holding their cartridges breast-high; and blades were glancing, and bayonets gleaming, and banners waving; and, under glancing blades, and gleaming bayonets and waving banners, the dark mass rushed high upon the beach!

Then arose a cheer—loud, long, and exulting. It pealed along the whole line, uttered from five thousand throats, and answered by twice that number from the anchored ships. It echoed along the shores, and back from the distant battlements.

A color-sergeant, springing forward, rushed up the steep sides of a sandhill, and planted his flag upon its snowy ridge.

As the well-known banner swung out upon the breeze, another cheer, wild and thrilling, ran along the line; a hundred answering flags were hauled up through the fleet; the ships of war saluted with full broadsides, and the guns of San Juan, now for the first time waking from their lethargic silence, poured forth their loudest thunder!

The sun was just setting, as our column commenced its advance inward. After winding, for a short distance, through the defiles of the hills, we halted for the night—our left wing resting upon the beach.

The soldiers bivouacked without tents—sleeping upon their arms, with the soft sand for their couch, and a cartridge-box for their pillow

I had brought with me a light rifle. It was but the work of a moment to unsling and level it. The sharp crack followed, and the ball impinged harmlessly between the monster's eyes, glancing from its hard skull as though it had been a plate of steel. The shot was an idle one—perhaps worse—for, stung to madness with the stunning shock, the reptile sprang far out into the water, and made directly for his victims.—Page 51.

CHAPTER VIII.

THE INVESTMENT OF VERA CRUZ.

At break of day on the 10th, the army took up its line of march, through hills of sand-drift. Division lapped upon division, regiment upon regiment, extending the circle of investment by an irregular échellon. Foot-rifles and light infantry drove the enemy from ridge to ridge, and through the dark mazes of the chapparal gorge. The column continued its tortuous track, winding through deep defiles, and over hot white hills, like a bristling snake. It moved within range of the guns of the city, screened by intervening heights. Now and then, the loud cannon of Santiago opened upon it, as some regiment displayed, crossing a defile, or pushing over the spur of a sand-hill. The constant rattling of rifles and musketry told that our skirmishers were busy in the advance. The Arsenal was carried, by a brilliant charge, and the American flag waved over the ruins of the convent Malibran. On the 11th, the Orizava road was crossed, and the light troops of the enemy were brushed from the neighboring hills. They retired sullenly under shelter of their heavy guns, and within the walls of the city.

On the morning of the 12th, the investment was complete. Vera Cruz lay within a semi-circle, around its centre. The circumference was a chain of hostile regiments that embraced the city in their concave arc. The right of the chain pitched its tents opposite the isle Sacrificios; while, five miles off, to the north, its left rested upon the hamlet, Vergara. The sea covered the complement of this circle, guarded by a fleet of dark and warlike ships.

The diameter hourly grew shorter. The lines of circumvallation lapped closer and closer, around the devoted city, until the American pickets appeared along the ridges of the nearest hills, and within range of the guns of Santiago Concepcion, and Ulloa.

Fort Concepcion defends the city on the north, Santiago on the south. The celebrated castle of San Juan de Ulloa stands out in the water at half-a-mile's distance from the *mole*.

A smooth sand-plain, only a mile in width, lay between the besiegers and the walls of the besieged.

After tatoo-beat, on the night of the 12th, with a party of my brother officers, I ascended the high hill around which winds the road leading to Orizava.

This hill overlooks the city of Vera Cruz.

Vera Cruz stands on the beach, on a smooth table of sand that runs back for nearly a mile, where it ends in high ridges of drift sand. The plain itself is perfectly naked, and often, during high tides, and "northers," the city becomes nearly insulated with the overflow of the sea.

The back coun ry, for miles inland, is a continuation of sandy spurs and ridges, more or less covered with chapparal. There are but few "settlements." — Here and there the "rancho" of a peasant or herdsman, and occasionally a "hacienda," or a small hamlet. It is thus up to the mountains, with some exceptions, as around Jalapa, or in the tobacco country of Cordova and Orizava.

After dragging ourselves wearily through the soft yielding sand, we reached the summit, and halted on a projecting ridge.

With the exception of a variety of exclamations expressing surprise and delight, not a word for a while was uttered by any of our party; each individual being wrapped up in the contemplation of a scene of surpassing interest. It was moonlight, and sufficiently clear to distinguish the minutest objects on the picture, that lay rolled out before us like a map.

Below our position, and seeming almost within reach of the hand, lay the "City of the True Cross," rising out of the white plain, and outlined upon the blue background of the sea.

The dark grey towers, and painted domes; the gothic turret, and Moorish minaret, impressed us with an idea of the antique; while here and there the tamarind nourished on some *azotea*,* or the fringed leaves of the palm-tree, drooping over the notched parapet, lent to the city an aspect at once southern and picturesque.

Domes, spires and cupolas rose over the old grey walls, crowned with

---

* The name given to the flat roofs of Spanish houses.

floating banners—the consular flags of France, and Spain, and Britain, waving alongside the eagle of the Aztecs.

Beyond, the blue waters of the gulf rippled lightly against the sea-washed battlements of San Juan, whose brilliant lights glistened along the combing of the surf.

To the south, we could distinguish the isles of Sacrificios, and the dark hulls that slept silently under the shelter of its coral reef.

Outside the fortified wall, which girt the city with its cincture of grey rock a smooth plain stretched rearward to the foot of the hill, on which we stood and right and left, along the crest of the ridge from Punta Hornos to Vergara, ranged a line of dark forms—the picket sentries of the American out-posts as they stood, knee-deep, in the soft yielding sand-drift.

[The view of Vera Cruz from the sand-ridges in the rear, is indeed, a picture of surpassing interest. The city looks as if it had been built to make a picture—so fine is the arrangement of its turrets and roofs, tied into a compact body by the wall that girdles it. It reminds one of the engravings we used to dream over, in Goldsmith's epitome of geography.

It was a picture of surpassing interest, and, as we stood gazing upon it, the moon suddenly disappeared behind a bank of clouds; and the lamps of the city, heretofore eclipsed by her brighter beam, now burned up and glistened along the walls.

Bells rung merrily from church-towers; and bugles sounded through the echoing streets. At intervals, we could hear the shrill cries of the guard. '*Centinela alerte!*" and the sharp challenge "*Quien viva?*"

Then the sound of sweet music, mingled with the soft voices of women, was wafted to our ears, and with beating hearts, we fancied we could hear the light tread of silken feet, as they brushed over the polished floor of the ball-room!

It was a tantalizing moment, and wistful glances were cast on the beleaguered town; while more than one of our party was heard impatiently muttering a wish, that it might be carried by assault.

As we continued gazing, a bright jet of flame shot out horizontally from the parapet over Puerto Nuevo.

"Look out!" cried Twing, at the same instant flinging his wiry little carcass squat under the brow of a sand-wreath.

Several of the party followed his example; but, before all had housed themselves, a shot came singing past, along with the loud report of a twenty-four.

The shot struck the comb of the ridge, within several yards of the group, and ricochetted off into the distant hills.

"Try it again!" cried one.

"That fellow has lost a champagne supper!" said Twing.

"More likely he has had it, or his aim would be more steady," suggested an officer.

"Oysters, too—only think of it!" said Clayley.

"Howld your tongue, Clayley, or by my sowl, I'll charge down upon the town!"

This came from Hennessy, upon whose imagination the contrast between champagne and oysters, and the gritty pork and biscuit he had been feeding upon for several days past, acted like a shock.

"There again!" cried Twing, whose quick eye caught the blaze upon the parapet.

"A shell, by the powers!" exclaimed Hennessy. "Let it dhrop first, or it may dhrop on yez!" he continued, as several officers were about to fling themselves on their faces.

The bomb shot up with a hissing, hurtling sound. A little spark could be seen, as it traced its graceful curves through the dark heavens.

The report echoed from the walls, and at the same instant was heard a dull sound, as the shell buried itself in the sand-drift.

It fell close to one of the picket sentinels, who was standing upon his post within a few paces of the group. The man appeared to be either asleep or stupefied, as he remained stock still. Perhaps he had mistaken it for the ricochet of a round shot.

"It's big shooting for them to hit the hill!" exclaimed a young officer.

The words were scarce passed, when a loud crash, like the bursting of a cannon, was heard under our feet—the ground opened like an earthquake; and, amidst the whistling of the fragments, the sand was dashed into our faces!

A cloud of dust hung for a moment above the spot.

The moon, at this instant, re-appeared; and, as the dust slowly settled away, the mutilated body of the soldier was seen upon the brow of the hill, at the distance of twenty paces from his post

A low cheer reached us from Concepcion—the fort whence the shell had been projected.

Chagrined at the occurrence, and mortified that it had been caused by our imprudence, we were turning to leave the hill, when the "whish" of a rocket attracted our attention

It rose from the chapparal, about a quarter of a mile in rear of the camp; and, before it had reached its culminating point, an answering signal shot up from the Puerto Nuevo.

At the same instant, a horseman dashed out of the thicket and headed his horse at the steep sand-hills. After three or four desperate plunges, the fiery mustang gained the crest of the ridge upon which lay the remains of the dead soldier.

Here the rider, seeing our party, suddenly reined up, balancing for a moment, as if uncertain whether to advance or retreat.

We, on the other hand, taking him for some officer of our own, and wondering who it could be galloping about at such an hour, stood silent and waiting.

"By heavens, that's a Mexican!" whispered Twing, as the ranchero dress became apparent under a brighter beam of the moon.

Before any one could reply, the strange horseman wheeled sharply to the left, and, drawing a pistol, fired into our midst. Then spurring his wild horse, he gallopped off into a deep defile of the hills!

"You're a set of Yankee fools!" he shouted back, as he reached the bottom of the dell.

Half-a-dozen shots replied to the taunting speech; but the retreating object was beyond pistol range, before our astonished party had recovered from their surprise at such an act of daring audacity!

In a few minutes we could see the horseman—a speck on the white plain below—and shortly after we heard the grating hinges of the Puerto Nuevo, as the huge gate swung open to receive him. No one was hit by the shot of his pistol. Several could be heard gritting their teeth with mortification, as we commenced descending the hill.

Did you know that voice Captain?" whispered Clayley to me, as we returned to camp.

"Yes."

"You think it was--?"

"Dubrosc."

CHAPTER XI.

MAJOR BLOSSOM.

On reaching the camp, I found a mounzed orderly in front of my tent.
"From the General," said the soldier, touching his cap, and handing me sealed note.
The orderly, without waiting a reply, leaped into his saddle and rode off.
I broke the seal, and read with delight:

"SIR—You will report with fifty men, to Major Blossom at 4 A. M. tomorrow. By order,
(Signed) A. A. A. G."
CAPTAIN HALLER, Commanding Co. Rifle Rangers.

"Old Blos, eh? quarter-master scouting I hope," said Clayley, looking over the contents of the note.
"Anything but the trenches; I am sick of them."
"Had it been anybody else but Blossom—fighting Daniels for instance—we might have reckoned on a comfortable bit of duty; but the old whale can hardly climb into his saddle—it *does* look bad."
I will not remain long in doubt. Order the sergeant to warn the men for four."
I walked through the camp in search of Blossom's marquee, which I found n an arbutus grove, and out of range of the heaviest metal in Vera Cruz. The Major himself was seated in a large campeachy* chair, that had been ' bor-

---

* A chair of a peculiar fashion, with a concave seat made of raw-hide, or leather. They are to be found in Mexico in almost every respectable house

rowed" from some neighboring ranche, and perhaps it was never so well filled, as by its present occupant.

It would be useless to attempt an elaborate description of Major Blossom. That would require an entire chapter.

Perhaps the best that can be done to give the reader an idea of him, is to say, that he was a great, fat, red man, and known among his brother officers as the "swearing major." If any one in the army loved good living, it was Major Blossom, and if any one hated hard living, that man was Major George Blossom. He hated Mexicans, too, and mosquitoes, and scorpions, and snakes, and sand-flies, and all enemies to his rest and comfort; and the manner in which he swore at these natural foes, would have entitled him to a high commission in the celebrated army of Flanders.

Major Blossom was a quarter-master in more senses than one; as he occupied more quarters than any two men in the army, not excepting the General-in-chief; and, when many a braver and better officer was cut down to "twenty-five pounds of baggage" the private lumber of Major Blossom, including himself, occupied a string of wagons like a siege train.

As I entered the tent, he was seated at supper. The viands before him were in striking contrast to the food, upon which the army was then subsisting. There was no gravel gritting between the Major's teeth as he masticated mess-pork or mouldy biscuit. He found no *debris* of sand and small rocks at the bottom of his coffee-cup No; quite the contrary.

A dish of pickled salmon, a side of cold turkey, several plates of sliced tongue, with a fine Virginia ham, were the striking features of the Major's supper; while a handsome French coffee-urn, containing the essence of Mocha, simmered upon the table. Out of this the Major, from time to time, replenished his silver cup. A bottle of *eau-de-vie* that stood near his right hand, assisted him likewise in swallowing his ample ration.

"Major Blossom, I presume?" said I.

"My name," ejaculated the Major, between two swallows, so short and quick, that the phrase sounded like a monosyllable.

"I have received orders to report to you, sir."

"Ah! bad business! bad business!" exclaimed the Major qualifying the badness of the business with an energetic oath.

"How, sir?"

"Atrocious business—dangerous service—can't see why they sent *me*."

"I came, Major, to inquire the nature of the service, so that I may have my men in order for it."

"Horrid, dangerous service!"

"It is?"

"Infernal cut-throats, thousands of 'em in the bushes—bore a man through without as much as a wink! Those yellow monsters are worse than—" and again the swearing Major wound up with an exclamation not proper to be repeated."

"Can't see why they picked *me* out; there's Myers, and Wayne, and Wood not half my size, and that thin scare-the-crows, Allen—but no; the General wants *me* killed. Die soon enough in this infernal nest of centipedes without being shot in the chapparal! I wish the chapparal was—" and again the Major's unmentionable words came pouring forth in a volley.

I saw that it was useless to interrupt him until the first burst was over. From his frequent anathemas on the "bushes" and the "chapparal," I could gather that the service I was called upon to perform lay at some distance from the camp; but beyond this I could learn nothing, until the Major had sworn himself into a degree of composure, which, after some minutes, he accomplished. I then re-stated the object of my visit.

"We're going into the country for mules," replied the Major; "mules, indeed! Heaven knows there is'nt a mule within ten miles, unless with a yellow Mexican on his back! and such mules we don't want, not a bit of it. The volunteers—" and here came another of the Major's anathemas, "have scared everything to the mountains; not a stick of celery, nor an onion to be had, at any price."

"How long do you think we will be gone?" I inquired.

"Long? Only a day! If I stay over night in the chapparal, may a wolf eat me! Oh, no! If the mules don't turn up soon, somebody else may go fetch 'em, that's all!"

"I may ration, them, for one day?" said I.

"Two—two; your fellow 'll be hungry. Roberts, of the Rifles, who's been out in the country, tells me there isn't enough forage to feed a cat. So you'd better take two days' biscuit; I suppose we'll meet with beef enough on the hoof; though I'd rather have a rumpsteak out of the Philadelphia market than all the beef in Mexico. Hang their beef! it's as tough as tan leather."

"At four o'clock, then, Major, I'll be with you," said I, preparing to take my leave.

"Make it a little later, Captain; I get no sleep with these cursed gallinippers and things—but stay; how many men have you got?"

"In my company eighty; but my order is to take only fifty."

"There again! I told you so; want me killed, they want old Blos killed.

Fifty men, when a thousand of them leather-skinned devils have been seen, not ten miles off! Fifty men! great heavens; fifty men! There's an escort to take the chapparal with!"

"But they are fifty men worth a hundred, I promise you."

"And if they were worth five hundred, it wouldn't be enough; I tell you the chapparal's full—full as —" (a certain place of torment familiar to th Major's lips).

"We will have to proceed with the more caution," I rejoined.

"Caution!" and caution was summarily sentenced to the same regions. 'Bring all, every son of a gun, drummer and all!"

"But that, Major, would be contrary to the General's orders."

"Hang the General's orders! Obey some General's orders in this army, and you would do queer things. Bring them all, take my advice. I tell you, if you don't our lives may answer for it. Fifty men!"

I was about to depart, when the Major stopped me with a loud "hilloa!"

"Why," cried he, "I have lost my senses—your pardon, Captain. This unlucky thing has driven me crazy. They must pick upon *me!* What will you drink? Here's some good brandy—infernal good—sorry I can't say as much for the water."

I mixed a glass of brandy and water. The Major did the same, and, pledging each other, we bade "good night," and separated.

CHAPTER X.

GOING ON THE SCOUT.

BEFORE daybreak, a head appeared between the flaps of my tent. It was that of Sergeant Bob Lincoln.

"The men er under arms, Cap'n."

"Very well," cried I, leaping from my bed, and hastily buckling on my accoutrements. I looked forth. The moon was still brightly shining, and I could see a number of uniformed men standing upon the company parade, in double rank. directly in front of my tent, a small boy was saddling a very small horse. The boy was "Little Jack," as the soldiers called him; and the horse was Little Jack's mustang, "Twidget."

Jack wore a tight-fitting green jacket, trimmed with yellow lace, and buttoned up to the throat; pantaloons of light green, straight cut and striped along the seams; a forage cap set jauntily upon a profusion of bright curls; a sabre with a blade of eighteen inches, and a pair of clinking Mexican spurs. Besides these, he carried the smallest of all rifles. Thus armed and accoutred, he presented the appearance of a miniature ranger.

Twidget had his peculiarities. He was a tight, wiry, little animal, that could live upon mezquite beans, or maguey leaves, for an indefinite time; and his abstemiousness was often put to the test. On one occasion, during the battles in the valley of Mexico, Jack and Twidget had somehow got separated, at which time the mustang had been shut up for four days in the cellar of a ruined convent with no other food than stones and mortar! How Twidget came by his name is not clear. Perhaps it was some waif of the rider's own fancy.

As I appeared at the entrance of my tent, Jack had just finished strapping on his Mexican saddle, and seeing me he ran to assist in serving my breakfast. This was hastily despatched, and we took the route in silence through the sleeping camp. Shortly after, we were joined by the Major, mounted on a tall, raw-looking horse; while a darkie, whom the Major addressed as "Doc," rode a snug looking cob, and carried a basket. This last contained the Major's commissariat.

We came out on the Orizava Road, the Major and Jack riding in the advance. I could not help smiling at the contrast between these two equestrians; the former with his great gaunt horse, looming up in the uncertain light of the morning like some huge centaur; while Jack and Twidget appeared like two representatives of the kingdom of Lilliput!

On turning an angle of the forest, a horseman appeared at some distance along the road. The Major gradually slackened his pace, until he was square with the head of the column, and then fell back into the rear. This manœuvre was executed in the most natural manner, but I could plainly see that the mounted Mexican had caused the Major no small degree of alarm.

The horseman proved to be a *zambo** in pursuit of some cattle that had escaped from a neighboring corral. The zambo pointed to the south, saying, in Spanish, that mules were plenty in that direction.

"*Hay muchos, muchissimos!*" (there are many) said he, as he indicated a road which led through a strip of woods on our left.

Following his direction, I struck into the new path, which soon narrowed into a bridle road, or trail. The men were thrown into single file, and marched *à l'Indienne*. The road darkened, passing under thick-leaved trees that met and twined over our heads.

At times, the hanging limbs and joining parasites, caused the Major to flatten his huge body upon the horn of the saddle; and once or twice he was obliged to alight, and walk under the light branches of the thorny acacia.

Our journey continued without noise; silence being interrupted only by an occasional oath from the Major, uttered, however, in a low tone, as we were now fairly "in the woods." The road, at length, opened upon a small prairie or glade, near the borders of which rose a high "butte,"* covered with thickets of nopal.

* A cross of the negro and mestize. There are many of this race along the coast of the Tierra Caliente.

* Knoll.

Leaving my men in ambuscade below, I ascended the butte, to obtain a view of the surrounding country. The day had now fairly broke, and the sun was just rising over the blue waters of the gulf.

His rays, prinkling over the waves, caused them to dance and sparkle with a metallic brightness; and, it was only after shading my eyes, that I could distinguish the tall masts of ships and the burnished towers of the city.

To the south and west stretched a wide expanse of champaign country glowing in all the brilliance of tropical vegetation. Fields of green, and forests of darker green, here and there patches of yellow, and belts of olive-colored leaves; at intervals, a sheet of silver—the reflection from a placid lake, or the bend of some silent stream—was visible upon the imposing picture at my feet.

A broad belt of forest, dotted with the life-like frondage of the palm,† swept up to the foot of the hill. Beyond this lay an open tract of meadow, or prairie, upon which were browsing thousands of cattle. The distance was too great to distinguish their species, but the slender forms of some of them convinced me that the object of our search would be found in this direction.

The meadow, then, was the point to be reached.

The belt of forest already mentioned must be crossed; and, to effect this I struck into a trail, which seemed to lead in the direction of the meadow.

The trail became lighter as we entered the heavy timber. Some distance further on, we reached a stream. Here the trail entirely disappeared. No "signs" could be found on the opposite bank. The underwood was thick, and vines, with broad green leaves and huge clusters of scarlet flowers, barred up the path like a wall.

It was strange! the path had evidently led to this point, but where beyond? Several men were detached across the stream to find an opening. After a search of several minutes, a short exclamation from Lincoln proclaimed success. I crossed over, and found the hunter standing near the bank, holding back a huge screen of boughs and vine-leaves, beyond which a narrow, but plain track was easily distinguished, leading on into the forest. The trellis closed like a gate; and it seemed as if art had lent a hand to the concealment of the track. The foot-prints of several horses were plainly visible in the sandy bottom of the road. The men entered in single file. With some difficulty, Major Blossom and his great horse squeezed themselves under, and we moved on through the dark and silent woods.

† I have been struck with this peculiarity of the palm-tree. As it rises over the jungle, the regularity of its structure imparts the idea of something animated, or belonging to a kingdom of nature different from that of its forest companions.

After a march of several miles, fording numerous streams, and working our way through tangled thickets of nopal and wild maguey,* an opening suddenly appeared through the trees. Emerging from the forest, a brilliant scene burst upon us. A large clearing, evidently once cultivated, but now in a state of neglect, stretched out before us. Broad fields, covered with flowers of every hue—thickets of blooming rose-trees—belts of the yellow helianthus—an patches of half-wild plantains, formed a picture singular and beautiful.

On one side, and close to the border of the forest, could be seen the roof of a house, peering above groves of glistening trees, and thither we marched.

We entered a lane, with its *guardarayas*† of orange trees planted in rows upon each side, and meeting overhead.

The sunlight fell through this leafy screen with a mellowed and delicious softness, and the perfumes of a thousand flowers were wafted on the air.

The rich music of birds was around us; and the loveliness of the scene was heightened by the wild neglect which had stamped itself on every object.

On approaching the house we halted, and charging the men to remain silent, I advanced alone to reconnoitre.

* The maguey spoken of in these sketches is not the celebrated plant from which *pulque* is extracted, but a species of aloes (agave) that flourishes in the *tierra caliente*. The other—the pulque—is only found upon the uplands—the tierra templada—where it is extensively cultivated for the refreshing beverage which it produces. Its leaves are invariably of a dark, uniform green, while those of the wild species are mottled with a bright scarlet. These are, besides, more slender and thorny. The wild maguey produces a species of fiery whiskey—the *mezcal* of travellers.

† Lanes shaded with tropical trees, such as palms, caymetos, shaddocks, are so called by the Spanish-Americans

CHAPTER XI.

ADVENTURE WITH A CAYMAN.

The lane suddenly opened upon a pasture, but within this a thick hedge of jessamines, forming a circle, barred the view.

In this circle was the house, whose roof only could be seen from without.

Not finding any opening through the jessamines, I parted the leaves with my hand, and looked through. The picture was dream-like. So strange, I could scarce credit my senses. " Was it real ?"

On the crest of the little hillock stood a house of rare construction—unique and unlike any thing I had ever seen.

The sides were formed of bamboos, closely picketed, and laced together by strips of the palmilla. The roof—a thatch of palm-leaves—projected far over the eaves, rising to a cone, and terminating in a small wooden cupola, with a cross. There were no windows. The walls themselves were translucent; and articles of furniture could be distinguished through the interstices of the bamboos.

The houses of the *tierra calients* are frail structures, similar to the one described, though generally ruder. In the forests clothing the sides of mountains, you meet with the log cabin, somewhat resembling that of the United States. On the elevated plains, you come to the endless adobes, or sun-dried bricks. Cottages of this material are nothing better than mud-cabins, such as appear in various parts of Ireland and other countries.

A curtain of green barege, supported by a rod and rings, formed the door. This was drawn, discovering an ottoman near the entrance, and an elegant harp.

The whole structure presented the *coup d'œil* of a huge bird-cage, with its wires of gold!

The grounds were in keeping with the house. In these, the evidence of neglect, which had been noticed without, existed no longer. Every object appeared to be under the training of a watchful solicitude.

A thick grove of olives, with their gnarled and spreading branches, and ark green leaves, stretched rearward, forming a back-ground to the picture. Right and left grew clumps of orange and lime trees. Golden fruit and flowers of brilliant hues mingled with their yellow leaves. Spring and autumn blended upon the same branches!

Rare shrubs—exotics—grew out of large vessels of japanned earthenware whose brilliant tints added to the voluptuous coloring of the scene.

A *jet d'eau*, crystalline, rose to the height of twenty feet, and returning in a shower of prismatic globules, stole away through a bed of water-lilies and other aquatic plants, losing itself in a grove of lofty plaintain trees. These growing from the cool watery bed, flung out their broad glistening leaves to the length of twenty feet.

No signs of human life met the eye. The birds alone seemed to revel in the luxuriance of this tropical paradise.

A brace of peafowl stalked over the *parterre* in all the pride of their rainbow plumage.

In the fountain appeared the tall form of a flamingo: his scarlet plumage contrasting with the green leaves of the water-lily.

Songsters were trilling in every tree.

The mock-bird perched upon the highest limb, was mimicking the monotonous tones of the parrot. The grakle and gold-bird flashed from grove to grove, or balanced their bodies under the spray of the *jet d'eau;* while the humming-bird hung upon the leaves of some honeyed blossom, or prinkled over the parterre like a straying sunbeam!

I was running my eye over this dreamlike picture, in search of a human figure, when the soft metallic accents of a female voice reached me from the grove of plaintains. It was a burst of laughter—clear and ringing. Then followed another, with short exclamations and the sound of water, as if dashed and sprinkled with a light hand.

What must be the Eve of a Paradise like this? The silvery tones were full of promise. It was the first female voice that had greeted my ears for a month, and chords long slumbering vibrated under the exquisite touch.

My heart bounded. My first impulse was "forward," which I obeyed by springing through the jessamines. But the fear of intruding upon a scene á la Diane changed my determination and my next thought was to make a quiet retreat.

I was preparing to return, and had thrust one leg back through the hedge, when a harsh voice—apparently that of a man—mingled with the silvery tones.

"*Anda—anda—hace mucho calor. Vamos a volver.*" ("Hasten—it is hot. Let us return.")

"*Ah, no! Pepe; un ratito mas.*" ("Ah, no! Pepe; a little while longer.")

"*Vaya, carrambo!*" ("Quick, then!")

Again the clear laughter rang out, mingled with the clapping of hands, and short exclamations of delight.

"Come," thought I, once more entering the parterre, "as there appears to be one of my own sex here already, it cannot be very *mal-à-propos* to take a peep at this amusement, whatever it be."

I approached the row of plantain-trees, whose leaves screened the speakers from view.

"*Lupe! Lupe! mira! que bonito!*" ("Lupe, Lupe! look here! What a pretty thing!")

"*Ah, pobrecito! echalo, Luz, echalo!*" ("Ah! poor little thing! fling it back, Luz!")

"*Voy luego!*" ("Presently!")

I stooped down, and silently parted the broad silken leaves. The sight was divine!

Within lay a circular tank, or basin, of crystal water, several rods in diameter, and walled in on all sides by the high screen of glossy plantains, whose giant leaves stretching out horizontally, sheltered it from the rays of the noonday sun.

A low parapet of mason-work ran around, forming the circumference of the circle. This was japanned with a species of porcelain—whose deep coloring of blue, and green, and yellow, was displayed in a variety of grotesque figures.

A strong jet boiled up in the centre, by the refraction of whose ripples the gold and red fish seemed multiplied into myriads.

At a distant point a bed of water-lilies hung out from the parapet; and the long, thin neck of a swan rose gracefully over the leaves. Another, his mate, stood upon the bank, drying her snowy pinions in the sun.

A different object attracted me, depriving me, for awhile, of the power of action.

In the water, and near the jet, were two beautiful girls, clothed in a sort of sleeveless green tunic, loosely girdled. They were immersed to the waist. So pellucid was the water, that their little feet were distinctly visible at the bottom, shining like gold.

Luxuriant hair fell down in broad flakes, partially shrouding the snowy development of their arms and shoulders. Their forms were strikingly similiar. Tall, graceful, fully developed, and characterized by that elliptical line of beauty that in the female form, more than any other earthly object illustrates the far-famed curve of Hogarth.

Their features, too, were alike. " Sisters!" one would exclaim, and yet their complexions were strikingly dissimilar. The blood mantling darker in the veins of one, lent an olive tinge to the soft and wax-like surface of her skin; while the red upon her cheeks and lips presented an admixture of purple. Her hair, too, was black; and a dark shading along the upper lip, soft and silken as the tracery of a crayon, contrasted with the dazzling whiteness of her teeth. Her eyes were black, large, and almond-shaped—with that expression which looks over one; and her whole appearance formed a type of that beauty which we associate with the Abencerrage and the Alhambra. This was evidently the elder. The other was the type of a distinct class of beauty—the golden-haired blonde. Her eyes were large, globular, and blue as turquoise. Her hair of a chastened yellow, long and luxuriant; while her skin, less soft and waxen than that of her sister, presented an effusion of roseate blushes, that extended along the snowy whiteness of her arms. These, in the sun, appeared as bloodless and transparent as the tiny goldfish that quivered in her uplifted hand!

I was rivetted to the spot. My first impulse was to retire, silently and modestly, but the power of a strange fascination for a moment prevented me. Was it a dream?

"*Ah! que barbara! pobrecito—ito—ito!*" (Ah! what a barbarian you are! poor little thing!)

"*Comeremos.*" (We will eat it.)

"*Por dios! no! echalo, Luz, o tirare la agua en sus ojos de V.*" (Goodness! no! fling it in, Luz, or I will throw water in your eyes.) And the speaker stooped, as if to execute the threat.

"*Ya—no.*" (Now I will not,) said Luz, resolutely.

"*Guarda te!*" (Look out.)

The brunette placed her little hands close together, forming with their united palms a concave surface, and commenced dashing water upon the perverse blonde.

The latter instantly dropped the goldfish, and retaliated.

An exciting and animated contest ensued. The bright globules flew around their heads, and rolled down their glistening tresses, as from the pinions of a swan; while their clear laughter rang out at intervals, as one or the other appeared victorious.

A hoarse voice drew my attention from this interesting spectacle. Looking whence it came, my eye rested upon a huge negress, stretched under a cocoa tree, who had raised herself on one arm, and was laughing at the contest.

It was her voice, then, I had mistaken for that of a man!

Becoming sensible of my intrusive position, I turned to retreat, when a shrill cry reached me from the pond.

The swans, with a frightened energy, shrieked and flapped over the surface—the goldfish shot to and fro like sunbeams, and leaped out of the water quivering and terrified—and the birds on all sides screamed and chattered.

I sprang forward to ascertain the cause of this strange commotion. My eye fell upon the negress, who had risen, and running out upon the parapet with uplifted arms, shouted in terrified accents:

"*Valgame dios—niñas? El cayman! el cayman!*"

I looked across to the other side of the pond. A fearful object met my eyes—the cayman of Mexico! The hideous monster was slowly crawling over the low wall, dragging his lengthened body from a bed of aquatic plants.

Already his short fore-arms, squammy and corrugated, rested upon the inner edge of the parapet—his shoulders projecting as if in the act to spring! His scale-covered back, with its long serrated ridge, glittered with a slippery moistness; and his eyes, usually dull, gleamed fierce and lurid from their prominent sockets.

I had brought with me a light rifle. It was but the work of a moment to unsling and level it. The sharp crack followed, and the ball impinged harmlessly between the monster's eyes, glancing from its hard skull as though it had been a plate of steel. The shot was an idle one—perhaps worse—for, stung to madness with the stunning shock, the reptile sprang far out into the water, and made directly for his victims.

The girls, who had long since given over their mirthful contest, seemed to have lost all presence of mind, and, instead of making for the bank stood locked in each other's arms terrified and trembling.

Their symmetrical forms fell into an agonized embrace, and their rounded arms, olive and roseate, laced each other, and twined across their quivering bodies.

Their faces were turned to Haven, as though they expected succor from above—a group that rivalled the Laocoon! With a spring I cleared the parapet, and drawing my sword, dashed madly across the basin.

The girls were near the centre; but the cayman had got the start of me, and the water, three feet deep, impeded my progress. The bottom of the tank, too, was slippery, and I fell once or twice on my hands. I rose again, and with frantic energy plunged forward—all the while calling upon the bathers to make for the parapet.

Notwithstanding my shouts, the terrified girls made no effort to save themselves. They were incapable from terror.

On came the cayman with the velocity of vengeance. It was a fearful moment. Already, at the distance of less than six paces from his prey, his long snout projected from the water, his gaunt jaws displaying their quadruple rows of sharp glistening teeth.

I shouted despairingly. I was baffled by the deep water. I had nearly twice the distance before I could interpose myself between the monster and his victims.

"I shall be too late?"

Suddenly I saw that the cayman had swerved. In his eagerness he had struck a subaqueous pipe of the jet!

It delayed him only a moment, but in that moment I had passed the statue-like group, and stood ready to receive his attack.

"*A la orilla—a la orilla!*" To the bank, to the bank!) I shouted, pushing the terrified girls with one hand, while with the other I held my sword at arm's length in the face of the advancing reptile.

The girls now, for the first time, awaking from their lethargy of terror, rushed toward the bank.

On came the monster, gnashing his teeth in the fury of disappointment, and uttering fearful human-like cries.

As soon as he had got within reach, I aimed a blow at his head; but the light sabre glinted from the fleshless skull with the ringing of steel to steel.

The blow, however, turned him out of his course, and, missing his aim, he passed me like an arrow. I looked around with a feeling of despair. "Thank Heaven, they are safe!"

I felt the clammy scales rub against my thigh; and I leaped aside to avoid the stroke of his tail, as it lashed the water into foam.

Again the monster turned, and came on as before.

This time I did not attempt to cut, but thrust the sabre directly for his throat.

The cold blade snapped between his teeth, like an icicle!

Not above twelve inches remained with the hilt; and with this I hacked and fought with the energy of despair

My situation had now grown critical indeed. The girls had reached the bank, and stood screaming upon the parapet.

At length, the elder seized upon a pole, and, lifting it with all her might, leaped back into the basin, and was hastening to my rescue, when a stream of fire was poured through the leaves of the plantains—a sharp crack—the short humming whiz of a bullet; and a large form, followed by half a dozen others, emerged from the grove, and, rushing over the wall, plunged into the pond.

A loud plashing in the water—the shouts of men—the clashing of bayonets—and the reptile rolled over, pierced by a dozen wounds!

CHAPTER XII.

DON COSME ROSALES.

"YER safe Cap'n." It was Lincoln's voice. Around me stood a dozen of the men, up to their waists. Little Jack, too, (his head and forage cap just appearing over the surface of the water) stood with his eighteen inches of steel buried in the carcass of the dead reptile! I could not help smiling at the ludicrous picture.

"Yes, safe," answered I, panting for breath, "safe—you came in good time though."

"We heern yer shot, Cap'n," said Lincoln, "an we guessed yer didn't shoot 'ithout a somethin ter shoot for; so I tuk a half a dozen files, and kim up."

"You acted right, Sergeant; but where—?"

I was looking toward the edge of the tank, where I had last seen the girls. They had disappeared.

"If yez mane the faymales," answered Chane, "they're *vamosed* through the threes. Be Saint Patrick, the black one's a thrump, any how! She looks for all the world like them bewtiful crayoles of Dimmerary."

Saying this, he turned suddenly round, and commenced driving his bayonet furiously into the dead cayman, exclaiming between the thrusts.

"Och! ye divil! bad luck to yer ugly carcase! You're a nate looking aste, to interfere with a pair of illigent craythers! By the crass! he's all shill, boys! Oh! mother o' Moses, I can't find a saft spot in him!"

We climbed out upon the parapet, and the soldiers commenced wiping their wet guns.

Clayley appeared at this moment, filing round the pond, at the head of the detachment.

As I explained the adventure to the lieutenant, he laughed heartily.

"By Jove! it will never do for a despatch!" said he; "one killed on the side of the enemy, and on ours not a wound. There is one, however, who may be reported 'badly scared.'"

"Who?" I asked.

"Why, who but the bold Blossom!"

"But where is he?"

"Heaven only knows! The last I saw of him, he was screening himself behind an old ruin. I wouldn't think it strange if he was off to camp,—that is, if he believes he can find his way back again!"

As Clayley said this, he burst into a loud yell of laughter.

It was with difficulty I could restrain myself, for, looking in the same direction indicated by the lieutenant, I saw a bright object, which I at once recognised as the Major's face.

He had drawn aside the broad plantain-leaves, and was peering cautiously through, with a look of the most ludicrous terror. His face only was visible, round and luminous, like the full moon; and like her, too, variegated with light and shade,—for fear had produced spots of white and purple over the surface of his capacious cheeks.

As soon as the Major saw how the "land lay," he came blowing and blustering through the bushes like an elephant; and it now became apparent that he carried his long sabre drawn and flourishing!

"Bad luck after all!" said he, as he marched round the pond with a bold stride; "that's all? Bah! in hopes we'd have a brush with the yellow fellows."

"No, Major," said I, trying to look serious; "we are not so fortunate."

"I have no doubt, however," said Clayley, with a malicious wink, "but that we'll have them here in a squirrel's jump. They must have heard the report of our guns."

A complete change became visible in the major's bearing. The point of his sabre dropped slowly to the ground, and the blue and white spots began to array themselves afresh on his huge red cheeks.

"Don't you think, captain," said he, "we've gone far enough into the curs'd country? There's no mules in it,—I can certify there's not—not a single mule."

Before I could reply, an object appeared that drew our attention, and heightened the mosaic upon the Major's cheeks.

A man, strangely attired, was seen running down the slope towards the spot where we were standing.

"Guerillas, by Jove!" exclaimed Clayley, in a voice of feigned terror; and he pointed to the scarlet sash, which was twisted round the man's waist.

The Major looked round for some object, where he might shelter himself in case of a skirmish. He was sidling behind a high point of the parapet, when the stranger rushed forward, and, throwing both arms about his neck, poured forth a perfect cataract of Spanish, in which the word *gracias* was of frequent occurence.

"What does the man mean with his grashes?" exclaimed the Major, struggling to free himself from the Mexican.

But the latter did not hear him, for his eye at that moment rested upon my dripping habiliments; and, dropping the Major, he transferred his embrace and *gracias* to me.

Señor Capitan,', he said, still speaking in Spanish, and hugging me like a bear, "accept my thanks. Ah sir! you have saved my children; how can I show you my gratitude?"

Here followed a multitude of those complimentary expressions, peculiar to the language of Cervantes, which ended by his offering me his house, and all it contained.

I bowed in acknowledgement of his courtesy, apologising for being so ill prepared to receive his "hug" as I observed that my saturated vestments had wet the old fellow to the skin.

I had now time to examine the stranger, who was a tall, thin, sallow old gentleman, with a face at once Spanish and intelligent. His hair was white and short, while a moustache, somewhat grizzled, shaded his fine lips. Jet black brows projected over a pair of keen and sparkling eyes. His dress was a round-about of the finest white linen, with vest and pantaloons of the same material—the latter fastened round the waist by a scarf of bright red silk. Shoes of green morocco covered his small feet; while a broad Guyaquil hat shaded his face from the sun.

Though his costume was trans-Atlantic—speaking in reference to Old Spain—there was that in his air and manner that bespoke him a hidalgo.

After a moment's observation, I proceeded, in my best Spanish, to express my regret for the fright which the young ladies—his daughters, I presumed—had suffered.

The Mexican looked at me with a slight appearance of surprise.

"Why, Señor Capitan," said he, "your accent—you are a foreigner?"

"A foreigner! To Mexico did you mean?"

"Yes Señor. Is it not so?"

"Oh! of course!" answered I, smiling, and somewhat puzzled in turn.

"And how long have you been in the army Señor Capitan?"

"But a short time."

"How do you like Mexico, Señor?"

"I have seen but little of it as yet."

"Why, how long have you been in the country then?"

"Three days," answered I, "we landed on the 9th."

"Por dios! three days, and in the army already!" muttered the Spaniard, throwing up his eyes in unaffected surprise.

I began to think I was interrogated by a lunatic.

"May I ask what countryman you are?" continued the old gentleman.

"What countryman? An American, of course."

"An American."

"*Un Americano*," repeated I; for we were conversing in Spanish.

"*Y son esos Americanos?*" (and are these Americans?) quickly demanded my new acquaintance.

"*Si, Señor*," replied I.

"*Carrambo!*" shouted the Spaniard, with a sudden leap, his eyes almost starting from their sockets.

"I should say, not exactly Americans," I added. "Many of them are Irish, and French, and Germans, and Swedes, and Swiss; yet, they are all Americans, now."

But the Mexican did not stay to hear my explanation. After recovering from the first shock of surprise, he had bounded through the grove; and, with a wave of his hand, and the ejaculation, "*esparte!*" disappeared among the plantains. The men, who had gathered around the lower end of the basin, burst out into a roar of laughter, which I did not attempt to repress. The look of terrified astonishment of the old Don had been too much for my own gravity; and I could not help being amused at the conversation that ensued among the soldiers. They were at some distance, yet I could overhear their remarks.

'That Mexikin's an unhospitable cuss!" muttered Lincoln, with an expression of contempt.

"He might av axed the Captain to dhrink, after havin such a pair of illigant craythers," said Chane.

"Sorra dhrap's in the house, Murt; the place looks dry."

"Och! an it's a beautiful cage, any how" returned the other, "and beautiful birds in it, too—it puts me in mind of ould Dimmerary ;* but there we had the liquor, the raal rum—oshins of it, allanna!"

"That ere chap's a greelye, I strongly 'spect," whispered one, a regular down-east Yankee.

"A what?" asked his companion.

"Why, a greelye—one o' them ere Mixikin robbers."

"Arrah, now! did yez see the rid sash?" inquired an Irishman.

"Thim's captin's," suggested the Yankee.

"He's a capten, or a kernel; I'll bet high on that."

"What did he say, Nath, as he was running off?"

"I don't know 'zactly—somethin that sounded mighty like 'spearin on us.'"

"He's a lanzeer then, by jingo."

He had better try on his speerin," said another; "there's shootin before spearin—mighty good ground, too, behind this hyar painted wall.

"The old fellow was mighty frindly at first; what got into him, any how?"

"Raoul says, he offered to give the Captain his house and all the furnishins."

"Oh, mother o' Moses! and thim illigant girls, too."

"Ov coorse."

"By my soul! an if I was the Captin, I'd take him at his word, and lave off fightin' intirely."

"It *is* delph," said a soldier, referring to the material of which the parapet was constructed.

"No, it aint."

"It's chaney, then."

"No, nor chaney, either."

"Well, what is it?"

"It's only a stone wall painted, you green-horn!"

"Stone-thunder! it's solid delph, I say."

"Try it with your bayonet, Jim."

"*Crick—crick—crick—crinell!*" and one of the men commenced breaking off the japanned work of the parapet with his bayonet.

"Stop that!" I shouted to the fellow.

"The captin don't want yez to destroy what'll be his own some day, when he marries one of thim young Dons. Here comes the ould one, and, by th powers! he's got a big paper; he's goin' to make over the property!"

* Chane had served in the British West Indies

Laughing, I looked around, and saw that the Don was returning sure enough. He hurried up, holding out a large sheet of parchment.

"Well, señor, what's this?" I inquired.

"*No soy Mexicano, soy Espagnol!*" (I am no Mexican, I am a Spaniard,) said he, with the expression of a true hidalgo.

Casting my eye carelessly over the document, I perceived that it was a safeguard from the Spanish Consul at Vera Cruz, certifying that the bearer, Don Cosme Rosales, was a native of Spain.

"Señor Rosales," said I, returning the paper, "this was not necessary. The interesting circumstances under which we have met should have secured you good treatment, even were you a Mexican, and we the barbarians we have been represented. We have come to make war not with peaceful citizens, but with a rabble soldiery."

"*Es verdad*—you are wet, señor? you are hungry?"

I could not deny but that I was both the one and the other.

"You need refreshment, gentlemen; will you come to my house?"

"Permit me, señor, to introduce to you Major Blossom—Lieutenant Clayley—Lieutenant Oakes: Don Cosme Rosales, gentlemen."

My friends and the Don bowed graciously. The Major had now recovered his complacency.

"*Vamonos caballeros!*" said the Don, starting towards the house.

"But your soldiers, capitan?" added he, stopping suddenly.

"They will remain here," I rejoined.

"Permit me to send them some dinner?"

"Oh! certainly," replied I, "use your own pleasure, Don Cosme but do not put your household to any inconvenience."

In a few minutes we found our way to the house, which was neither more nor less than the cage-looking structure already described.

CHAPTER XIII.

A MEXICAN DINNER.

"*Pasun a dentro, señores,*" said Don Cosme, drawing aside the curtain of the rancho, and beckoning us to enter.

"Ha!" exclaimed the Major, struck with the *coup d'œil* of the interior.

"Be seated, gentlemen—*ya vuelvo.*" (I will return in an instant.)

So saying, Don Cosme disappeared into a little porch in the back, partially screened from observation by a close network of cane.

"Very pretty, by Jove!" said Clayley, in a low voice.

"Pretty, indeed!" echoed the Major, with one of his customary asseverations.

"Stylish, one ought rather to say, to do it justice.

"Stylish!" again chimed in the Major, repeating his formula.

"Rosewood chairs and tables," continued Clayley; "a harp, guitar, piano, ottomans, carpets knee-deep—whew!"

Not thinking of the furniture, I looked around the room strangely bewildered.

"Ha! ha! what perplexes you, Captain?" asked Clayley.

"Nothing."

"Ah! the girls you spoke of—the nymphs of the pond; but where the deuce are they?"

"Ay, where?" I asked, with a strange sense of uneasiness.

"Girls! what girls?" inquired the Major, who had not yet learned the exact nature of our aquatic adventure.

Here the voice of Don Cosme was heard calling out:

"Pepe! Ramon! Francisca! bring dinner. *Anda, anda!*"

"Who on earth is the old fellow calling?" asked the Major with some concern in his manner. "I see no one."

Nor could we; so we rose up together, and approached that side of the building that looked rearward.

The house to all appearance, had but one apartment—the room in which we then were. The only point of this screened from observation was the little veranda into which Don Cosme had entered; but this was not large enough to contain the number of persons who might represent the names he had called upon!

Two smaller buildings stood under the olive-trees in the rear; but these, like the house were transparent, and not a human figure appeared within them! We could see through the trunks of the olives a clear distance of a hundred yards. Beyond this, the mezquite and the scarlet leaves of the wild maguey marked the boundary of the forest.

It was equally puzzling to us, whither the girls had gone, or whence "Pepe, Ramon, and Francisca," where to come!

The tinkling of a little bell startled us from our conje―― ―nd the voice of Don Cosme was heard inquiring:

"Have you any favorite dish, gentlemen?"

Some one answered, "No."

"Curse me!" exclaimed the Major, "I believe he can get anything ―― call for—raise it out of the ground by stamping his foot, or ringing ―― Didn't I tell you?"

This exclamation was uttered in consequence of the appearance of ―― of well-dressed servants—five or six in number—bringing waiters wi―― and decanters! They entered from the porch; but how did they ―― Certainly not from the woods without, else we should have seen th―― approached the cage.

The Major uttered a terrible invocation, adding in a hoarse whisper, "This must be the Mexican Aladdin!"

I confess I was not less puzzled than he. Meanwhile, the servants came and went, going empty, and returning loaded. In less than ten minutes, the table fairly cracked under the weight of a sumptuous dinner. This is no figure of speech. There were dishes of massive silver, with huge flagons of the same metal, and even cups of gold!

"*Señores vamos a comer*" (let us eat, gentlemen), said Don Cosme, poately motioning us to be seated. I fear that you will not be pleased with my cuisine:—it is purely Mexican, *estilo del pais*."

To say that the dinner was not a good one, would be to utter a falsehood, and contradict the statement of Major George Blossom, of the U. S. quartermaster's department, who afterwards declared that it was the best dinner he had ever eaten in his life.

Turtle soup first.

"Perhaps you would prefer *Julienne*, or *vermicelli*, gentlemen?" inquired the Don.

"Thank you; your turtle is very fine," replied I, necessarily the interpreter of the party.

"Try some of the *aguacate*—it will improve the flavor of your soup."

One of the waiters handed around a dark olive-colored fruit of an oblong shape about the size of an apple.

"Ask him how it is used, Captain" said the Major to me.

"Oh! I beg your pardon, gentlemen. I had forgotten that some of our edibles may be strange to you; simply pare off the rind, and slice it thus."

We tried the experiment, but could not discover any peculiar improvement in the flavor of the soup. The pulp of the aguacate seemed singularly insipid to our Saxon palates.

Fish, fresh from us, and of the finest quality, formed the second course.

A variety of dishes were now brought upon the table; most of them new to us, all piquant, pleasant to the taste, and peculiar.

The Major tried them all, determined to find out which he might like best—a piece of knowledge that he said would serve him upon some future occasion. The Don seemed to take a pleasure in helping the Major, whom he honored with "Señor Coronel!"

"No, Señor Coronel!"

"Thank you, sir," grunted the Major, and tried the puchero, which is a mixed dish of meat and vegetables, boiled. It is generally composed of chicken, ham, beef, cabbage, garbanzos (a species of pea), turnips, boiled pears, and calabash. Sometimes, there are other ingredients in the compound. It is a dish entirely distinct from the famous *olla podrida*, which latter, by the way, notwithstanding the representations of traveller, is rarely to be met with in Mexico.

"Allow me to help you to a spoonful of *molé*?" Another favorite dish—a stew of fowl, in a red-colored, peppery sauce.

"With pleasure, Don Cosme."

The molé suddenly disappeared down the Major's capacious throat.

"Try some of this *chilé rilleno.*" Another stew of chilé and meats. It would be likely to skin the throat of any one not used to eating such fiery viands.

"By all means," answered the Major. "Ah! by Jove! hot as fire—whew!"

"*Pica, pica,*" answered Don Cosme, pointing to his thorax, and smiling at the wry faces the Major was making. "Wash it down, Señor, with a glass of this claret—or here, Pepe! Is the chambertin cool yet? Bring it in, then! Perhaps you prefer champagne, Señores?"

"Thank you, do not trouble yourself, Don Cosme."

"No trouble, Captain—bring champagne. Here, Señore Coronel try the *guisado de pato.*" (Duck cooked in the same red-hot style.)

"Thank you; you are very kind. Curse the thing! how it burns!"

"Do you think he understands English?" inquired Clayley of me, in a whisper.

"I should think not," I replied.

"Well, then, I wish to say aloud, that this old chap's a superb old gent. What say you, Major? Don't you wish we had him on the lines?"

"I wish his kitchen was a little nearer the lines," replied the other, with a wink.

"Señor Coronel, permit me—."

"What is it, my dear Don?" inquired the Major.

"*Pasteles de Moctezuma.*" Small patties peculiar to the Mexican cui[sine]

"Oh, certainly! I say, lads, I don't know what the plague I'm eating—[n]ot bad to take though."

"Señor Coronel, allow me to hand you to a guana steak."

"A guana steak!" echoed the Major, in some surprise.

"Si Señor," replied Don Cosme holding the steak on his fork

"A guana steak—do you think, lads, he means the ugly things we saw at Lobos?"

"To be sure—why not?"

"Then, by Jove, I'm through. I can't go lizards. Thank you, my dear Don Cosme, I believe I have dined."

"Try this; it is very tender, I assure you," insisted Don Cosme

"Come, try it Major, and report," cried Clayley.

"Good—you're like the apothecary that poisoned his dog, to try the effect of his nostrums. Well—" with an oath—" here goes; it can't be very bad, seeing how our friend gets it down. Delicious, by Jupiter! tender as chicken

—good good;"—and amidst sundry similar ejaculations, the Major ate his first guana steak.

"Gentlemen, here is an ortolan pie. I can recommend this—the birds are in season."

"Reed-birds, by Jove!" said the Major recognising his favorite dish.

An incredible number of these creatures disappeared in an incredibly short time.

The dinner-dishes were at length removed, and dessert followed,—cakes and creams, and jellies of various kinds, and blanc-mange, and a profusion of the most luxurious fruits. The golden orange, the ripe pine, the pale green lime, the juicy grape, the custard-like cherimolla, the zapoté, the granadilla, the pitahaya, the tuna, the mamay. with dates, figs, almonds, plantains, bananas, and a dozen orher species of fruits, piled upon salvers of silver, were set before us. In fact, every product of the tropical clime, that could excite a new nerve of the sense of taste. We were fairly astonished at the profusion of luxuries that came from no one knew were.

"Come, gentlemen, try a glass of Curaçoa. Señor Coronel, allow me the pleasure?"

"Sir, your very good health!"

"Señor Coronel, would you prefer a glass of Majorca?"

"Thank you."

"Or, perhaps, you would choose *Pedro Ximenes*. I have some very old *Pedro Ximenes*?"

"Either, my dear Don Cosme,—either."

"Bring both, Ramon; and bring a couple of bottles of the Madeira—*sella verde*."

"As I'm a Christian, the old gentleman's a conjuror!" muttered the Major now in the best humor possible.

"I wish he would conjure up something else than his infernal wine bottles," thought I, becoming impatient at the non-appearance of the ladies.

"Cáfé señores? a servant entered.

Coffee was handed round in cups of Sèvres china.

"You smoke, gentleman? Would you prefer a Havanna? Here are some sent me from Cuba by a friend. I believe they are good; or, if you would amuse yourself with a cigarrito, here are Campeacheanos; these are the country cigars—*puros*, as we call them. I would not recommend them.'

"A Havanna for me," said the major, helping himself at the same time to a fine looking regalia.

I had fallen into a somewhat painful reverie.

I began to fear that, with all his hospitality, the Mexican would allow us to depart without an introduction to his family; and I had conceived a strong desire to speak with the two lovely beings whom I had already seen, but more particulary with the brunette, whose actions had impressed me. So strange is the mystery of love! My heart had already formed its preference.

I was suddenly aroused by the voice of Don Cosme, who had risen, and was inviting myself and comrades to join the ladies in the drawing-room.

I started up so suddenly, as almost to overturn one of the waiters.

"Why, captain, what's the matter? said Clayley. "Don Cosme is about to introduce us to the ladies. You're not going to back out?"

"Certainly not," stammered I, somewhat ashamed at my *gaucherie*.

"He says they're in the drawing-room," whispered the Major, in a voice that betokened a degree of suspicion; "but where the plague that is Heaven only knows. Stand by, my boys!—are your pistols all right?"

"Pshaw Major! for shame!"

CHAPTER XIV.

A SUBTERRANEAN DRAWING-ROOM.

THE mystery of the drawing-room, and the servants and the dishes, was soon over. A descending stairway explained the enigma.

"Let me conduct you to my cave, gentlemen," said the Spaniard, "I am half a subterranean. In the hot weather, and during the northers, we find it more agreeable to live under the ground. Follow me, señores!"

We descended, with the exception of Oakes, who returned to look after the men.

At the foot of the staircase, we entered a hall brilliantly lighted. The floor was without a carpet, and exhibited a mosaic of the finest marble. The walls were painted of a pale blue color, and embellished by a series of pictures, from the pencil of Murillo.* These were framed in a costly and elegant manner. From the ceiling were suspended chandeliers of a curious and unique construction, holding in their outstretched branches wax candles of an ivory whiteness.

Large vases of waxen flowers, covered with crystals, stood around the hall upon tables of polished marble. Other articles of furniture, candelabras, girandoles, gilded clocks, filled the outline. Broad mirrors reflected the

---

* I have seen many paintings in Mexico by the old Spanish masters. When the former wealth of the Mexican nobles is taken into consideration, this will not appear strange Even yet there are connoiseurs of art in this decayed Republic. While in its capital city a gentleman of my acquaintance received several paintings from Madrid, that had cost him 1,000 dollars each.

different objects; so that, instead of one apartment, this hall appeared
one of a continuous suite of splendid drawing-rooms!

And yet, upon closer observation, there seemed to be no door leading from
this hall, which, as Don Cosme informed his guests, was the waiting-room.

Our host approached one of the large mirrors, and silently touched a
spring. The tinkling of a small bell was heard within; and, at the same
instant, the mirror glided back, reflecting in its motion a series of brilliant
objects, that for a moment bewildered our eyes, with a blazing light.

"*Pasan a dentro, señores,*" said Don Cosme, stepping aside, and waving
us to enter.

We walked into the drawing-room. The magnificence that greeted us
seemed a vision—a glorious and dazzling hallucination—more like the gilded
brilliance of some enchanted palace, than the interior of a Mexican gentleman's
habitation.

As we stood gazing with irresistible wonderment, Don Cosme opened a
side-door, and called aloud, "*Niñas, niñas, ven aca!*" (children come here.)
This beautiful word of endearment is pronounced "neenya." It signifies
child, but is used in speaking to grown-up girls, and often, in complimentary
phraseology, to grey-haired old ladies.

Presently we heard several female voices, blending together, like a medley
of singing birds.

They approached. We heard the rustling of silken dresses—the falling
of light feet in the doorway—and three ladies entered—the Señora of Don
Cosme, followed by her two beautiful daughters, the heroines of our aquatic
adventure.

These hesitated a moment—scanning our faces—then with a cry of "*Neustro
salvador,*" both rushed forward and knelt, or rather crouched at my feet,
each of them clasping one of my hands and covering it with kisses!

Their panting agitation—their flashing eyes—the silken touch of their
delicate fingers, sent the blood rushing through my veins, like a stream of
lava; but in their gentle accents, the simple ingenuousness of their expressions, the childlike innocence of their faces. I regarded them only as two
beautiful children kneeling in the *abandon* of gratitude.

Meanwhile, Don Cosme had introduced Clayley and the Major to his
Señora, whose baptismal name was Joaquina, and, taking the young ladies
one in each hand, he presented them as his daughters, Guadalupe and Maria
de la Luz (Mary of the light).

The names given in the text are the real surnames of the ladies who figured as described in these adventures. The family name has been changed, for obvious reasons, by the author.

"Mamma," said Don Cosme, "the gentlemen had not quite finished their cigars."

"Oh, they can smoke here," replied the Señora.

"Will the ladies not object to that?" I inquired.

"No—no—no—!" ejaculated they simultaneously.

"Perhaps you will join us?—we have heard that such is the custom of your country."

"It *was* the custom," cried Don Cosme. "At present the young ladies of Mexico are rather ashamed of the habit."

This is a fact, notwithstanding the assertions of travellers that smoking is fashionable among the young ladies of Mexico. Few of them smoke at all, and those who do, perform the operation "behind the door."

"We no smoke—mamma, yes;" added the elder, whose name was Guadalupe.

"Ha! you speak English?"

"Little Englis speak—no good Englis?" was the reply.

"Who taught you English?" I inquired, prompted by a mysterious curiosity.

"Un American us teach—Don Emilio."

"Ha! an American?"

"Yes, Señor," said Don Cosme, "a gentleman from Vera Cruz, who formerly visited our family."

I thought I could perceive a desire upon the part of our host, not to say more on this subject, and I felt a strange and painful curiosity. I can only explain this by asking the reader, if he or she has not experienced a similar feeling, while endeavoring to trace the unknown past of some being, in whom they have lately taken an interest—stronger than friendship?

That mamma smoked, was clear, for the old lady had already gone through the process of unrolling one of the small cartouche-like cigars. Although these little cigars are ready made, a Mexican never smokes one without taking it down and re-making it to suit himself. This is done, partly, to pass the time; but more, because the fresh rolled cigar smokes better. Having re-rolled it between her fingers, she placed it within the grip of a pair of small golden pincers.

This done, she held one end to the coals that lay upon the *brazero*, and ignited the paper. Then taking the other end between her thin purlish lips, she breathed forth a blue cloud of aromatic vapor.

After a few whiffs, she invited the Major to participate, offering him a cigarrito from her beaded cigar case.

This being considered an especial favor, the Major's gallantry would not permit him to refuse. He took the cigarrito, therefore; but, once in possession, he knew not how to use it.

Imitating the Señora, he opened the diminitive cartridge, speading out the edges of the wrapper; but attempted in vain to re-roll it.

The ladies, who had watched the process, seemed highly amused, particularly the younger, who laughed outright.

"Permit me, Señor Coronel," said the Dona Joaquina, taking the cigarrito, from the Major's hand, and giving it a turn through her nimble fingers, which brought it all right again.

"Thus—now—hold your fingers thus. Do not press it—*suare—suave*. This end to the light—so—very well!"

The Major lit the cigar, and putting it between his great, thick lips, began to puff in a most energetic style.

He had not cast off half-a-dozen whiffs, when the fire reaching his fingers burned them severely, causing him to remove them suddenly from the cigar The wrapper then burst open, and the loose, pulverized tobacco, by a sudden inhalation, rushed into his mouth, and down his throat, causing him to cough and sputter in the most ludicrous manner.

This was too much for the ladies, who, encouraged by the cachinnations of Clayley, laughed outright; while the Major, with tears in his eyes, could be heard interlarding his coughing solo with all kinds of oaths and expressions.

The scene ended by one of the young ladies offering the Major a glass of water. which he drank off, effectually clearing the avenues of his throat.

"Will you try another, Señor Coronel?" asked Dona Joaquina with a smile.

"No, ma'am, thank you," replied the Major, and then a sort of an internal subterraneous curse could be heard in his throat.

The conversation continued in English, and we were highly amused at the attempts of our new acquaintances to express themselves in that language.

After failing, on one occasion, to make herself understood, Guadalupe said, with some vexation in her manner—

"We wish brother was home come; brother speak ver better Englis."

"Where is he?" I inquired.

"In the ceety—Vera Cruz."

"Ha! and when did you expect him?"

"Thees day—to-night—he home come."

"Yes," added the Señora, in Spanish. "He went to the city to spend a few days with a friend; but he was to return to-day, and we are looking for him to arrive in the evening."

"But how is he to get out?" cried the Major, in his coarse, rough manner.

"How?—why, Señor?" asked the ladies, in a breath, turning deadly pale.

"Why, he can't pass the pickets, ma'am;" answered the Major.

"Explain, Captain, explain!" said the ladies, appealing to me with looks of anxiety.

I saw that concealment would be idle. The Major had fired the train.

"It gives me pain, ladies," said I, speaking in Spanish, "to inform you that you must be disappointed. I fear the return of your brother to-day is impossible."

"But why, Captain?—why?"

"Our lines are completly around Vera Cruz, and all intercourse, to and from the city, is at an end."

Had a shell fallen into Don Cosme's drawing-room, it could not have caused a greater change in the feelings of its inmates. Knowing nothing of military life, they had no idea that our presence there had drawn an impassable barrier between them and a much-loved member of their family. In a seclusion almost hermitical, they knew that a war existed between their country and the United States; but that was far away upon the Rio Grande. They had heard, moreover, that our fleet lay off Vera Cruz; and the pealing of the distant thunder of San Juan, had from time to time reached their ears. But they had not dreamed, on seeing us, that the city was invested by land. The truth was now clear; and the anguish of the mother and daughters became afflicting, when we informed them what we were unable to conceal—that it was the intention of the American commander to bombard the city.

The scene was to us deeply distressing.

Doña Joaquina wrung her hands, and called upon the Virgin, with all the earnestness of entreaty. The sisters clung alternately to their mother, and

Don Cosme, weeping and crying aloud, "*Pobre Narcisso! nuestro hermanito—le asesinaron!*" (Poor Narcisso—our little brother—they will murder him!—) In the midst of this distressing scene, the door of the drawing-room was thrown suddenly open, and a servant, in an agitated voice, rushed in, shouting, "*El Norte—el Norte!*"

CHAPTER XV.

THE NORTHER.

WE hurried after Don Cosme toward the *ante-sala*, both myself and my companions as ignorant of this new object of dread.

When we emerged from the stairway, the scene that hailed us was one of terrific sublimity. Earth and heaven had undergone a sudden and convulsive change. The face of nature, not a moment since gay with summer smiles, was now hideously distorted. The sky had changed suddenly from its blue and sunny brightness, to an aspect dark and portentous.

Along the north-west a vast volume of black vapor rolled up over the Sierra Madre, and rested upon the peaks of the mountains. From this, ragged masses, parting in fantastic forms and groupings, floated off against the concavity of the sky, as though the demons of the storm were breaking up from an angry council. Each of these, as it careered across the heavens, seemed bent upon some spiteful purpose!

An isolated fragment hung lowering above the snowy cone of Orizava, like huge vampire suspended over his sleeping victim!

From the great " parent cloud" that rested upon the Sierra Madre, lightning-bolts shot out, and forked hither and thither, and sank into the detached masses—the messengers of the storm-king bearing his fiery mandates across the 5!

Away along the horizon of the east, moved yellow pillars of sand, whirled upward by the wind, like vast columnal towers leading to heaven.

The storm had not yet reached the rancho. The leaves lay motionless, under a dark and ominous calm; but the wild screams of many birds—the shrieks of swans—the discordant notes of the frightened pea-owl—the chattering of parrots, as they sought the shelter of the thick olives in terrified flight—all betokened the speedy advent of some fearful convulsion.

The rain, in large drops, fell upon the broad leaves, with a soft, plashing sound; and now and then a quick, short puff came snorting along, and, seizing the feathery frondage of the *palma redonda*—a beautiful species of the palm-tree—shook it with a spiteful and ruffian energy.

The long, green stripes, after oscillating a moment, would settle down again in graceful and motionless curves.

A low sound, like the "sough" of the sea, or the distant falling of water, came from the north; while, at intervals, the hoarse bark of the *coyote*, or prairie wolf, and the yelling of terrified monkeys, could be heard afar off in the woods.

"*Tapa la casa—tapa la casa!*" ("Cover the house!") cried Don Cosme, as soon as he had fairly got his head above ground.

"*Anda—anda con los macates!*" ("Quick with the cords!")

With lightning quickness a roll of palmetto mats came down on all sides of the house, completely covering the bamboo walls, and forming a screen impervious to both wind and rain. This was speedily fastened at all corners and strong stays were carried out, and warped around the trunks of trees. In five minutes the change was complete. The cage-looking structure had disappeared, and a house with walls of yellow *petaté* stood in its place. This petaté is a thin, light mat, woven from a species of palm. They are found in every house; and, in the rancheros of the poorer classes, the petaté spread on the floor is considered a bed. I have observed that in the valley of Mexico the palm leaf petaté is rarely met with. The article is there constructed of tulé, or bulrush, which grows in great plenty along the borders of the lakes Chalco and Tezcoco.

"Now, Señores, all is secured," said Don Cosme. "Let us return to the drawing-room."

"I should like to see the first burst of this tornado," I remarked, not wishing to intrude upon the scene of sorrow we had left.

"So be it, Captain. Stand here under the shelter, then!"

"Hot as thunder!" growled the Major, wiping the perspiration from his broad, red cheeks.

"In five minutes, Señor Coronel, you will be chilled. At this point the heated atmosphere is now compressed. Patience! it will soon be scattered."

"How long will the storm continue?" I asked.

"Por dios! Señor, it is impossible to tell how long the '*norté*' may rag —sometimes for days; perhaps only for a few hours. This appears to be the '*huracana*.' If so, it will be short, but terrible while it lasts. Carrambo!"

A puff of cold, sharp wind came whistling past like an arrow. Another followed, and another, like the three seas that roll over the stormy ocean. Then, with a loud, rushing sound, the broad, full blast went sweeping—strong, dark, and dusty—bearing upon its mane the screaming and terrified birds, mingled with torn and flouted leaves!

The olives creaked and tossed about. The tall palms bowed and yielded, flinging out their long pinions like streamers. The broad leaves of the plantains flapped and whistled, and, bending gracefully, allowed the fierce blast to pass over.

Then a great cloud came rolling down; a thick vapor seemed to fill the space; and the air felt hot, and dark, and heavy. A choking sulphurous smell rendered the breathing difficult; and, for a moment, day seemed changed to night.

Suddenly the whole atmosphere blazed forth in a sheet of flame, and the trees glistened as though they were on fire! An opaque darkness succeeded. Another flash, and, along with it the crashing thunder—the artillery of Heaven—deafening all earthly sounds!

Peal followed peal; the vast cloud was breached and burst by a hundred fiery bolts; and, like an avalanche, the heavy tropical rain was precipitated to the earth.

It fell in torrents; but the strength of the tempest had been spent on the first onslaught. The dark cloud passed on to the south, and a piercing cold wind swept after it.

"*Vamos a bajar, Señores!*" (Let us descend, gentlemen), said Don Cosme, with a shiver; and he conducted us back to the stairway.

Clayley and the Major looked towards me with an expression that said— "Shall we go in?" There were several reasons why our return to the drawing-room was unpleasant to myself and companions. A scene of domestic affliction is ever painful to a stranger. How much more painful to us; know ing, as we did, that our countrymen—that *we* had been the partial agents of this calamity. We hesitated a moment on the threshold.

"Gentlemen, we must return for a moment, we have been the bearers of evil tidings—let us offer such consolation as we may think of. Come!"

We descended after our host.

CHAPTER XVI.

A LITTLE FAIR WEATHER AGAIN.

On re-entering the sala, the picture of woe was again presented, but in an altered aspect. A change, sudden as the atmospheric one we had just witnessed, had taken place: and the scene of wild weeping was now succeeded by one of resignation and prayer.

On one side was Dona Joaquina, holding in her hands a golden rosary, with its crucifix. The girls were kneeling in front of a picture—a portrait of Dolores, with the fatal dagger; and the "Lady of Grief" looked not more sorrowful from the canvass, than the beautiful devotees that bent before her.

With their heads slightly leaning—their arms crossed upon their swelling bosoms—and their long loose hair trailing upon the carpet—they formed a picture at once painful and prepossessing.

The saints most popular in Mexico are Dolores', Remedios, and Guadalupe. The latter is the Saint patroness of the nation, and paintings, representing her as very beautiful, may be met with in almost every Mexican house.

Not wishing to intrude upon this sacred sorrow, we made a motion to retire.

"No, Señores," said Don Cosme, interrupting us, "be seated; let us talk calmly—let us know the worst!"

We then proceeded to inform Don Cosme of the landing of the American troops, and the manner in which our lines were drawn around the city; and pointed out to him the impossibility of any one passing either in or out.

"There is still a hope, Don Cosme," said I, "and that, perhaps, rests with yourself."

The thought had struck me that a Spaniard, of Don Cosme's evident rank and wealth, might be enabled to procure access to the city by means of his Consul, and through the Spanish ship of war, that I recollected was lying off San Juan.

"Oh! name it, Captain, name it!" cried he; while, at the word 'hope' he ladies had rushed forwards, and stood clinging around me.

"There is a Spanish ship of war lying under the walls of Vera Cruz."

"We know it, we know it," replied Don Cosme, eagerly.

"Ah! you know it, then?"

"Oh, yes," said Guadalupe, "Don Santiago is on board of her."

"Don Santiago?" inquired I; "who is he?"

"He is a relation of ours, captain," said Don Cosme; "an officer in the Spanish navy."

This information pained me, although I scarcely knew why.

"You have a friend, then, aboard the Spanish ship," said I to the elder of the sisters; "tis well; it will be in his power to restore to you your brother."

A ring of brightening faces was around me, while I uttered these cheering words; and Don Cosme, grasping me by the hand, entreated me to proceed.

"This Spanish ship," I continued, "is still allowed to keep up a communication with the town. You should proceed aboard at once then, and by the assistance of this friend, you may bring away your son before the bombardment commences. I see no difficulty; our batteries are not yet formed."

"I will go this instant," said Don Cosme, leaping to his feet, while Dona Joaquina and her daughters ran out to make preparations for his journey.

Hope—sweet hope—was again in the ascendant.

"But how, Señor?" asked Don Cosme, as soon as they were gone' "how can I pass your lines? Shall I be permitted to reach the ships?"

"It will be necessary for me to accompany you, Don Cosme," I replied, "and I regret, exceedingly, that my duty will not permit me to return with you at once."

"Oh, Señor!" exclaimed the Spaniard, with a painful expression.

"My business here," continued I, "is to procure pack-mules for the American army.

"Mules?"

"Yes. We were crossing for that purpose to a plain on the other side of the woods, where we had observed some animals of that description."

"'Tis true, Capitan—there are a hundred or more—they are mine—take them all."

"But it is our intention to pay for them, Don Cosme. The Major, here, has the power to contract with you."

"As you please, gentlemen; but you will then return this way, and proceed to your camp."

"As soon as possible," I replied; "how far distant is this plain?"

"Not more than a league. I would go with you, but—" Here Don Cosme hesitated, and approaching, said, in a lower tone, "the truth is, Señor Capitan, I should be glad if you could take them without my consent. I have mixed but little in the politics of this country; but Santa Anna is my enemy—he would ask no better motive for despoiling me."

"I understand you," said I. "Then, Don Cosme, we will take your mules by force, and carry yourself a prisoner to the American camp—a Yankee return for your hospitality."

"It is good," replied the Spaniard, with a smile.

"Señor Capitan," continued he, "you are without a sword! will you favor me by accepting this?"

Don Cosme held out to me a rapier of Toledo steel,[*] with a golden scabbard richly chased, and bearing on its hilt the eagle and nopal of Mexico. "It is a family relic, and once belonged to the brave Guadalupe Victoria."[†]

"Ha! indeed." I exclaimed, taking the sword, "I shall value it much. Thanks, Señor, thanks. Now, Major, we are ready to proceed."

"A glass of maraschino, gentlemen?" said Don Cosme, as a servant appeared with a flask and glasses.

"Thank you—yes," grunted the Major; "and while we are drinking it, Señor Don, let me give you a hint. "You appear to have plenty of pewter." Here the Major significantly touched a gold sugar-dish, which the servant was carrying upon a tray of chased silver, "take my word for it, you can't bury it too soon."

---

[*] This weapon was manufactured in London, and presented to Guadalupe Victoria. It cost £300. For reasons best known to his descendants, the precious relic is now in tranger hands.

[†] The First President of Mexico, and generally known as the Washington of that country, a name to which he is most fully entitled. He was truly a hero of many virtues; and his adventurous life, spent in fighting for his country's freedom, was a romance of itself.

"It is true, Don Cosme," said I, translating to him the Major's advice," we are not French, but there are robbers who hang on the skirts of every army."

Don Cosme promised to follow the hint with alacrity; and we prepared to take our departure from the rancho.

"I will give you a guide, Señor Capitan; you will find my people with the *milada*. Please *compel* them to lasso the cattle for you. You will obtain what you want in the *corral*. Adios, señores."

"Farewell, Don Cosme."

"Adieu, ladies, adieu."

"Adios, Capitan! adios! adios!"

I held out my hand to the younger of the girls, who instantly caught it, and pressed it to her lips. It was the action of a child. Guadalupe followed the example of her sister, but evidently with a degree of reserve. What, then, should have caused this difference in their manner.

In the next moment, we were ascending the stairway.

"Lucky dog!" growled the Major, "Take a ducking myself for that."

"Both beautiful, by Jove." said Clayley; "but of all the women I ever saw, give me 'Mary of the Light.'"

CHAPTER XVII.

THE SCOUT CONTINUED, WITH A VARIETY OF REFLECTIONS.

Love is a rose growing upon a thorny bramble. There is jealousy in the very first blush of a passion. No sooner has a fair face made its impress on the heart, than hopes and fears spring up in alternation. Every action, every word, every look, is noted and examined with a jealous scrutiny; and the heart of the lover, changing like the cameleon, takes its hues from the latest sentiment that may have dropped from the loved one's lips. And then the various looks, words, and actions—the favorable with the unfavorable—are recalled, and, by a mental process, classified and marshalled against each other, and compared and balanced with as much exactitude as the *pros* and *cons* of a miser's bank-book, and in this process we have a new alternation of hopes and fears.

Ah, love! we could write a long history of thy rise and progress; but it is doubtful whether any of our readers would be a jot the wiser for it. Most of them, ere this, have read that history in their own hearts.

I felt and knew that I was in love. It had come like a thought, as it comes upon all men whose souls are attuned to vibrate under the mystical impressions of the beautiful. And well I knew *she* was beautiful. I saw its unfailing index in those oval developments—the index, too, of the intellectual; for experience had taught me that *intellect takes a shape;* and that those peculiarities of form that we admire, without knowing why, are but the material illustrations of the diviner principles of mind.

The eye, too, with its almond outline, and wild, half-Indian, half-Ara' expression—the dark tracery over the lip, so rarely seen in the lineaments of her sex—even these were attractions. There was something picturesque, something strange, something almost fierce, in her aspect; and yet it was this indefinable something, this very fierceness, that had challenged my love! For I must confess mine is not one of those curious natures that I have read of, whose love is based only upon the goodness of the object. THAT *is not one*.

My heart recognised in her *the heroine of extremes!* One of those natures gifted with all the tenderness that belongs to the angel idea—woman; yet soaring above her sex in the paralyzing moments of peril and despair. Her feelings, in relation to her sister's cruelty to the goldfish, proved the existence of the former principle; her actions, in attempting my own rescue, when battling with the monster, were evidence of the latter. One of those natures that may err from the desparate intensity of one passion, that knows no limit to its self-sacrifice short of destruction and death! One of those beings that may fall—but *only once*.

"What would I give—what would I do—to be the hero of such a heart?" These were my reflections, as I quitted the house.

I had noted every word, every look, every action, that could lend me a hope; and my memory conjured up, and my judgment canvassed, each little circumstance in its turn.

"How strange her conduct at bidding adieu! How unlike her sister—less friendly and sincere!" and yet from this very circumstance I drew my happiest omens.

Strange, is it not? My experience had taught me that love and hate, for the *same* object, can exist in the *same* heart, and at the *same* time. If this be a paradox, I am a child of error.

I believed it then; and her apparent coldness, which would have rendered many another hopeless, produced with me an opposite effect.

Then came the cloud—the thought of Don Santiago, and a painful feeling shot through my heart.

Don Santiago, a naval officer, young, handsome. Bah! hers is not a heart o be won by a face,—Such were my reflections and half-uttered expressions, as I slowly led my soldiers through the tangled path.

Don Santiago's age and his appearance were the creations of a jealous fancy I had bidden adieu to my new acquaintances, knowing nothing of Don Santiago beyond the fact that he was an officer on board the Spanish ship of war and a relation of Don Cosme.

"Oh, yes! Don Santiago is on board!" Ha! there was an evident interest,

Her look, as she said it; her manner—furies! But he is a relation; a cousin—*a cousin. I hate cousins.*

I must have pronounced the last words aloud, as Mr. Lincoln, who walked in my rear, stepped hastily up, and asked—

"What did yer say Capt'n?"

"Oh! nothing, Serjeant," stammered I, in some confusion.

Notwithstanding my assurance, I overheard Mr. Lincoln whisper to his nearest comrade,

"What ther old Harry he's got into the Cap'?"

He referred to the fact, that I had unconsciously hooked myself half-a-dozen times on the thorny claws of the wild maguey, and my overalls began to exhibit a most tattered condition.

Our route lay through a dense chapparal, now crossing a sandy spur, covered with mezquit and acacia; then sinking into the bed of some silent creek shaded with old cork trees, whose gnarled and venerable trunks were laced together by a thousand parasites. Two miles from the rancho we reached the banks of a considerable stream, which we conjectured was a branch of the Tamapa river.

On both sides, a fringe of dark forest trees flung out long branches, extending half way across the stream. The water flowed darkly underneath. Huge lilies stood out from the banks; their broad, wax-like leaves trailing upon the glassy ripple.

Here and there were pools, fringed with drooping willows, and belts of green *tulé.* Other aquatic plants rose from the water to the height of twenty feet; their tall, spear-like stems, ending in a dark brown cylinder, like the pompon of a grenadier's cap.

As we approached the banks, the pelican scared from his lonely haunt, rose upon heavy wing, and, with a shrill scream, flapped away through the dark aisles of the forest. The cayman plunged sullenly into the sedgy water; and the sapajou, suspended by the tail from some overhanging bough, oscillated to and fro, and filled the air with his hideous half-human cries.

Halting for a moment to re-fill the canteens, we crossed over, and ascended the opposite bank. A hundred paces farther on, the guide, who had gone ahead, cried out from an eminence—"*Mira la caballada!*"

CHAPTER XVIII.

ONE WAY OF TAMING A BULL.

PUSHING through the jungle, we ascended the eminence. A brilliant picture opened before us. The storm had suddenly lulled, and the tropical sun shone down upon the flowery surface of the earth, bathing its verdure in a flood of yellow light.

It was several hours before sunset, but the bright orb had commenced descending towards the snowy cone of Orizava; and his rays had assumed that golden red, which characterizes the ante-twilight of the tropics. The short lived storm had swept the heavens, and the blue roof of the world was without a cloud. The dark masses had rolled away over the south-eastern horizon, and were now spending their fury upon the dye-wood forests of Honduras and Tabasco.

At our feet lay the prairie, spread before us like a green carpet; bounded upon the farther side by a dark wall of forest-trees. Several clumps of timber lay like islands on the plain, adding to the picturesque character of the landscape.

Near the centre of the prairie stood a small *rancho*, surrounded by a high picket fence. This we at once recognised as the *corral* mentioned by Don Cosme.

At some distance from this enclosure, thousands of cattle were now browsing upon the grassy level, their spotted flanks and long upright horns showing their descent from the famous race of Spanish bulls. Some of them, straggling from the herd, rambled through the "mottes," or lay stretched out under the shade of some isolated palm-tree. Ox-bells were tinkling their cheerful but monotonous music. Hundreds of horses and mules mingled with the herd and we could distinguish a couple of leather-clad herdsmen, gallopping from point to point on their swift "mustangs."

These, as we appeared upon the ridge, dashed out after a wild bull that had just escaped from the corral.

All five—the vaqueros, the mustangs, and the bull—swept over the prairie like wind, the bull bellowing with rage and terror; while the vaqueros were yelling in his rear, and whirling their long lassos. Their straight black hair floating in the wind—their swarthy, Arab-like faces—their high Spanish hats —their red leather "calzoneros," buttoned up the sides—their huge, jingling spurs, and the ornamental trappings of their deep saddles—all these, combined with the perfect *manège* of their dashing steeds, and the wild excitement of the chase in which they were engaged, rendered them objects of picturesque interest; and we halted a moment to witness the result.

The bull came rushing past, within fifty paces of where we stood, snorting with rage, and tossing his horns high in the air—his pursuers close upon him. At this moment, one of the vaqueros launched his lariat, which, floating gracefully out, settled down over one horn. Seeing this, the vaquero did not turn his horse, but sate facing the bull, and permitted the rope to run out. It was soon carried taut; and, scarcely checking the animal, it slipped along the smooth horn, and spun out into the air.

The second vaquero now flung his lasso with more success. The heavy loop, skilfully projected, shot out like an arrow, and embraced both horns in its curving noose. With the quickness of thought, the vaquero wheeled his horse, buried his spurs deep into his flanks, and, pressing his thighs to the saddle, gallopped off in an opposite direction. The bull dashed on as before. In a moment, the lariat was stretched. The sudden jerk caused the thong to vibrate like a bowstring, and the bull lay motionless on the grass! The shock almost dragged the mustang upon his flanks.

The bull lay for some time where he had fallen; then, making an effort, he sprang up, and looked around him with a bewildered air. He was not yet conquered. His eye, flashing with rage, rolled around until it fell upon the rope leading from his horns to the saddle, and, suddenly lowering his head with a furious roar he rushed upon the vaquero.

The latter, who had been expecting this attack, drove the spurs into his mustang, and started in full gollop across the prairie. On followed the bull sometimes shortening the distance between him and his enemy; while at intervals the lariat tightening, would almost jerk him upon his head.

After running for a hundred yards or so, the vaquero suddenly wheeled and gallopped out at right angles to his former course. Before the bull could turn himself, the lariat again tightened with a jerk, and flung him upon his side. This time he lay but an instant, and again springing to his feet, he dashed off in fresh pursuit.

The second vaquero now came up, and, as the bull rushed past, launched his lariat after, and snared him around one of the legs,* drawing the noos upon his ankle.

This time the bull was flung completely over, and with such a violent shock, that he lay as if dead. One of the vaqueros rode cautiously up, and, bending over in the saddle, unfastened both of the lariats, and let the animal free.

The bull rose to his feet, and, looking around in the most cowed and pitiful manner, walked quietly off, driven unresistingly toward the corral.*

We commenced descending into the plain, and the vaqueros, catching a glimpse of our uniforms, simultaneously reined up their mustangs with a sudden jerk. We could see from their gestures that they were frightened at the approach of our party. This was not strange, as the Major, mounted upon his great, gaunt charger, loomed up against the blue sky like a Colossus. The Mexicans, doubtless, had never seen anything in the way of horseflesh bigger than the mustangs† they were riding; and this apparition, with the long line of uniformed soldiers descending the hill, was calculated to alarm them severely.

"Them fellers is gwine to put, Cap'n," said Lincoln, touching his cap respectfully.

---

* I have seen the vaquero seize a bull's tail while both were in full gallop, and, twitching it under one of his legs, toss him over on his back This is a common exploit.

* This description is as correct as my notes and memory can make it. I have witnessed the lazoing of wild cattle fifty times, and it is true that the bull must be caught both by the horns and heels, and almost drawn asunder between the two mustangs before he surrenders.

† The Mexican horses—known among us by the name of mustangs—are, in fact, nothing more than large-sized ponies. They are the descendants of the Spanish breed, elegant and active, but deficient in weight.

Mustang is the name applied to the wild horses on the great prairies of Texas; but as those are directly sprung from Mexican progenitors, we give the name to all horses of that country.

"You're right, Sergeant,' I replied, "and without them we might as well think of catching the wind as one of these mules."

"If yer'll just let me draw a bead on the near mustang, I kin kripple him 'ithout hurtin' the thing thet's in the saddle."

"It would be a pity; no Sergeant," answered I. "I might stop them by sending forward the guide," continued I, addressing myself rather than Lincoln; "but no, it will not do; there must be the appearance of force. I have promised. Major, would you have the goodness to ride forwaad, and prevent those fellows from gallopping off?"

"Lord, Captain," said the Major, with a terrified look, "you don't think I could overtake such Arabs as them? Hercules is slow—slow as a crab."

Now this was a lie, and I knew it, for "Hercules," the Major's great rawboned steed, was as fleet as the wind.

"Then, Major, perhaps you will allow Mr. Clayley to make trial of him?". I suggested. "He is light weight. I assure you that, without the assistance of these Mexicans, we shall not be able to catch a single mule."

The Major, seeing that all eyes were fixed upon him, suddenly straightened himself up in his stirrups, and, swelling with courage and importance, declared, if that was the case, he would go himself. Then, calling upon "Doc" to follow him, he struck the spurs into Hercules, and rode forward at a gallop. It proved that this was just the very course to start the vaqueros, as the Major had inspired them with more terror than all the rest of our party. They showed evident symptoms of taking to their heels; and I shouted to them at the top of my voice,

"*Alto! somos amigos*"—(Halt, we are friends.)

The words were scarcely out of my mouth, when the Mexicans drove the rowels into their mustangs, and gallopped off as if for their lives, in the direction of the corral.

The Major followed at a slashing pace, Doc bringing up the rear; while the basket which the latter carried over his arm, began to eject its contents, scattering the commissariat of the Major over the prairie. Fortunately, the hospitality of Don Cosme had already provided a substitute for this loss.

After a run of about half a mile, Hercules began to gain rapidly upon the mustangs; whereas Doc was losing distance in an inverse ratio. The Mexicans had got within a couple of hundred yards of the rancho—the Major not over a hundred in their rear—when I observed the latter suddenly pull up and, jerking the long body of Hercules around, commence riding slowly back, all the while looking over his shoulder towards the enclosure.

The vaqueros did not halt at the corral, as we expected, but kept across the prairie, and disappeared among the trees on the opposite side.

"What the deuce got into Blossom?" inquired Clayley; "he was nearly gaining on them. The old bloat must have burst a blood-vessel."

CHAPTER XIX.

A BRUSH WITH THE GUERILLEROS.*

"Why, what was the matter, Major?" inquired I, as the Major rode up, blowing like a porpoise.

"Matter," replied he, with one of his direst imprecations; "matter, indeed! you wouldn't have me ride plump into their works, would you?"

"Works?" echoed I, in some surprise; "what do you mean by that, Major?"

"I mean works—that's all. There's a stockade ten feet high, as full as it can stick of them."

"Full of what?"

"Full of the enemy—full of rancheros. I saw their ugly copper faces—a dozen of them, at least—looking at me over the pickets; and, sure as heaven, if I had gone ten paces further, they would have riddled me like a target."

"But, Major, they were only peaceable rancheros—cow-herds –nothing more."

"Cow-herds? I tell you, Captain, that those two mahogany-colored devils that galloped off had a sword apiece, strapped to their saddles. I saw them when I got near—they were decoys to bring us up to that stockade, I'll bet my life upon it."

"Well, Major," rejoined I, "they're far enough from the stockade now, and the best we can do in their absence, will be to examine it, and see what chances it may offer to corral these mules; for, unless they can be driven into it, we shall have to return to camp empty-handed."

Saying this, I moved forward with the men, the Major keeping in the rear

We soon reached the formidable stockade, which proved to be nothing more than a regular corral, such as are found on the great *Haciendas de ganados* (cattle farms) of Spanish America. In one corner was a house, constructed of upright poles, with a thatch of palm-leaves. This contained the lassos, *alparejos*, saddles, &c., of the vaqueros; and, in the door of this house, stood a decrepid old zambo, the only human thing about the place. The zambo's woolly head over the pickets, had reflected itself a dozen times on th Major's terrified imagination.

* Guerilla is a band of guerilleros—guerillero an individual of the band.

After examining the corral, I found it excellent for our purpose, provided we could only succeed in driving the mules into it; and, throwing open the bars, we proceeded to make the attempt. The mules were browsing quitely at the distance of a quarter of a mile from the corral.

Marching past the drove, I deployed the company in the form of a semicircle, forming a complete cordon outside the animals; then closing in upon them slowly, the soldiers commenced driving them toward the pen.

We were somewhat awkward at this new duty; but by means of a shower of small rocks, pieces of *bois de vache,* and an occasional "heigh, heigh," the mules were soon in motion, and in the required direction.

The Major, with Doc and Little Jack, being the mounted men of the party, did great service; especially Jack, who was highly delighted with this kind of thing, and kept Twidget in a constant gallop, from right to left.

As the *mulada* neared the gates of the enclosure, the two extremes of the semi-circumference gradually approached each other, closing in toward the corral.

The mules were already within fifty paces of the entrance, the soldiers coming up about two hundred yards in the rear, when a noise like the tramping of many hoofs arrested our attention. The quick, sharp note of a cavalry bugle rang out across the plain, followed by a wild yell, as though a band of Comanches were swooping down upon the foe.

In an instant, every eye was turned, and we beheld, with consternation, a cloud of horsemen springing out from the woods, and dashing along in the headlong velocity of a charge.

It required but a single glance to satisfy me that they were *guerilleros*. Their picturesque attire—their peculiar arms—and the particolored bannerets upon their lances—were not to be mistaken.

We stood for a moment as if thunderstruck; a sharp cry rose along the deployed line.

I signalled to the bugler, who gave the command: "Rally upon the centre!"

As if by one impulse, the whole line closed in with a run upon the gates of the enclosure.

The mules, impelled by the sudden rush, dashed forward pell mell, blocking up the entrance.

On came the guerilleros, with streaming pennons, and lances couched, shouting their wild cries:

"*Andela—andela! mueran los Yankees!*"

The foremost of the soldiers were already upon the heels of the mulada, pricking them with bayonets.

The animals began to kick and plunge in the most furious manner, causing a new danger in front.

"Face about—fire!"

An irregular, but well-directed volley emptied half-a-dozen saddles, and, for a moment, staggered the charging line; but, before my men could re-load, the guerilleros had leaped clear over their fallen comrades, and were swooping down with cries of vengeance.

A dozen of their bravest men were already within shot range, firing thei escopettes and pistols as they came down.

Our position had now grown fearfully critical. The mules still blocked up the entrance, preventing the soldiers from taking shelter behind the stockade; and, before we could re-load, the rearmost would be at the mercy of the enemy's lances.

Seizing the Major's servant by the arm, I dragged him from his horse; and, leaping into the saddle, flung myself upon the rear. Half-a-dozen of my bravest men, among whom were Lincoln, Chane, and the Frenchman Raoul, rallied around the horse, determined to receive the cavalry charge on the short bayonets of their rifles. Their pieces were all empty.

At this moment, my eye rested upon one of the soldiers, a brave, but slow-footed German, who was still twenty paces in the rear of his comrades, making every effort to come up. Two of the guerilleros were rushing upon him with couched lances. I gallopped out to his rescue, but before I could reach him the lance of the foremost Mexican crashed through the soldier's skull, shivering it like a shell. The barb and bloody pennon came out on the opposite side. The man was lifted from the ground, and carried several paces upon the shaft of the lance!

The guerillero dropped his entangled weapon, but before he could draw any other, the sword of Victoria was through his heart.

His comrade turned upon me with a cry of vengeance. I had not yet disengaged my weapon to ward off the thrust. The lance's point was within three feet of my breast, when a sharp crack was heard from behind—the lancer threw out his arms with a spasmodic jerk—his long spear was whirled into the air—and he fell back in his saddle, dead!

"Well, done, Jack! Fire and scissors! who showed yer that trick? whooray-whoop!" and I heard the voice of Lincoln, in a sort of Indian yell, rising high above the din.

At this moment a guerillero, mounted upon a powerful black mustang, came gallopping down. This man, unlike most of his comrades, was armed with the sabre, which he evidently wielded with great dexterity. He came dashing on, his white teeth set in a fierce smile.

"Ha! Monsieur le Capitaine," shouted he, as he came near, "still alive? I thought I had finished you on Lobos; not too late yet."

I recognised the deserter, Dubrosc!

"Villain!" I ejaculated, too full of rage to utter another word.

We met at full speed, but with my unmanageable horse, I could only ward off his blow as he swept past me. We wheeled again, and gallopped toward each other, both of us impelled by hatred, but my horse again shied, frightened by the gleaming sabre of my antagonist. Before I could rein him around, he had brought me close to the pickets of the corral, and on turning to meet the deserter, I found that we were separated by a band of dark objects.

It was a detachment of mules, that had backed from the gates of the corral, and were escaping to the open plain. We reined up, eyeing each other with impatient vengeance; but the bullets of my men began to whistle from the pickets; and Dubrosc, with a threatening gesture, wheeled his horse, and gallopped off to his comrades. They had retired beyond range, and were halted in groups upon the prairie, chafing with disappointment, and rage.

CHAPTER XX.

A HERCULEAN FEAT.

The whole skirmish did not occupy two minutes. It was like most charges of Mexican cavalry—a dash—a wild yelling—half-a-dozen empty saddies—and a hasty retreat.

The guerilleros had swerved off as soon as they perceived that we had gained a safe position, and the bullets of our re-loaded pieces began to ring around their ears. Dubrosc, alone, in his impetuosity, galloped close up to the enclosure, and it was only on perceiving his danger, that he followed his party. They were now out upon the prairie, beyond the range of small arms grouped around their wounded comrades, or gallopping to and fro, with yells of disappointed vengeance.

I entered the corral, where most of my men had sheltered themselves behind the stockades. Little Jack sat upon Twidget, re-loading his rifle, and trying to appear insensible to the flattering encomiums that hailed him from all sides. A compliment from Lincoln, however, was too much for Jack, and a proud smile passed over the face of the boy.

"Thank you, Jack," said I, as I passed him, "I see you can use a rifle to some purpose."

Jack held down his head, without saying a word, and appeared to be very busy about the lock of his piece.

In the skirmish, Lincoln had received the scratch of a lance—at which he was chafing, in his own peculiar way, and vowing revenge upon the giver. It might be said that he had taken this, as he had driven his short bayonet through his antagonist's arm, and sent him off with this member hanging by his side.

The hunter was not content; and, as he retired sullenly into the enclosure he turned round, and, shaking his fist at the Mexicans, muttered savagely—

"Yer darned skunk! I'll know yer agin   See if I don't git yer yit."

Gravenitz, a Prussian soldier, had also been too near a lance; and several others had received slight wounds. The German was the only one killed. He was still lying out on the plain, where he had fallen, the long shaft of the lance standing up out of his skull! Not ten feet distant lay the corpse of his slayer, glistening in its gaudy and picturesque attire!

The other guerillero, as he fell, had noosed one of his legs in the lariat that hung from the horn of his saddle, and was now dragged over the prairie after his wild and snorting mustang. As the animal swerved, at every jerk his limber body bounded to the distance of twenty feet, where it would lie motionless until slung into the air by a fresh pluck on the lasso!

As we were watching this horrid spectacle, several of the guerilleros gallopped after, while half-a-dozen others were observed spurring their steeds towards the rear of the corral. On looking in this direction, we perceived a huge red horse, with an empty saddle, scouring at full speed across the prairie. A single glance showed us that this horse was Hercules.

"Good Heavens! the Major?"

"Safe somewhere," replied Clayley; "but where the deuce can he be? He is not 'hors de combat' on the plain, or one could see him ten miles off. Ha, ha, ha! look yonder!"

Clayley, yelling with laughter, pointed to the corner of the ranche.

Though after a scene so tragic, I could hardly refrain from joining Clayley in his boisterous mirth. Hanging by the belt of his sabre upon a high picket was the Major, kicking and struggling with all his might! The waist strap, tightly drawn by the bulky weight of the wearer, separated his body into two vast rotundities, while his face was distorted and purple with the agony of suspense and suspension. He was loudly bellowing for help, and several soldiers were running towards him; but, from the manner in which he jerked his body up, and screwed his neck, so as to enable him to look over the stockade, it was evident that the principal cause of his uneasiness lay on the "other side of the fence."

The truth was, the Major, on the first appearance of the enemy, had gallopped towards the rear of the corral, and, finding no entrance had thrown himself from the back of Hercules upon the stockade, intending to climb over; but, catching a glance of some guerilleros, he suddenly let go his bridle, and attempted to precipitate himself into the corral.

His waist-belt caught upon a sharp picket, and held him suspended midway, still under the impression that the Mexicans were close upon his rear. He was soon unhooked, and waddled across the corral, uttering a thick and continuous volley of his choicest oaths.

Our eyes were now directed towards Hercules. The horsemen had closed upon him within fifty yards, and were winding their long lassos in the air. The Major, to all appearance, had lost his horse.

After gallopping to the edge of the woods, Hercules suddenly halted, and hrew up the trailing bridle, with a loud neigh. His pursuers, coming up, flung out their lariats. Two of them settling over his head, noosed him around the neck. The huge brute, as if aware of the necessity of a desperate effort to free himself, dropped his nose to the ground, and stretched himself in full gallop.

The lariats, one by one tightening over his bony chest, snapped like threads, almost jerking the mustangs from their feet. The long fragments sailed out like streamers as he careered across the prairie, far ahead of his yelling pursuers. He now made directly for the corral. Several of the soldiers ran toward the stockade, in order to seize the bridle when he should come up but Hercules, spying his old comrade—the horse of the "doctor"—within the enclosure, neighed loudly; and throwing all his nerve into the effort sprang high over the picket fence!

A cheer rose from the men, who had watched with interest his efforts to escape; and who now welcomed him as if he had been one of themselves.

"Two months' pay for your horse, Major!" cried Clayley.

"Och, the bewtifull baste! He's worth the full of his skin in goold. By my sowl! the Capten ought to have 'im," ejaculated Chane; and various other encomiums were uttered in honor of Hercules.

Meanwhile, his pursuers, not daring to approach the stockade, drew off towards their comrades, with gestures of disappointment and chagrin.

CHAPTER XXI

RUNNING THE GAUNTLET.

I BEGAN to reflect upon the real danger of our situation: *corralled* upon a naked prairie, ten miles from camp, with no prospect of escape. I knew that we could defend ourselves against twice the number of our cowardly adversaries. Those would never dare to come within range of our rifles; but how to get out? how to cross the open plain? Fifty infantry against four times that number of mounted men—lancers at that—and not a bush to shelter the foot soldier from the long spear and the iron hoof.

The nearest motte was half a mile off, and that another half mile from the edge of the woods. Even could the motte be reached by a desperate run, it would be impossible to gain the woods, as the enemy would certainly cordon our new position, and thus completely cut us off. At present, they had halted in a body about four hundred yards from the corral, and, feeling secure of having us in a trap, most of them had dismounted, and were running out their mustangs upon the lariat. It was plainly their determination to take us by siege.

To add to our desperate circumstances, we discovered that there was not a drop of water in the corral. The thirst that follows a fight had nearly exhausted the scanty supply of our canteens, and the heat was excessive.

As I was running over, in my mind, the perils of our position my eye rested upon Lincoln, who stood with his piece at a carry; his left hand crossed over his breast, in the attitude of a soldier waiting to receive orders

I leaped from my horse, and followed Lincoln through the bushes, upon the border of a small glade. The moon was shining full upon the face. I had never seen the features before. He was a Zambo, and, from the half-military equipments that clung around his body, I saw that he had been a guerillero. Lincoln was right.—Page 117.

our search, upon the border of a small glade. The moon was shining full upon the face. I stooped down to examine it. A single glance was sufficient. I had never seen the features before. They were coarse and swart, and the long black locks were matted and woolly. He was a Zambo, and, from the half-military equipments that clung around his body, I saw that he had been a guerillero. Lincoln was right.—Page 117.

"Well, Sergeant, what is it?" I inquired.

"Will yer allow me, Cap'n, ter take a couple o'files, and fetch in the Dutchman; the men ud like ter put a sod upon him, afore them thievin' robbers kin git at him."

"Certainly. But will you be safe? He's at some distance from the stockade."

"I don't think them fellers 'll kum down—they've had enuf. We'll run out quick, and the boys kin kiver us with their fire."

"Very well, then; set about it."

Lincoln returned to the company, and selected four of the most active of his men, with whom he proceeded towards the entrance. I ordered the soldiers to throw themselves on that side of the enclosure, and cover the party, in case of an attack; but none was made. A movement was visible among the Mexicans, as they perceived Lincoln and his party rush out towards the body; but seeing they would be too late to prevent them from carrying it off, they wisely kept beyond the reach of the American rifles.

The body of the German was brought into the enclosure, and buried with due ceremony; although his comrades believed that, before many hours, it would be torn from its "warrior-grave;" dragged forth to feed the coyote and vulture, and his bones left to whiten upon the naked prairie. Which of us knew that it might not, in a few hours, be his own fate?

"Gentlemen," said I, to my brother officers, as we came together, "can you suggest any mode of escape?"

"Our only chance is to fight them where we stand. There are four to one," replied Clayley.

"We have no other chance, Captain," said Oakes, with a shake of the head.

"But, it is not their intention to fight *us*. Their design is to starve us. See! they are picketing their horses, knowing they can easily overtake us, if we attempt to leave the enclosure."

"Cannot we move in a hollow square?"

"But what is a hollow square of fifty men? and against four times that number of cavalry, with lances and lassos? No, no, they would shiver it with single charge. Our only hope is, that we may be able to hold out, until our bsence from camp may bring a detachment to our relief."

"And why not send for it?" inquired the Major, who had scarcely been asked for his advice, but whose wits had been sharpened by the extremity of his danger. "Why not send for a couple of regiments?"

"How are we to send, Major?" asked Clayley, looking on the Major's proposition as ludicrous under the circumstances. "Have you a pigeon in your pocket?"

"Why, how? there's Hercules runs like a hare; stick one of your fellows in the saddle, and I'll warrant him to camp in an hour."

"You are right, Major," said I, catching at the Major's proposal; thank you for the thought. If he could only pass that point in the woods I hate it! but it is our only chance."

The last sentence I muttered to myself.

"Why do you hate it, Captain?" inquired the Major, who had overheard me.

"You might not understand my reasons, Major."

I was thinking upon the disgrace of being trapped as I was, and on my first scout too.

"Who will volunteer to ride an express to camp?" I inquired, addressing the men.

Twenty of them leaped out simultaneously.

"Which of you remembers the course, that you could follow it in a gallop?" I asked.

The Frenchman Raoul stood forth, touching his cap.

"I know a shorter one, Captain, by Mata Cordera."

"Ha! Raoul, you know the country? you are the man."

I now remembered that the Frenchman joined us at Sacrificios, just after the landing of the expedition.

"Are you a good horseman?"

"I have lived in Mexico five years."

"True; do you think you can pass them; they are nearly in your track."

"As we entered the prairie, Captain; but my route will lie past this motte to the left."

"This will give you several points, do not stop a moment after you have mounted, or they will take the hint, and intercept you."

"With the red horse there will be no danger, Captain."

"Leave your gun; take these pistols. Ha! you have a pair in the holsters. See if they are loaded. These spurs—so—cut loose that heavy piece from the saddle; the cloak, too; you must have nothing to encumber you. When you come near the camp, leave your horse in the chapparal. Give this to Colonel C——."

I wrote the following words on a scrap of paper:

"Dear Colonel,—two hundred will be enough. Could they be stolen out after night? If so, all will be well—if it gets abroad . . . . .
"Yours,
"H. H."

As I handed the paper to Raoul, I whispered in his ear:
"To Colonel C——'s own hand. Privately, Raoul—privately do yo 1ear?"

Colonel C—— was my friend, and I knew that he would send a *private* party to my rescue.

"I understand, Captain," was the answer of Raoul.

"Ready, then; now mount and be off."

The Frenchman sprang nimbly to the saddle; and, driving his spurs into the flanks of his horse, shot out from the penn like a bolt of lightning. For the first three hundred yards or so, he galloped directly towards the guorilleros. These stood leaning upon their saddles, or lay stretched along the green sward.

Seeing a single horseman riding towards them, none of them moved—believing him to be some messenger sent to treat for our surrender.

Suddenly, the Frenchman swerved from his direct course, and went sweeping around them in the curve of an ellipse!

They now perceived the ruse, and, with a yell, leaped into their saddles. Some fired their escopettes; others, unwinding their lassos, started in pursuit.

Raoul had, by this time, set Hercules' head for the clump of timber, which he had taken as his guide; and now kept on in a track almost rectilinear. Could he reach the motte or clump in safety he knew that there were straggling trees beyond, and these would secure him, in some measure, from the lariats of his pursuers. We stood watching his progress with breathless silence. Our lives depended on his escape. A crowd of his pursuers was between him and us; but we could see the green jacket of the soldier, and the great red flanks of Hercules, as he bounded on towards the edge of the woods. Then we saw the lariats launched out, and, spinning around Raoul's head, and straggling shots were fired; and we fancied, at one time, that our comrade sprang up in the saddle, as if he had been hit! Then he appeared again, all safe, rounding the little islet of timber, and the next moment he was gone. There followed a while of suspense—of terrible suspense—for the motte hid from view both pursuers and pursued. Every eye was straining towards the point where the horseman had disappeared, when Lincoln, who had climbed to the top of the ranche, cried out:

"He's safe Cap'n." Ther dod-rotted skunks air kummin 'ithout him."

It was true. A minute after, the horsemen appeared round the motte riding slowly back, with that air and attitude that betoken disappointment

CHAPTER XXII.

A SHORT FIGHT AT "LONG SHOT."

The escape of Raoul and Hercules produced an effect almost magical upon the enemy. Instead of the listless, defensive attitude, lately assumed, the guerilleros were now in motion like a nest of roused hornets, scouring over the plain and yelling like a war party of Indians.

They did not surround the corral, as I had anticipated they would. They had no fear that we should attempt to escape; but they knew that, instead of the three days, in which they expected to kill us with thirst at their leisure, they had not three hours left to accomplish that object. Raoul would reach the camp in little more than an hour's time, and either infantry or mounted men would be on them in two hours after.

Scouts were seen gallopping off in the direction taken by Raoul; and others dashed into the woods on the opposite side of the prairie. All was hurry and scurry.

Along with Clayley I climbed upon the roof of the ranche, to watch the motions of the enemy and to find out, if possible his intentions. We stood for some time without speaking, both of us gazing at the manœuvres of the guerilleros. They were gallopping to and fro over the prairie, excited by the escape of Raoul.

"Splendidly done!" exclaimed my companion, struck with their graceful horsemanship. "One of those fellows, Captain, as he sits at this m.. .e, would——"

"Ha! what——?" shouted he, suddenly turning and pointing towards th woods.

I looked in the direction indicated. A cloud of dust was visible at the debouchement of the Medellin road. It appeared to hang over a small body c troops upon the march. The sun was just setting; and, as this cloud lay towards the west, I could distinguish the sparkling of bright objects through its dun volume. The guerilleros had reined up their horses, and were eagerly gazing towards the same point.

Presently the dust was wafted aside, a dozen dark forms became visible, and, in their midst, a bright object flashed under the sun like a sheet of gold. At the same instant, an exulting shout broke from the guerilleros, and a voice was heard exclaiming,

"*Cenobio, Cenobio! Los cañones!*" (Cenobio Cenobio, the cannon!)

Clayley turned towards me with an inquiring look.

"It is true, Clayley; by heavens—we'll have it now."

"What did they say?"

"Look for yourself—well?"

"A brass piece, as I live; a six-pound carronade!"

"We are fighting the guerilla of Cenobia—a small army of itself. Neither stockade nor motte will avail us now."

"What is to be done?" asked my companion.

"Nothing, but die with arms in our hands. We will not die without a struggle, and the sooner we prepare for it the better."

I leaped from the roof, and ordered the bugler to sound the *assembly*.

In a moment, the clear notes rang out, and the soldiers formed before me in the corral.

"My brave comrades!" cried I, "they have got the advantage of us at last. They are bringing down a piece of artillery; and, I fear, these pickets will offer us but poor shelter. If we are driven out, we will strike for that island of timber; and, mark us, if we are broken, let every man fight his way as he best can, or die over a fallen enemy."

A determined cheer followed this short harangue, and I continued

"But we will first see how they use their piece. It is a small one, and will not destroy us all at once. Fling yourselves down as they fire. By lying flat on our faces, we may not suffer so badly. Perhaps we can hold the corral until our friends reach us. At all events, we will try."

Another cheer rang along the line.

"Great Heaven. Captain, it's terrible!" whispered the Major.

"What is terrible?" I asked, feeling at the moment a contempt for the blaspheming coward.

"Oh! this—this business—such a fix to be—"

"Major! remember you are a soldier."

"Yes; and I wish I had resigned, as intended to do, before this cursed war commenced."

"Never fear," said I, tempted to smile at the candor of his cowardice; "you'll drink wine at Hewlett's in a month. Get behind this log, it's the only point shot-proof in the whole stockade."

"Do you think, Captain, it will stop a shot?"

"Ay, from a siege-gun. Look out, men, and be ready to obey orders!"

The six-pounder had now approached within five hundred yards of the stockade, and was leisurely being unlimbered in the midst of a group of the enemy's artillerists.

At this moment, the voice of the Major arrested my attention.

"Great Heaven, Captain! Why do you allow them to come so near?"

"How am I to prevent them?" I asked, with some surprise.

"Why, my rifle will reach farther than that. It might keep them off, I think."

"Major, you are dreaming!" said I. "They are two hundred yards beyond range of our rifles. If they would only come within that, we would soon send them back for you."

"But, Captain, mine will carry twice the distance."

I looked at the Major, under the belief that he had taken leave of his senses.

"It's a Zünd-nadel, I assure you, and will kill at eight hundred yards."

"Is it possible!" cried I, starting; for I now recollected the curious-looking piece which I had ordered to be cut loose from the saddle of Hercules. "Why did you not tell me that before? Where is Major Blossom's rifle?" I shouted, looking around.

"This yeer's the Major's *gun*," answered Sergeant Lincoln. "But if it's a rifle, I never seed sich. It looks more like a two-year-old kannon."

It was, as the Major had declared, a conical ball-rifle—a new invention—of which I had heard something.

"Is it loaded, Major?" I asked, taking the piece from Lincoln.

"It is."

"Can you hit that man with the sponge?" said I, returning the piece to the hunter.

"If this yeer thing 'll carry fur enuf, I kin," was the reply.

"It will kill a thousand yards, point blank," cried the Major, with energy.

"Ha! are you sure of that, Major?" I asked.

"Certainly, Captain. I got it from the inventor. We tried it at Washington. It is the best Prussian conical ball. It bored a hole through an inch plank at that distance."

"Well. Now, Sergeant, take sure aim; this may save us yet."

Lincoln planted himself firmly on his feet, choosing a notch of the stockade that ranged exactly with his shoulder. He then carefully wiped the dust from the sights; and, placing the heavy barrel in the notch, laid his cheek slowly against the stock.

"Sergeant, the man with the shot!" I called out.

As I spake, one of the artillerists was stooping to the muzzle of the six-pounder, holding in his hand a spherical case-shot. Lincoln pressed the trigger. The crack followed, and the artillerist threw out his arms, and doubled over on his head without giving a kick.

The shot rolled out upon the green sward. A wild cry, expressive of extreme astonishment, broke from the guerilleros. At the same instant, a cheer rang through the corral.

"Well done!" cried a dozen voices at once.

In a moment, the rifle was wiped and re-loaded.

"This time, Sergeant, the fellow with the firelock."

During the re-loading of the rifle, the Mexicans around the six-pounder had somewhat recovered from their surprise, and had rammed home the cartridge. A tall artillerist stood, with linstock and fuse, near the breech, waiting for the order to fire. Before he received that order, the rifle again cracked—his arm flew up with a sudden jerk, and the smoking rod, flying from his grasp, was projected to the distance of twenty feet. The man, himself, spun round, and, staggering a pace or two, fell into the arms of his comrade.

"Cap'n jest allow me ter take that ere skunk, next time."

"Which one, Sergeant?" I asked.

"Him—thet's him on the black, makin sich a dod-rotted muss."

I recognised the horse and figure of Dubrosc.

"Certainly, by all means," said I, with a strange feeling at my heart, as I gave the order.

But, before Lincoln could reload, one of the Mexicans, apparently an officer had snatched up the burning fuse, and, running up, applied it to the touch

"On your faces, men!"

The ball came crashing through the thin pickets of the corral, and, whizzing across the enclosure, struck one of the mules on the flank, tearing open its hip, causing it to kick furiously as it tumbled over the ground. Its companions, stampeding, gallopped, for a moment, through the penn; then co-

..ecting in a corner, stood cowered up and quivering. A fierce yell announced the exultation of the guerilleros.

Dubrosc was sitting on his powerful mustang, facing the córral, and watching the effects of the shot.

"If he wur only 'ithin range ev my own lead," muttered Lincoln, as he glanced along the sights.

The crack soon followed—the black horse reared, staggered, and fell back on his rider!

"Ten strike! set 'em up!" exclaimed a soldier.

"Missed the skunk—curse him," cried Lincoln, gritting his teeth, as the horseman was seen to struggle from under the fallen animal. Rising to his feet, Dubrosc sprang out to the front, and shook his fist in the air, with a shout of defiance.

The guerilleros galloped back; and the artillerists, wheeling the six-pounder dragged it after, and took up a new position, about three hundred yards farther to the rear.

A second shot from the piece again tore through the pickets, striking one of our men, and killing him instantly.

'Aim at the artillerists, Sergeant. We have nothing to fear from the others."

Lincoln fired again. The shot hit the ground in front of the enemy's gun; but glancing, it struck one of the cannoniers, apparently wounding him badly, as he was carried back by his comrades.

The Mexicans, terror-struck at this strange instrument of destruction, took up a new position, two hundred yards still farther back. Their third shot ricochetted, striking the top of the strong plank, behind which the Major was screening himself, and only frightening the latter by the shock upon the timber.

Lincoln again fired. This time his shot produced no visible effect; and a taunting cheer from the enemy told that they felt themselves beyond range.

Another shot was fired from the rifle, apparently with a similar result.

"It's beyond her carry, Cap'n," said Lincoln, bringing the butt of his piece to the ground, with an expression of reluctant conviction.

"Try one more shot. If it fail, we willl reserve the others for closer work Aim high!"

This resulted as the two preceding ones; and a voice from the guerilleros was heard, exclaiming:

" *Yankes bobos! mas adelante!*" (A little farther, you Yankee fools.")

Another shot from the six-pounder cracked through the planks, knocking his piece from the hands of a soldier, and shivering the dry stock-wood into fifty fragments.

"Sergeant, give me the rifle," said I. 'They must be a thousand yards off; but, as they are as troublesome with that carronade, as if they were only ten. I will try one more shot."

I fired, but the ball sank at least fifty paces in front of the enemy.

"We expect too much. It is not a twenty-four pounder. Major, I envy you two things—your rifle and your horse."

"Hercules?"

"Of course."

"Lord, Captain, you may do what you will with the rifle; and, if ever we get out of the reach of these infernal devils, Hercules shall be—

At this moment, a cheer came from the guerilleros, and a voice was heard shouting above the din:

"*La metralla! la metralla!*" The howitzer!)

I leaped upon the roof, and looked out upon the plain. It was true. A howitzer-carriage, drawn by mules, was debouching from the woods, the animals dragging it along at a gallop.

It was evidently a piece of some size, large enough to tear the light picketing to pieces.

I turned towards my men with a look of despair. My eye at this moment rested on the drove of mules that stood crowded together in a corner of the pen. A sudden thought struck me. Might we not mount them and escape? There were more than enough to carry us all, and the ranche was filled with bridles and lariats. I instantly leaped from the roof, and gave the order to the men.

"Speedily, but without noise," cried I, as the men proceeded to fling bridles upon the necks of the animals.

In five minutes each soldier, with his rifle slung, stood by a mule, some of them having buckled on *tapadas*,* to prevent the animals from kicking.

The Major stood ready by his horse.

"Now, my brave fellows," shouted I in a loud voice, "we must take it cavalry fashion—Mexican cavalry, I mean." The men laughed. "Once in the woods, we will retreat no farther. At the words '*mount and fellow*,' spring

---

* The tapada is a blind of leather, that covers the whole face of a mule. It is used to tame them, and prevent their kicking when being loaded. With his tapada over his head, the most vicious *macho* becomes quite gentle.

to your seats and follow Mr. Clayley. I will look to your rear—dont't stop to fire—hold on well. If any one fall, let his nearest comrade take him up. Ha! any one hurt there? A shot had whistled through the ranks. "Only a scratch," was the reply.

"All ready, then, are you? Now, Mr. Clayley, you see the high timber—make direct for it. Down with the bars! '*Mount and fellow!*'"

As I uttered the last words, the men leaped to their seats; and Clayley, riding the bell-mule, dashed out of the corral, followed by the whole train, some of them plunging and kicking, but all gallopping forward at the sound of the bell upon their guide.

As the dark cavalcade rushed out upon the prairie, a wild cry from the guerilleros told that this was the first intimation they had had of the singular ruse. They sprung to their saddles with yells, and gallopped in pursuit. The howitzer, that had been trailed upon the corral, was suddenly wheeled about, and fired; but the shot, ill-directed in their haste, whistled harmlessly over our heads.

The guerilleros, on their swift steeds, soon lessened the distance between us.

With a dozen of the best men I hung in the rear, to give the foremost of the pursuers a volley, or pick up any soldier who might be tossed from his mule. One of these, at intervals, kicked as only a Mexican mule can; and, when within five hundred yards of the timber, his rider, an Irishman, was flung upon the prairie.

The rearmost of our party stopped to take him up. He was seized by Chane, who mounted him in front of himself. The delay had nearly been fatal. The pursuers were already within a hundred yards, firing their pistols and escopettes, without effect. A number of the men turned in their seats and blazed back. Others threw their rifles over their shoulders, and pulled trigger at random. I could perceive that two or three guerilleros dropped from their saddles. Their comrades, with shouts of vengeance, closed upon us nearer and nearer. The long lariats, far in advance, whistled around our heads.

I felt the slippery noose light upon my shoulders. I flung out my arms to throw it off, but, with a sudden jerk, it tightened around my neck. I clutched the hard thong, and pulled with all my might. It was all in vain. The animal I rode, freed from my *manège*, seemed to plunge under me, and gather up its back with a vicious determination; and I was launched in the air, and dashed to the earth with a stunning violence.

I felt myself dragged along the gravelly ground. I grasped the weeds, but they came away in my hands, torn up by the roots. There was a struggle above and around me. I could hear loud shouts, and the firing of guns.

I was choking.

A bright object glistened before my eyes. I felt myself seized by a strong rough hand, and swung into the air, and rudely shaken, as if in the grasp of some giant's arm.

Something twitched me sharply over the cheeks. I heard the rustling of trees. Branches snapped and crackled, and leaves swept across my face. Then came the flash—flash—and the crack—crack—crack—of a dozen rifles, and, under their blazing light, I was dashed a second time with violence to the earth!

CHAPTER XXIII.

THE RESCUE.

"Rough handlin' Cap'n. Yer must excuse haste."

It was the voice of Lincoln.

"Ha! in the timber? Safe, then!" ejaculated I, in return.

"Two or three wounded—not bad neither. Chane has got a stab in the hip—he gin the feller goss. Let me louze the darned thing off your neck. It kum mighty near chokin' yer, Cap'n."

Bob proceeded to unwind the noose end of a lariat, that, with some six feet of a rawhide thong, was still tightly fastened around my neck.

"But who cut the rope?" demanded I.

"I did, with this yere tooth-pick. Yer see, Cap'n, it warn't yer time to be hung jest yet."

I could not help smiling, as I thanked the hunter for my safety.

"But where are the guerilleros?" asked I, looking around, my brain somewhat confused.

"Yander they are, keeping safe out 'o range of this yere long gun'—just listen to 'em—what a hiller-balloo!"

The Mexican horsemen were galloping out on the prairie, their arms glistning under the clear moonlight.

"Take to the trees, men!" cried I, seeing that the enemy had again unlimbered, and were preparing to discharge their howitzer.

In a moment the iron shower came whizzing through the branches, without doing any injury, as each of the men had covered his body with a tree. Several of the mules that stood tied and trembling, were killed by the discharge.

Another shower hurtled through the bushes with a similar effect.

I was thinking of retreating further into the timber, and was walking back to reconnoitre the ground, when my eye fell upon an object that arrested my attention. It was the body of a very large man, lying flat upon his face, his head buried among the roots of a cork-tree. The arms were stiffly pressed against his sides, and the legs projected at full stretch, exhibiting an appearance of motionless rigidity, as though a well-dressed corpse had been rolled over on its face. I at once recognised it as the body of the Major, whom I supposed to have fallen dead where he lay.

"Good heavens! Clayley, look here!" cried I, "poor Blossom's killed!"

"No, I'll be hanged if I am," growled the latter, screwing his neck round like a lizard, and looking up without changing the attitude of his body. Clayley was convulsed with laughter. The Major sheathed his head again, as he knew that another shot from the howitzer might soon be expected.

"Major," cried Clayley, "that right shoulder of yours projects over at least six inches."

"I know it," answered the Major, in a frightened voice; "curse the tree; it's hardly big enough to cover a squirrel;" and he squatted closer to the earth, pressing his arms tighter against his sides. His whole attitude was so ludicrous, that Clayley burst into a second yell of laughter. At this moment a wild shout was heard from the guerilleros.

"What next?" cried I, running toward the front, and looking out upon the prairie.

"Them wild cats are gwine to clar out, Cap'n," said Lincoln, meeting me 'I kin see them hitchin' up."

"It is as you say! What can be the reason?"

A strange commotion was visible in the groups of horsemen. Scouts were gallopping across the plain to a point of the woods about half a mile distant, and I could see the artillerists fastening their mules to the howitzer-carriage. Suddenly, a bugle rang out, sounding the recal, and the guerilleros, with wild yells gallopped off towards Medellin!

A loud cheer, such as was never uttered by Mexican throats, came from the opposite edge of the prairie; and looking in that direction, I beheld a long line of dark forms debouching from the woods at a gallop. Their sparkling blades, as they issued from the dark forest, glistened like a cordon of fire-flies; and I recognised the heavy foot-fall of the American horse. A cheer from my men attracted their attention; and the leader of the dragoons, seeing that the guerilleros had got far out of reach, wheeled his column to the right, and came gallopping down.

"Is that Colonel Rawley?" inquired I, recognising a dragoon officer

"Why, bless my soul!" exclaimed he, "how did you get out? We heard you were jugged. All alive yet?"

"We have lost two," I replied.

"Pah! that's nothing. I came out expecting to bury the whole kit of you. Here's Clayley, too. Clayley, your friend Twing's with us; you'll find him in the rear."

"Ha! Clayley, old boy," cried Twing, coming up, "no bones broke; al right. Take a pull; do you good—don't drink it all, though—leave a thimbleful for Haller, there. How do you like that?"

"Delicious, by Jove!" ejaculated Clayley, tugging away at the Major's flask.

'Come, Captain, try it.'

"Thank you."

'But where is old Blos; killed, wounded, or missing?"

"I believe the Major is not far off, and still uninjured."

I despatched a man for the Major, who presently came up blowing and swearing like a Flander's trooper.

"Hilloa, Blos!" shouted Twing, grasping him by the hand.

"Why, bless me, Twing, I'm glad to see you," answered Blossom, throwing his arms around the diminutive Major. "But where on earth is your pewter?" for during the embrace he had groped all over Twing's body for the flask.

"Here, Cudgo! that flask boy."

"Faith, Twing, I'm near choked; we've been fighting all day—a devil of a fight. I chased a whole squad of the cursed scoundrels on Hercules, and came within a squirrel's jump of riding right into their nest. We've killed dozens; but Haller will tell you all. He's a good fellow, that Haller, but he's too rash—rash as blazes. Hilloa, Hercules! glad to see you again, old fellow; you had a sharp brush for it."

"Remember your promise, Major," said I, as the Major stood patting Hercules upon the shoulder.

"I'll do better, Captain. I'll give you a choice between Hercules and a splendid black I have. Faith! it's hard to part with you, old Herky, but I know the Captain will like the black better; he's the handsomest horse in the whole army—bought him from poor Ridgely, who was killed at Monterey."

This speech of tha Major's was delivered partly in soliloquy, partly in an apostrophe to Hercules, and partly to myself.

"Very well, Major," I replied. "I'll take the black. Mr. Clayley, mount the men on their mules,—you will take command of the company, and proceed with Colonel Rawley to camp. I shall go myself for the Don."

The last was said in a whisper to Clayley.

"We may not get in before noon to-morrow. Say nothing of my absence to any one. I will make my report at noon to-morrow."

"And Captain——" said Clayley.

"Well Clayley?"

"You will carry back my——"

"What? To which, friend?"

"To Mary, of the Light."

"Oh! certainly!"

"In your best Spanish."

"Rest assured," said I, smiling at the earnestness of my friend.

I was about moving from the spot, when the thought occurred to me to send the company to camp, under command of Oakes and take Clayley along with me.

"Clayley, by the way," said I calling the Lieutenant back; "I don't see why you may not carry your compliments in person. Oakes can take the men back. I will borrow half-a-dozen dragoons from Rawley."

"With all my heart," replied Clayley.

"Come then, get a horse, and let us be off."

Taking Lincoln and Raoul, with half-a-dozen of Rawley's dragoons, I bade my friends "good night."

These started for camp by the road of Mata Cordera, while I, with my little party brushed for some distance round the border of the prairie, and climbed the hill, over which lay the path to the house of the Spaniard.

As I reached the top of the ridge, I turned to look upon the scene of our late skirmish.

The cold round moon, looking down upon the prairie of la Virgen, saw none of the victims of the fight.

The Jarochos, in their retreat had carried off their dead and wounded comrades; and the Americans slept under ground, in the lone corral; but I could not help fancying that gaunt wolves were skulking round the enclosure, and that the claws of the *coyote* were already tearing up the red earth that had been hurriedly heaped over their graves!

CHAPTER XXIV.

THE COCUYO.

A NIGHT ride through the golden tropical forest, when the moon is bathing its broad and wax-like frondage—when the winds are hushed, and the long leaves hang drooping and silent—when the path conducts through dark aisles and arbors of green vine leaves, and out again into bright and flowery glades—is one of those luxuries that I wish we could obtain without going beyond the limits of our own land.

But, no. The romance of our northern forest—the romance that lingers around the gnarled limbs of the oak, and the maple, and the elm—that sighs with the wintry wind high up among the twigs of the shining sycamore—that flits along the huge fallen trunks—that nestles in the brown and rustling leaves—that hovers above the bold cliff, and sleeps upon the grey rock—that sparkles in the diamond stalactites of the forest, or glides along the bosom of the cold black river—is a feeling or a fancy of a far different character.

These objects—themselves the emblems of the stony and iron things of nature—call up associations of the darker passions: strange scenes of strife and bloodshed; struggles between red and white savages—and struggles hardly less fierce with the wild beasts of the forest. The rifle, the tomahawk and the knife, are the visions conjured up, while the savage whoop and the dread yell, echo in your ear; and you dream of *war*.

Far different are the thoughts that suggest themselves as you glide along under the aromatic arbors of the southern forest; brushing aside the silken foliage, and treading upon the shadows of picturesque palms.

It was here we first met with the *cocuyo*, the beautiful firefly of the tropics. Its body is about the size of an almond, and its eyes (from whence issues the peculiar light) rather smaller than swan shot. Nothing can be conceived richer than the color of these, combining the three elements of green, gold, and light. With regard to their use as a lamp to read by, the mode hereafter described is the correct one. But this beautiful insect fills a much higher post of honor. It is used as an ornament for the dark tresses of the "doncellas" of Vera Cruz, I have seen a pair of them *pinned* to their hair—one glancing over each temple—like sentinels, watcing over the beauties that lay beneath. No diamond can display half the effulgence of these insect ornaments. Once at a *réunion* in Jalapa, I was particularly struck with the coiffeur of a very beautiful lady, that fairly gleamed with cocuyos—exhibiting a perfect constellation of them. I was struck not less with the cruelty (as I supposed) of thus wantonly impaling the harmless little creatures, for the gratification of a mere vanity. During the evening, I took occasion to hint my sentiments on the subject to the lady herself, who burst into a fit of laughter, and whisking one of the cocuyos from her head, held it before my eyes, and slowly disengaged the long, golden pin, upon which, as I thought, the insect had been impaled. My astonishment equalled my delight on seeing that this pin, instead of piercing the animal's body, had merely passed through a small loop under the breast, and the only pain to which the insect was subjected by the operation, was that of captivity. I could not help thinking that this singular loop was a provision of nature for this very purpose. When laid aside, after being used in this manner, the cocuyos are kept in a small wicker-basket, or cage, and fed upon flowers and chips of sugar cane. Cocuyos are brought to the market of Vera Cruz by the country people, who take them in the chapparal.

The *cocuyo* lights your way through the dark aisles, and the nightingale cheers you with his varied and mimic song. A thousand sights and sounds, that seem to be possessed of some mysterious and narcotic power, lull you into silence and sleep—a sleep whose dream is *love*.

Clayley and I felt this, as we rode silently along. Even the ruder hearts of our companions seemed touched by the same influence.

We entered the dark forest that fringed the arroyo; and the stream was crossed in silence. Raoul rode in advance, acting as our guide.

After a long silence, Clayley suddenly awoke from his reverie, and straightened himself up in the saddle.

"What time is it, Captain?" he inquired.

"Ten—a few minutes past," answered I, holding my watch under the moonlight.

"I wonder if the Don's in bed, yet!"

Not likely, he will be in distress; he expected us an hour ago"

"True, he will not sleep till we come; all right then."

"How all right then?"

"For our chances of a supper; a cold pasty, with a glass of Barsac. What think you?"

"I do not feel hungry."

"But I do—as a hawk. I long to sound the Don's larder."

"Do you not long more to see—?"

"Not to-night—no—that is until after supper. Everything in its own time and place; but a man with a hungry stomach, has no stomach for anything but eating. I pledge you my word, Haller, I would rather at this moment see that grand old stewardess Pepe, than the loveliest woman in Mexico, and that's 'Mary of the Light.'"

"Monstrous!"

"That is, until after I have supped. Then my feelings will doubtless take a turn."

"Ah! Clayley, you can never love!"

"Why so, Captain?"

"With you, love is a sentiment, not a passion. You regard the fair blonde as you would a picture, or a curious ornament."

"You mean to say, then, that my love is 'all in my eye'?"

"Exactly so, in a literal sense. I do not think it has reached your heart, else you would not be thinking of your supper. Now, I could go for days without food—suffer any hardship!—but—no—you cannot understand this."

"I confess not. I am too hungry."

"You could forget—nay, I should not be surprised if you have already forgotten all but the fact that your mistress is a blonde, with bright golden hair. Is it not so?"

"I confess, Captain, that I should make but a poor portrait of her from memory."

"And were I a painter, I could throw her features upon the canvass as truly as if they were before me. I see her face outlined upon these broad leaves—her dark eyes burning in the flash of the cocuyo—her long black hair drooping from the feathery fringes of the palm—and her—"

"Stop!" You are dreaming, Captain! Her eyes are not dark—her hair is not black!"

"What! Her eyes not dark?—as ebony, or night!"

"Blue as a turquois!"

"Black. What are you thinking of?"

"Mary of the Light."

"Oh, that is quite a different affair;" and my friend and I laughed heartily at our mutual misconceptions.

We rode on, again relapsing into silence. The stillness of the night was broken only by the heavy hoof bounding back from the hard turf, the jingling of spurs, or the ringing of the iron scabbard, as it struck against the moving flanks of our horses.

We had crossed the sandy spar, with its chapparal of cactus and mezquite, and were entering a gorge of heavy timber, when the practised eye of Lincoln detected an object in the dark shadow of the woods.

"Halt!" cried I, in a low voice.

The party reined up at the order. A rustling was heard in the bushes a-head.

"*Quien viva?*" challenged Raoul, in the advance."

"*Un amigo,*" was the response.

I sprang forward to the side of Raoul, and called out,

'*Acercate, ace vite?*"—(Come near.)

A figure moved out of the bushes, and approached.

"*Esta el Capitan?*"—(Is it the Captain?)

I recognised the guide given me by Don Cosme.

The Mexican approached, handed me a small piece of paper. I rode into an opening, and held it up to the moonlight, but the writing was in pencil, and I could not make out a single letter.

"Try this, Clayley. Perhaps your eyes are better than mine."

"No," said Clayley, after examining the paper. "I can hardly see the writing upon it."

"*Esperate, mi amo,*" (Wait, my master,) said the guide, making me a sign. We remained motionless.

The Mexican took from his head his heavy *sombrero,* and stepped into a darker recess of the forest. After standing for a moment, hat in hand, a brilliant object shot out from the leaves of the palma redonda. It was the *cuyo*—the fire-fly of the tropics. With a low, humming sound, it came istening along at the height of seven or eight feet from the ground. The an sprang up, and, with a sweep of his arm, jerked it suddenly to the earth, overing it with his hat, and, inverting his hand, caught the gleaming insect, nd presented it to me, with the ejaculation·

"*Ya!*" (Now.)

"*No muerde,*" (It does not bite,) added he, as he saw that I hesitated to touch the beetle-shaped insect.

I took the cocuyo in my hand, the green golden fire flashing from its great round eyes. I held it up before the writing, but the faint glimmer was scarcely discernable upon the paper.

"Why, it would require a dozen of these to make sufficient light?" I said to the guide.

"*No, Señor, uno basta—asi,*" (No, sir, one is enough—thus—) and the Mexican, taking the cocuyo in his fingers, pressed it gently against the surface of the paper. It produced a brilliant light, radiating over a circle of several inches in diameter.

Every point in the writing was plainly visible.

"See, Clayley!" cried I, admiring this lamp of nature's own making. "Never trust the tales of travelers. I have heard that half a dozen of these insects in a glass vessel would enable you to read the smallest type. Is that true?" added I, repeating what I had said in Spanish.

"*No, Señor; ni cincuenta,*" (No, sir; nor fifty,) replied the Mexican.

"And yet, with a single cocuyo, you may—but we have forgotten—let us see what's here."

I bent my head to the paper, and read in Spanish:—

"*I have made known your situation to the American commander.*"

There was no signature nor other mark upon the paper.

"From Don Cosme?" I inquired in a whisper to the Mexican.

"Yes, Señor," was the reply.

"And how did you expect to reach us in the corral?"

"*Asi,*" (so) said the man holding up a shaggy bull's hide, which he carried over his arm.

"We have friends here, Clayley. Come, my good fellow, take this!" and I handed a gold eagle to the *péon.*

"Forward!"

The tinkling of canteens, the jingling of sabres, and the echo of bounding hoofs, recommenced. We were again in motion, filing up through the shadowy woods.

CHAPTER XXV

LUPE AND LUZ.

THESE are the familiar abbreviations of Guadalupe and Maria de la Luz. The names themselves (especially the former) are common in Mexican families. Guadalupe is the name of the Saint Patroness of Mexico; and she has been daily honored at the baptismal font, scarcely a family in Mexico being without its Guadalupe. Lupita, Guadalupita, are familiar forms of the same appellation.

Shortly after, we debouched from the forest, entering the open fields of Don Cosme's plantation. There was a flowery brilliance around us full of novelty. We had been accustomed to the ruder scenes of a northern clime. The tropical moon threw a gauzy veil over objects that softened their outlines; and the notes of the nightingale were the only sounds that broke the stillness of what seemed a sleeping elysium.

Once a vanilla plantation—here and there the aromatic bean grew wild—its ground usurped by the maguey, the acacia, and the thorny cactus. The dry reservoir and the ruined *acequia* proved the care that had, in former times, been bestowed on its irrigation. *Guarda-rayas* of palms and orange trees, choked up with vines and jessamines—marked the ancient boundaries of the fields. Clusters of fruit and flowers hung from the drooping branches; and the aroma of a thousand shrubs was wafted upon the night air. We felt its narcotic influence as we rode along. The helianthus bowed its golden head, as if weeping at the absence of its god; and the cereus spread its snowy blossom, joying in the more mellow light of the moon.

Having in the preceding paragraph spoken of the maguey, perhaps our readers would like a more full description of that valuable plant:

The wild maguey, or aloe, is found all through the woods of the *tierra caliente*. From this the mezcal is distilled. Its root and part of its leaves, when roasted in a peculiar way, known to the natives, are a delicious esculent, not unlike citron preserve. It produces a strange prinkling upon the tongues of those who are not used to it. The cactus grows in all parts of Mexico, and n a hundred varieties, with as many different names. A description of the different species and their peculiarities would fill a volume. Some of them attain the height of twenty or thirty feet, and assume the appearance of trees; others, as the *pitahaya*, shoot up in straight regular columns, lending a most picturesque character to the landscape. The fruits of several species, as the tuna and pitahaya, are much valued, and brought to market in large quantities.] We will now resume the thread of our story.

The guide pointed to one of the guarda-rayas that led to the house. We struck into it, and rode forward. The path was pictured by the moonbeams, as they glanced through the half-shadowing leaves. An antelope bounded away before us, brushing his soft flanks against the rustling thorns of the mesquite.

Farther on we entered the grounds, and, halting behind the jessamines, dismounted. Clayley and myself entered the enclosure.

As we pushed through a copse, we were saluted by the hoarse bark of a couple of mastiffs; and we could perceive several forms moving in front of the ranche. We stopped a moment to observe them.

"*Quitate, Carlo! Pompo!*" (Be off, Carlo, Pompo!) The dogs growled fiercely, barking at intervals.

"*Papa—mandalos!*" (Papa—order them off.)

We recognised the voices, and pressed forward.

"*Afuera! malditos perros, abajo!*" (Out of the way, wicked dogs—down!) shouted Don Cosme, chiding the fierce brutes, and driving them back.

The dogs were secured by several domestics, and we advanced.

"*Quien es?*" inquired Don Cosme.

"*Amigos*" (friends), I replied.

"*Papa—papa—es el Capitan*" (papa, it is the captain), cried one of the sisters, who had run out in advance; and whom I recognised as the elder one.

"Do not be alarmed, Señorita," said I, approaching.

"Oh! you are safe—you are safe!—papa, he is safe!" cried both the girls at once; while Don Cosme exhibited his joy by hugging my comrade and myself alternately.

Suddenly letting go, he threw up his hands, and inquired, with a look of anxiety,

"*Y el Señor gordo?*" (and the fat gentleman?)

"Oh! he's all right," replied Clayley, with a laugh: "he has saved his bacon, Don Cosme; though, I imagine about this time, he wouldn't object to a little of yours."

I translated my companion's answer. The latter part of it seemed to act upon Don Cosme as a hint; and we were immediately hurried to the dining-oom, where we found the Doña Joaquina preparing supper.

During our meal, I recounted the principal events of the day. Don Cosme knew nothing of these guerilleros, although he had heard that there were bands in the neighborhood. Learning from the guide that we had been attacked, he had dispatched a trusty servant to the American camp, and Raoul had met the party coming to our rescue.

After supper, Don Cosme left us to give some orders relative to his departure in the morning. His lady set about preparing the sleeping apartments, and my companion and I were left for several hours in the sweet companionship of *Lupé* and *Luz*.

Both were exquisite musicians—playing the harp and guitar with equal cleverness. Many a pure Spanish melody was poured into the delighted ears of my friend and myself. The thoughts that arose in our minds, were doubtless of a similar kind, and yet how strange that our hearts should have been warmed to love by beings so different in character. The gay, free spirit of my comrade seemed to have met a responsive echo. He and his brilliant partner laughed, chatted, and sang in turns. In the incidents of the moment, this light-hearted creature had forgotten her brother, yet, the next moment, she would weep for him. A tender heart—a heart of joys and sorrows—of ever-changing emotions—coming and passing like shadows thrown by straggling clouds upon the sun-lit stream!

Unlike was our converse. More serious. "We may not laugh, lest we should profane the holy sentiment that is stealing upon us. There is no mirth in love. There are joy, pleasure, luxury; but laughter finds no echo in the heart that loves. Love is a feeling of anxiety—of expectation. The harp is set aside. The guitar lies untouched for a sweeter music—the music that vibrates from the strings of the heart. Are our eyes not held together by some invisible chain? Are our souls not in communion through some mysterious means? It is not language—at least not the language of words; for we are conversing upon indifferent things—not indifferent, either. Narcisso, Narcisso a theme fraternal. His peril casts a cloud over our happiness.

'Oh! that he were here, then we could be happy indeed."

"He will return; fear not—grieve not; to-morrow your father will easily find him. I will leave no means untried to restore him to so fond a sister."

"Thanks, thanks; oh! we are already indebted to you so much."

Are those eyes swimming with love? or gratitude? or both at once? Surely gratitude alone does not speak so wildly? Could this scene not last or ever?

"Good night—good night!"

"*Señores, dasan Vds. buena noche!*" (Gentlemen may you pass a pleasant night.)

They are gone; and those oval developments of face and figure are floating before me, as though the body itself were still present. It is the soft memory of love in all its growing distinctness!

* * * * * * * * *

We were shown to our sleeping apartments. Our men picketed their horses under the olives, and slept in the bamboo ranche, a single sentry walking his rounds during the night.

CHAPTER XXVI.

A TOUGH NIGHT OF IT AFTER ALL.

I ENTERED my chamber—to sleep? No. And yet it contained a bed fit for Morpheus. A bed canopied and curtained, with clothes from the looms of Damascus. Shining rods roofed upwards, and met in an ornamental design, where the god of sleep, fanned by virgins of silver, reclined upon a couch of roses.

I drew aside the curtains—a bank of snow—pillows, as if prepared for the cheek of a beautiful bride. I had not slept in a bed for two months. A close crib in a transport-ship; a "shake down" among scorpions and spiders upon Lobos—a single blanket among the sand-hills, where it was not unusual to wake up half buried by the drift.*

These were my souvenirs. Fancy the prospect. It certainly invited repose. And yet I was in no humor to sleep. My brain was in a whirl. The strange incidents of the day—some of them were mysterious—crowded into my mind. My whole system, mental as well as physical, was flushed; and thought followed thought with nervous rapidity.

My heart shared the excitement—chords long silent, had been touched—the divine element was fairly enthroned. I was in love!

It was not the first passion of my life, and I easily recognised it. Even jealousy had begun to distil its poison—" Don Santiago!"

I was standing in front of a large mirror, when I noticed two small miniatures hanging against the wall, one on each side of the glass.

---

* This was a common occurrence. On one occasion, my company were employed for twenty-four hours on outpost duty. When we returned to our former bivouack, the soldiers found their knapsacks completely buried in the drift. Even hills of fifty feet high are thrown up in a single night, and others of equal altitude disappear as quickly. The tops of tall trees are often trodden under foot as you pass along these sandy ridges

I bent over to examine, first, that which hung upon the right. I gazed with emotion. They were *her* features; "and yet," thought I, "the painter has not flattered her; it might better represent her, ten years hence; still the likeness is there—stupid artist!" I turned to the other. "Her fair sister, no doubt—gracious heaven! Do my eyes deceive me? No! the black wavy hair—the arching brows—the sinister lip—*Dubrosc*."

A sharp pang shot through my heart. I looked at the picture again and again, with a kind of incredulous bewilderment; but every fresh examination only strengthened conviction. "There is no mistaking those features—they are his!" Paralyzed with the shock, I sank into a chair; my heart filled with the most painful emotions.

For some moments I was unable to think, much less to act.

"What can it mean? Is this accomplished villain a fiend?—the fiend of my existence?—thus to cross me at every point, perhaps in the end to —"

Our mutual dislike at first meeting—Lobos—his re-appearance upon the sand-hills—the mystery of his passing the lines, and again appearing with the guerilla—all came forcibly upon my recollection, and now——I seized the lamp, and rushed back to the pictures.

'Yes, I am not mistaken; it is he—it is she, her features—all—all. And thus, too!—the position—side by side—counterparts! There are no others on the wall—matched—mated—perhaps betrothed! His name, too, Don Emilio! The American who taught them English! *His* is Emile—the voice cried 'Emile!' Oh! the coincidence is complete. This villain—handsome and accomplished as he is—has been here before me! Betrothed—perhaps married—perhaps——Torture horrible!"

I reeled back to my chair, dashing the lamp recklessly upon the table. I know not how long I sate, but a world of wintry thoughts passed through my heart and brain. A clock striking from a large picture awoke me from my reverie. I did not count the hours. Music began to play behind the picture. It was a sad, sweet air, that chimed with my feelings, and, to some extent, soothed them. I arose at length, and hastily undressing, threw myself upon the bed, mentally resolving to forget all—to forget that I had ever seen her.

"I will rise early—return to camp without meeting her; and. once there, my duties will drive away this painful fancy. The drum and the fife, and the roar of the cannon, will drown remembrance. Ha! it was only a passing thought at best—the hallucination of a moment. I shall easily get rid of it. Ha! ha!"

I laid my fevered cheek upon the soft, cool pillow. I felt composed—almost happy.

"A creole of New Orleans! How could he have been here? Oh! have I not the explanation already? Why should I dwell on it?"

A jealous heart—it is easy to say "forget."

I tried to prevent my thoughts from returning to this theme. I directed them to a thousand things. To the ships—to the landing—to the army—to the soldiers—to the buttons upon their jackets, and the swabs upon their shoulders—to every thing I could think of—all in vain. Back, back, back, in painful throes it came, and my heart throbbed, and my brain burned with bitter memories freshly awakened.

I turned, and tossed upon my couch for many a long hour. The clock in the picture struck, and played the same music again and again, still soothing me as before! Even despair has its moments of respite; and worn with fatigue—mental as well as physical—I listened to the sad strain until it died away into my dreams.

CHAPTER XXVII.

THE LIGHT AFTER THE SHADE.

When I awoke, all was darkness around me. I threw out my arms, and opened the damask curtains. Not a ray of light entered the room. I felt refreshed, and from this I concluded I must have slept long. I slipped out upon the floor, and commenced groping for my watch. Some one knocked.

"Come in," I called.

The door opened, and a flood of light gushed into the apartment. It was a servant, bearing a lamp.

"What is the hour?" I demanded.

"Nine o'clock, my master," was the reply.

The servant set down the lamp, and went out. Another immediately entered, carrying a salver with a small gold cup.

"What have you there?"

"*Chocolate*,* master, Dona Joaquina has sent it."

I drank off the beverage, and hastened to dress myself. I was reflecting whether I should pass on to camp, without seeing any one of the family. Somehow, my heart felt less heavy. I believe the morning always brings relief to pain, either mental or bodily. It seems to be a law of nature—at

---

* The first thing a Mexican does after getting up, is to swallow a very small cup of chocolate made very thick and sweet. This is called *desayunar*, and corresponds to th French déjeûner. Your Mexican lives on this till half-past ten or eleven, when he takes breakfast (almuerzo), although this breakfast bears far more resemblance to a dinner than to the meal whose name it bears.

least so my experience tells me. The morning air, buoyant and balmy. dulls the edge of anguish. New hopes arise, and new projects appear with the sun. The invalid, couch-tossing through the long watches of the night, will acknowledge this truth. I did not approach the mirror. I dared not.

"I will not look upon the loved, the hated face—no, on to the camp—let Lethe— Has my friend arisen?"

"Yes, master; he has been up for hours."

"Ha! where is he?"

"In the garden, master."

"Alone?"

"No, master; he is with the *niñas*."

"Happy, light-hearted Clayley! No jealous thoughts to torture him," mused I, as I buckled on my stock.

I had observed that the fair-haired sister and he were kindred spirits—sympathetic natures, who only needed to be placed, *en rapport*, to "like each other mightily"—who could laugh, dance, and sing together, romp for months, and then get married, as a thing of course; but should any accident prevent this happy consummation, could say "good bye," and part, without a broken heart on either side. An easy thing for natures like theirs; a return exchange of numerous *billets doux*—a laugh over the past, and a light heart for the future! Such is the history of many a love. I can vouch for it. How different with —

"Tell my friend, when he returns to the house, I would desire to see him."

"Yes, master."

The servant bowed, and left the room.

In a few minutes, Clayley made his appearance, gay as a grasshopper.

"So, good lieutenant, you have been improving your time, I hear?"

"Haven't I, though? Such a delicious stroll! Haller—this *is* a paradise.'

"Where have you been?

"Feeding the swans," replied Clayley, with a laugh.

"But, by the way, your *chère amie* hangs her pretty head this morning. She seems hurt that you have not been up. She kept constantly looking toward the house."

"Clayley, will you do me the favor to order the men to their saddles?"

"What! going so soon? Not before breakfast, though?"

"In five minutes."

"Why, Captain what's the matter? And such a breakfast as they ar getting! Oh Don Cosme will not hear of it."

"Don Cosme——."

Our host entered at that moment, and, listening to his remonstrances, the order was rescinded, and I consented to remain.

I saluted the ladies with as much courtesy as I could assume. I could not help the coldness of my manner; and I could perceive that, with her it did not pass unobserved.

We sate down to the breakfast-table, but my heart was full of bitterness; and I scarcely touched the delicate viands that were placed before me.

"You do not eat, Capitan. I hope you are well?" said Don Cosme, observing my strange and somewhat rude demeanor.

"Thank you, Señor. I never enjoyed better health."

I studiously avoided looking towards her, paying slight attentions to her sister. This is the game of piques. Once or twice, I ventured a side glance. Her eyes were bent upon me with a strange, inquiring look.

They are swimming in tears—and soft—and forgiving. They are swollen. She has been weeping. That is not strange. Her brother's danger is, no doubt, the cause of her sorrow.

Yet is there not reproach in her looks? Reproach? How ill does my conduct of last night correspond with this affected coldness—this rudeness! Can she, too, be suffering?

I arose from the table, and, walking forth, ordered Lincoln to prepare the men for marching.

I strolled down among the orange-trees. Clayley followed soon after, accompanied by both the girls. Don Cosme remained at the house to superintend the saddling of his mule, while Doña Joaquina was packing the last articles into his portmanteau.

Following some silent instinct, we came together. Clayley and his mistress had strayed away, leaving us alone. I had not yet spoken. I felt a strange impulse,—a desire to know the worst. I felt as one looking over a fearful precipice.

Then I will brave the danger; it can be no worse than this agony of suspicion—of suspense.

I turned towards her. Her head was bent to one side. She was crushing an orange-flower between her fingers, and her eyes seemed to follow the dropping fragments.

How beautiful was she at that moment!

"The artist has not certainly flattered you."

She looked at me with a bewildered expression. Oh! those swimming eyes!

She did not understand me.

I repeated the observation.

"Señor Captain, what do you mean?"

"That the painter has not done you justice. The portrait is certainly a likeness, yet the expression, I think, should have been younger."

"The painter! What painter? The portrait! What portrait, Señor?"

"I refer to your portrait, which I accidentally found hanging in my apartment."

"Ah! by the mirror?"

"Yes; by the mirror," I answered sullenly.

"But it is not mine, Señor Capitan."

"Ha!—how? Not yours?"

"No; it is the portrait of my cousin, Maria de Mereed. They saw we were much alike."

My heart expanded. My whole frame quivered under the influence of joyful emotions.

"And the gentleman?" I faltered out.

"Don Emilio? He was cousin's lover—*huyeron.*"*

As she repeated the last word, she turned her head away, and I thought there was a sadness in her manner.

I was about to speak, when she continued:—

"It was her room,—we have not touched anything."

"And where is your cousin, now?"

"We know not."

"There is a mystery," thought I. I pressed the subject no farther. It was nothing to me, now. My heart was happy.

"Let us walk farther, Lupita."

She turned her eyes upon me with an expression of wonder. The change in my manner—so sudden—how was she to account for it? I could have knelt before her, and explained all. Reserve disappeared; and the confidence of the preceding night was fully restored.

We wandered along under the *guarda-rayas* amidst sounds and scenes suggestive of love and tenderness. Love! We heard it in the songs of a thousand birds—in the humming of the bees—in the voices of all nature around us. We felt it in our own hearts. The late cloud had passed, making the sky still brighter than before—the re-action had heightened our mutual

---

* Literally, "they fled;" figuratively, "they eloped."

passion to the intensity of non-resistance; and we walked on, her hand clasped in mine. We had eyes only for each other.

We reached a clump of cocoa-trees—one of them had fallen, and its smooth trunk offered a seat, protected from the sun, by the shadowy leaves of its fellows. On this we sate down. There was no resistance—no reasoning process—no calculation of advantages, and chances—such as is too often mingled with the noble passion of love. We felt nothing of this—nothing but that undefinable impulse which had entered our hearts, and against whose mystical power neither of us dreamed of struggling. Delay and duty were alike forgotten.

"I shall ask that question now—I shall know my fate at once."

In the changing scene of a soldier's life, there is but little time for the slow formalities—the zealous vigils—the complicated finesse of courtship. Perhaps this consideration impelled me. I have but little confidence in the cold heart that is won by a series of assiduities. There is too much calculation of after-events—too much selfishness. These reflections passed through my mind. I bent towards my companion, and whispered to her in that language—rich above all others in the vocabulary of the heart—

"*Guadalupe, tu me amas?*" (Guadalupe, do you love me?)

"*Yo te amo!*" was the simple reply.

The confession rendered her sacred in my eyes; and we sate for some time silent—enjoying that transport only known to those who have truly, purely loved.

The trampling of hoofs! It was Clayley at the head of the troop. They were mounted, and waiting for me. Don Cosme was impatient; so was the Doña Joaquina. I could not blame them, knowing the cause.

"Ride forward! I will follow presently."

The horsemen filed off into the fields, headed by the lieutenant, beside whom rode Don Cosme, on his white mule.

"You will soon return, Enrique?"

"I will lose no opportunity; I shall long for the hour more than you, I fear."

"Oh! no, no!"

"Believe me yes, Lupita! Say again you will never cease to love me!"

"Never, never! *Tuya, tuya, hasta la muerte!*" (Yours till death.)

How often has this question been asked! How often answered as above!

I sprang into the saddle. A parting look—another from a distance—a wave of the hand—and the next moment I was urging my horse in full gallop along under the shadowy palms.

CHAPTER XXVIII.

A DISAPPOINTMENT AND A NEW PLAN.

I OVERTOOK my companions as they were entering the woods. Clayley, who had been looking back from time to time, brushed alongside, as if wishing to enter into conversation.

"Hard work, Captain, to leave such quarters. By Jove, I could have stayed for ever."

"Come, Clayley, you are in love."

"Yes; they who live in glass houses—Oh! if I could only speak the lingo as you do."

I could not help smiling, for I had overheard him through the trees making the most he could of his partner's broken English. I was curious to know how he had sped, and whether he had been as "quick upon the trigger" as myself. My curiosity was soon relieved.

"I tell you, Captain," he continued, "if I could only have talked it, I would have put the question on the spot. I did try to git a "yes" or a "no" out of her; but she either couldn't. or wouldn't understand me. It was all bad luck."

"Could you not make her understand you? Surely she knows English enough for that?"

"I thought so, too; but, when I spoke about love, she only laughed, and slapped me on the face with her fan. Oh! no, the thing must be done in Spanish, that's plain; and you see I am going to set about it in earnest. She loaned me these." So saying, he pulled out of the crown of his foraging cap a couple of small volumes, which I recognised as a Spanish grammar and dictionary. I could not resist laughing aloud.

"Comrade, you will find the best dictionary to be the lady herself."

"That's true; but how the deuce are we to get back again? A mule hunt don't happen every day."

"I fancy there will be some difficulty in it."

I had already thought of this. It was no easy matter to steal away from camp. One's brother-officers are so solicitous about your appearance at drills and parades. The ranche was at least ten miles from the lines, and the road would not be the safest for the solitary lover. The prospect of frequent returns was not at all flattering.

"Can't we steal out at night?" suggested Clayley. "I think we might mount half-a-dozen of our fellows, and do it snugly. What do you say, Captain?"

"Clayley, I cannot return without this brother. I have almost given my word to that effect."

"You have? That is bad! I fear there is no prospect of getting him out as you propose."

My companion's prophetic forboding proved but too correct; for, on nearing the camp, we were met by an aide-de-camp of the commander-in-chief, who informed me that, on that very morning, all communication between the foreign ships of war and the besieged city, had been prohibited.

Don Cosme's journey, then, would be in vain. I explained this, advising him to return to his family.

"Do not make it known—say that some time is required, and you have left the matter in my hands. Be assured I shall be among the first to enter the city, and I shall find him, and bring him to his mother in safety."

This was the only consolation I could offer

"You are kind, Capitan—very kind; but I know that nothing can now be done. We can only hope and pray."

The old man had dropped into a bent attitude, his countenance marked by he deepest melancholy. Taking the Frenchman, Raoul, along with me, I ode back until I had placed him beyond the danger of the straggling plunderer, when we shook hands, and parted. As he left me, I turned to look after him. He still sate in that attitude that betokens deep dejection, his shoulders bent forward over the neck of his mule, while he gazed vacantly on the path! My heart sank at the spectacle, and, sad and dispirited, I rode at a lagging pace towards the camp.

Not a shot had as yet been fired against the town, but our batteries were nearly perfected, and several mortars were mounted and ready to fling in their deadly missiles. I knew that every shot and shell would carry death into the devoted city; for there was not a point within its walls out of range of a ten-inch howitzer. Women and children must perish along with armed soldiers; and the boy—he, too—might be a victim. Would this be the tidings I should carry to his home? And how should I be received by her with such a tale upon my lips? Already have I sent back a sorrowing father.

"Is there no way to save him, Raoul?"

"Captain?" answered the man, starting at the vehemence of my manner.

A sudden thought had occurred to me.

"Are you well acquainted with Vera Cruz?"

"I know every street, Captain."

"Where do those arches lead that open from the sea? There is one on each side of the *mole*."

I had observed these when visiting a friend—an officer of the navy—on board his ship.

"They are conductors, Captain, to carry off the overflow of the sea after a norther; they lead under the city, opening at various places. I have had the pleasure of passing through them."

"Ha! how?"

"On a little smuggling expedition."

"It is possible, then, to reach the town by these?"

"Nothing easier—unless they may have a guard at the mouth; but that is not likely. They would not dream of any one's making the attempt."

"How would *you* like to make it?"

"If the Captain wishes it, I will bring him a bottle of wine from the Café de Santa Anna."

"I do not wish you to go alone. I would accompany you."

"Think of it, Captain; there is risk for *you*. *I* may go safely. No one knows that I have joined you, I believe. If *you* are taken—"

"Yes, yes. I know well the result."

"The risk is not great either," continued the Frenchman, in a half soliloquy "Disguised as Mexicans, you speak the language as well as I. If you wish it, Captain."

"I do."

"I am ready then."

I knew the fellow well. One of those dare-devil spirits ready for anything that promised adventure. A child of fortune—astray waif tumbling about among the waves of chance—gifted with head and heart of no common order—ignorant of books, yet educated in experience. There was a dash of the heroic in his character, that had won my admiration, and I was fond of his company.

It was a desperate adventure. I knew that; but I felt stronger interest than common in the fate of this boy. My own future fate, too, was, in a great degree connected with his safety. There was something in the very danger that lured me. I felt that it would be adding another chapter to a life which I have termed adventurous.

CHAPTER XXIX.

A FOOL-HARDY ADVENTURE.

At night, Raoul and I—disguised in the leathern dresses of two rancheros—stole around the lines; and reached Punta Hornos, a point beyond our own pickets.

Here we "took the water," wading waist deep. This was about ten o'clock. The tide was just setting out—and the night, by good fortune, was as dark as pitch.

As the swell rolled in, we were buried to the neck; and, when it rolled back again, we bent forward, so that at no time could much of our bodies be seen above the surface.

In this manner—half wading, half swimming—we kept up to the town.

It was a toilsome journey; but the water was warm, and the sand on the bottom firm and level. We were strengthened—I at least—by hope, and the knowledge of danger. Doubtless my companion felt the latter stimulant as much as I. We soon reached the battlements of Santiago. Here we proceeded with increased caution. We could see the sentry up against the sky, pacing along the parapet. His shrill cry startled us. We thought we had been discovered. The darkness alone prevented this. At length we passed him, and came opposite the city, whose battlements rested upon the water's edge. The tide was at ebb, and a bed of black weed-covered rocks lay between the sea and the bastion. We approached these with caution; and, crawling over the slippery sides a hundred yards or so, found ourselves in the entrance of the conductor. Here we halted to rest ourselves, sitting upon a ledge of rock. We were in no more danger here than in our own tents; yet within twenty feet were men, who, had they known our proximity, would have strung us up like a pair of dogs. But our danger was far from lying at this end of the adventure. After a rest of half an hour, we kept up the conductor My companion seemed perfectly at home in this subterranean passage, walking along as boldly as if it had been brilliantly lighted with gas. We approached a grating, where a light shot in from above.

"Can we pass out here?" I inquired.

"Not yet, Captain," answered Raoul, in a whisper. "Farther on."

We passed the grating—then another, and another—and at length reached one, where only a feeble ray struggled downward through the bars. Here my guide stopped, and listened attentively, for several minutes. Then stretching out his hand, he undid the fastening of the grate, and silently turned it upon its hinge. He next swung himself up, until his head projected above ground. In this position, he again listened, looking cautiously on all sides. Satisfied, at length, he drew his body through the grating, and disappeared. After a short interval, he returned, and called down—

"Come, Captain?"

I swung myself up to the street. Raoul shut down the trap with care.

"Take marks, Captain!" whispered he; "we may get separated"

It was a dismal suburb. No living thing was apparent, with the exception of a gang of prowling dogs—lean and savage—as all dogs are during a siege. An image, decked in all the glare of gaud and tinsel, looked out of a glazed niche in the opposite wall! A dim lamp burned at its feet, showing to the charitable a receptacle for their offerings. A quaint old steeple loomed in the darkness overhead.

"What church?" I asked Raoul

"La Magdalene."

"That will do. Now onward."

"*Buenas noches! Señor,*" said Raoul to a soldier, who passed us, wrapped in his great coat.

"*Buenas noches!*" returned the man, in a gruff voice.

We stole cautiously along the streets, keeping in the darker ones to avoid observation. The citizens were mostly in their beds; but groups of soldiers were straggling about, and patrols met us at every corner. It became necessary to pass through one of the streets, that was brilliantly lighted. When about half way up, a fellow came swinging along, and, noticing our strange appearance, stopped and looked after us. Our dresses, as I have said, were of leather. Our calsoneros, as well as jackets, were shining with the sea water, and dripping upon the pavement at every step.

Before we could walk beyond reach, the man shouted out—

"Carajo! Cabelleros, why don't you strip before entering the baño?"

"What is it?" cried a soldier, coming up and stopping us.

A group of his comrades joined him, and we were hurried into the light.

"*Mil diablos!*" exclaimed one of the soldiers, recognising Raoul; "our ld friend the Frenchman! *Parlez-vous Français, Monsieur?*"

"Spies!" cried another.

"Arrest them!" shouted a sergeant of the guard, at the moment coming up with a patrol, and we were both jumped upon, and held by about a dozen men.

In vain Raoul protested our innocence, declaring that we were only two poor fishermen, who had wet our clothes in drawing the nets!

"It's not a fisherman's costume, Monsieur," said one.

"Fishermen don't usually wear diamonds on their knuckles," cried another, snatching a ring from my finger.

On this ring, inside the criclet, were engraven my name and rank!

Several men now coming forward, recognised Raoul, and stated, moreover, that he had been missing for some days.

"He must, therefore," said they, "have been with the Yankees."

We were soon handcuffed, and marched off to the guard-prison. There we were closely searched, but nothing further was found, except my purse, conaining several gold eagles—an American coin that would have condemned me of itself. We were now heavily chained to each other, and the guard left us to our thoughts. They could not have left us in much less agreeab'e companionship.

CHAPTER XXX.

HELP FROM HEAVEN.

"I would not care a claco for my own life," said Raoul, as the gate closed upon us, "but that you, Captain—hélas! hélas!" and the Frenchman groaned and sank upon the stone bench, dragging me down also. I could offer no consolation. I knew that we should be tried as spies; and, if convicted—a result almost certain—we had not twenty hours to live. The thought that I had brought this brave fellow to such a fate enhanced the misery of my situation. To die thus ingloriously was bitter indeed. Three days ago, I would have spent my life recklessly; but now, how changed were my feelings! I had found something worth living to enjoy; and to think I should never again—"Oh! I have become a coward." I cursed my rashness bitterly.

We passed the night in vain attempts at mutual consolation. Even our present sufferings occupied us. Our clothes were wet through, and the night had become piercing cold. Our bed was a bench of stone; and upon this we lay, as our chains would allow us, sleeping close together, to generate warmth It was, to us, a miserable night; but morning came at last; and at an early hour we were examined by the officer of the guard.

Our court-martial was fixed for the afternoon, and before this tribunal w were carried, amidst the jeers of the populace. We told our story, giving the name of the boy, Narcisso, and the house where he was lodged. This was verified by the court; but declared to be a *ruse* invented by my comrade. hose knowledge of circumstances rendered the thing probable enough. Raoul, moreover, was identified by many of the citizens, who proved his disappearance, coincident with the landing of our expedition. Besides, my ring and purse were sufficient of themselves to condemn us—and condemned we were. We were to be *gurotted* on the following morning! Raoul was offered life, if he would turn traitor, and give information of the enemy. The brave soldier indignantly spurned the offer. It was extended to me, with a similar result.

All at once, I observed a strange commotion among the people. Citizens and soldiers rushed from the hall, and the court hastily pronouncing our sentence, ordered us to be carried away. We were seized by the guard, and pulled into the street, and dragged back towards our late prison. Our conductors were evidently in a great hurry. As we passed along, we were met by citizens running to and fro, apparently in great terror. Women and children uttering shrieks, and suddenly disappearing behind walls and battlements. Some fell upon their knees, beating their breasts and praying loudly. Others, clasping their infants, stood shivering and speechless!

"It is just like the way they go in an earthquake; but there is none. What can it be, Captain?"

Before I could reply, the answer came from another quarter.

Far above, an object was hissing and hurtling through the air.

"A shell from ours! Hurrah!" cried Raoul.

I could scarcely refrain from cheering, though we ourselves might be its victims.

The soldiers who were guarding us had flung themselves down behind walls and pillars, leaving us alone in the open street.

The bomb fell beyond us, and, striking the pavement, burst. The fragments went crashing through the side of an adjoining house; and the wall that came back, told how well the iron missiles had done their work. This was, the second shell that had been projected from the American mortars. The first had been equally destructive; and hence the extreme terror of both citizen and soldier. Every missile seemed charged with death!

Our guard now returned, and dragged us onward, treating us with the greatest brutality. They were enraged at the exhultation visible in our manner; and one, more ferocious than the rest, drove his bayonet into the fleshy part of my comrade's thigh. After several acts of inhumanity we were thrown into our prison, and locked up as before.

Since our capture, we had tasted neither food nor drink, and hunger and thirst added to the misery of our situation.

The insult had maddened Raoul, and the pain of his wound now rendered him furious. He had not hands to touch it, or dress it. Frenzied by anger and pain to a strength almost superhuman, he twisted off his iron manacles as if they had been straws. This done, the chain that bound us together was soon broken, and our ankle "jewelry" followed.

"We will live our last hours, Captain, as we have our lives—free and un fettered!"

I could not help admiring the spirit of my brave comrade.

We placed ourselves close to the door to listen.

We could hear the heavy cannonade all around, and now and then the distant shots from the American batteries. We would wait for the bursting of the bombs, and, as the hoarse thunder of crumbling walls reached our ears, Raoul would spring up, shouting his wild, half French, half-Indian " Hurrah!"

A thought occurred to me.

"We have arms, Raoul." I held up the fragments of the heavy chain that had yoked us. "Could you reach the trap on a run, without the danger of mistaking your way?"

Raoul started.

"You are right, Captain—I can. It is barely possible they may visit us to-night. If so, any chance for life is better than none at all."

By a tacit understanding each of us took a fragment of the chain—there were but two—and sat down by the door to be ready in case our guards should open it. We sat for over an hour, without exchanging a word. We could hear the shells as they burst upon the house-tops, and the crashing of torn timbers, the rumbling of walls rolling over, struck by the heavy shot We could hear the shouts of men, and the wailing of woman, with now an then a shriek louder than all others, as some missile carried death into th terror-struck crowd.

Sacré!" said Raoul; "if they had only allowed us a couple of days, our friends would have opened these doors. *Sacré!*"

This exclamation was uttered in a shriek. Simultaneously, a heavy object burst through the roof, tearing the bricks and plaster, and falling with the ring of iron on the floor.

Then followed a deafening crash. The whole earth seemed to shake, and the whizzing of a thousand particles filled the air. A cloud of dust and lime, mixed with the smoke of sulphur, was around us. I gasped for breath, nearly suffocated. I endeavored to cry out, but my voice, husky and hoarse, was scarcely audible to myself. I succeeded, at length, in ejaculating:

"Raoul—Raoul!"

I felt myself grappling with the tawny monsters, and hurling them over the cliff. They sprang at my throat, and I threw out my arms, thrusting them fearlessly between the shining rows of teeth. Then I was free again, and, seizing a leg, or a tail, or the loose flaps of the neck, I dragged a savage brute towards the brink, and, summoning all my strength, dashed him against the brow, that he might tumble howling over.—PAGE 186.

I heard the voice of my comrade, seemingly at a great distance. I threw out my arms and groped for him. He was close by me, but, like myself, choking for want of air.

"*Sacré!* it was a shell," said he, in a wheezing voice. "Are you hurt, Captain?"

"No," I replied; "and you?"

"Sound as a bell—our luck is good—it must have struck every other part of the cell."

"Better it had not missed us," said I, after a pause; "we are only spared for the *garotte*."

"I am not so sure of that, Captain."

"Where that shell came in, something else may go out. Let us see—was it the roof."

"I think so."

We groped hand in hand towards the centre of the room, looking upwards.

"Waugh!" ejaculated Raoul, "I can't see a foot before me—my eyes are filled—*Bah!*"

So were mine. We stood waiting. The dust was gradually settling; and we could perceive a faint glimmer from above. *There was a hole through the roof!*

Slowly its outlines became defined, and we could see that it was large enough to pass the body of a man; but it was at least fourteen feet from the floor, and we had not timber enough to make a walking-stick!

"What is to be done? we are not cats, Raoul. We can never reach it!"

My comrade, without making a reply, lifted me up in his arms, telling me to climb. I mounted upon his shoulders, balancing myself like a Bedouin; but with my utmost stretch, I could not touch the roof.

"Hold!" cried I, a thought striking me. "Let me down, Raoul. Now, if they will only give us a little time."

"Never fear for them; they've enough to do taking care of their own carcasses."

I had noticed that a beam of the roof formed one side of the break; and I proceeded to twist our handcuffs into a clamp, while Raoul peeled off his leather breeches and commenced tearing them into strips. In ten minutes our tackle was ready; and mounting my comrade's shoulders, I flung it carefully at the beam. It failed to catch, and I came to the floor, my balance being lost. I repeated the attempt. Again it failed, and I staggered down as before.

"*Sacré !*" cried Raoul through his teeth. The iron had struck him on the head.

"Come, we will try, and try—our lives depend upon it."

The third attempt, according to popular superstition, should be successful It *was* so with us. The clamp caught, and the string hung dangling downwards. Mounting again upon my comrade's shoulders, I grasped the thong high up, to test its hold. It was secure; and, cautioning Raoul to hold fast, lest the hook might be detached by my vibration, I climbed up, and seized hold of the beam. By this, I squeezed myself through the roof. I crawled cautiously along the *azotea*,* which, like all others in Spanish houses, was flat, and bordered by a low parapet of mason-work. I peeped over the parapet, looking down into the street. It was night, and I could see no one below; but up against the sky upon distant battlements, I could distinguish armed soldiers, busy around their guns. These blazed forth at intervals, throwing their sulphury glare over the city.

I returned to assist Raoul; but, impatient at my delay, he had already mounted; and was dragging up the thong after him.

We crawled from roof to roof, looking for a dark spot to descend into the street. None of the houses, in the range of our prison, were more than one story; and, after passing several, we let ourselves down into a narrow alley. It was still early, and the people were running to and fro, amidst the frightful scenes of the bombardment. The shrieks of women were in our ears, mingled with the shouts of men; the groans of the wounded, and the fierce yelling of an excited rabble. The constant whizzing of bombs filled the air, and parapets were hurled down. A round shot struck the cupola of a church, as we passed nearly under it, and the ornaments of ages came tumbling down, blocking up the thoroughfare. We clambered over the ruins, and went on. There was no need of our crouching into dark shadows. No one thought of observing us now.

"We are near the house—will you take him along?" inquired Raoul, referring to the object of our enterprise.

"By all means! show me the place."

Raoul pointed to a large house, with portals, and a great door in the centre.

---

* The name of the flat roofs of Spanish houses These roofs are, usually, enclosures surrounded by a wall, or parapet, that separates one from another. They are tiled, but more usually plastered with cement that casts off the water into gutters along the sides. They form a pleasant resort when the sun is low, and especially when the owner has had the good taste to stock them with plants and flower-pots.

" There, Captain—there it is."

" Go under that shadow, and wait. I shall be better alone."

This was said in a whisper. My companion did as directed.

I approached the great door, and knocked boldly.

" *Quien !*" cried the porter within the *saguan*.

" *Yo*," I responded.

[This is the exact dialogue which passes before you can gain admission t a Mexican dwelling; and, although the " Yo," which simply signifies I, gives no very definite information to the porters within, it always operates as an 'Open Sesame." It is certainly more grammatical than the answer " Me," so frequently given to " Who's there ?" by people of a fair respectability in our land. Saguan is the gateway, or entrance, to a Spanish house.]

The door was opened slowly, and with caution.

" Is the Señorito Narcisso within ?" I inquired.

The man answered in the affirmative.

" Tell him, a friend wishes to speak with him."

After a moment's hesitation, the porter dragged himself lazily up the stone steps. In a few seconds, the boy—a fine, bold-looking lad, whom I had seen during our trial—came leaping down. He started on recognising me.

" Hush !" I whispered, signing to him to be silent. " Take leave of your friends, and meet me in ten minutes behind the church of La Magdalena."

" Why, Señor," inquired the boy without listening, " how have you got out of prison ? I have just been to the governor on your behalf, and—"

" No matter how," I replied, interrupting him; " follow my directions— remember your mother and sisters are suffering."

" I will come," said the boy resolutely.

" *Hasta luego !*" [Literally, until a little while — a beautiful form of expression much used in Spanish, for which we have no synonyme in English. *Hasta mañana, hasta la tarde*—until the morning, until the evening—imply that the person using these expressions will not see you until the morning or evening; and *hasta despues*, until hereafter, means that the time when you may come together again is unknown, or indefinite.]

We parted. I rejoined Raoul, and we walked on towards La Magdalena. We passed through the street where we had been captured on the preceding night: but it was so altered, we should not have known it. Fragments of walls were thrown across the path; and here and there lay masses of bricks and mortar, freshly torn down.

Neither patrol nor sentry thought of troubling us now; and our strange appearance did not strike the attention of the passengers. We reached the church, and Raoul descended, leaving me to wait for the boy, The latter was true to his word, and his slight figure soon appeared rounding the corner. We entered the subterranean passage, but the tide was still high, and we had to wait for the ebb. This came at length, and, clambering over the rocks, we entered the surf, and waded as before. After an hour's toil, we reached Punta Hornos; and a little beyond, I was enabled to hail one of our own pickets, and pass the lines in safety.

At ten o'clock, I was in my own tent; just twenty-four hours from the time I had left it; and, with the exception of Clayley, not one of my brother officers knew anything of our adventure.

Clayley and I agreed to "mount" a party the next night, and carry the boy to his friends. This we accordingly did, stealing out of camp after tatoo It would be impossible to describe the rejoicing of our new acquaintances— the gratitude lavishly expressed—the smiles of love that thanked us.

We could have repeated our visits nightly but the guerilleros now swarmed in the back country; and small parties, straggling from camp, were cut off daily. It was necessary, therefore, for my friend and myself to chafe under a prudent impatience; and wait for the fall of Vera Cruz.

CHAPTER XXXI

A SHOT IN THE DARK.

The City of the " True Cross" fell upon the 29th of March; and the American flag waved over the castle of San Juan de Ulloa. The enemy's troops marched out upon parole; most of them taking their way to their distant homes, upon the table-lands of the Andes.

The great body of the Mexican population is to be found on the elevated plains and valleys, the *tierra templada*, as these districts are called. The vegetation of the *tierra templada* is entirely distinct from that of the *tierra caliente*, and Nature wears a different aspect. *Tierra fria* is a title given to mountainous tracts that rise still higher than the table-lands.

The American garrison entered the town; but the body of our army encamped upon the green plains to the south.

Here we remained for several days, awaiting the order to march into the interior.

A report had reached us that the Mexican forces, under the celebrated Santa Anna, were concentracing at Puente Nacional; but, shortly after, it was ascertained that the enemy would make his next stand in the pass of the Cerro Gordo, about half way between Vera Cruz and the mountains.

After the surrender of the city, we were relieved from severe duty; and Clayley and I, taking advantage of this, resolved upon paying another stolen visit to our friends.

Several parties of light horse had been sent out to scour the country; and it had been reported that the guerilleros had gone farther up towards the Puente Nacional. We did not anticipate any danger from that source.

We started after nightfall, taking with us three of our best men—Lincoln Chane and Raoul. The boy Jack was also of the party. We were mounted on such horses as could be had. The Major had kept his word with me; and I bestrode the black—a splendid thorough-bred Arab.

It was a clear moonlight, and, as we rode along, we could not help noticing many changes. War had left its black mark upon the objects around. The ranches by the road were tenantless, many of them wrecked—not a few entirely gone—where they had stood, a ray of black ashes marking the outlines of their walls. Some were represented by a heap of half-burned rubbish, still smoking and smouldering!

Various pieces of household furniture lay along the path, torn or broken—articles of little value—strewed by the wanton hand of the ruthless robber. Here a *petaté*, or a palm hat—there a broken *olla*. A stringless *bandolon* * the fragments of a guitar, crushed under the angry heel, or some flimsy articles of female dress, cuffed into the dust. Leaves of torn books—*Misas*, or lives of the *Santissima Maria*—the labors of some zealous *padre*. Old paintings of the saints, Guadalupe, Remedios, and Dolores—of the niño of Guatepec—rudely torn from the walls, and perforated by the sacrilegious bayonet—flung into the road—kicked from foot to foot—the dishonored Penates of a conquered people!

A painful presentiment began to harass me. Wild stories had lately circulated through the army—stories of the misconduct of straggling parties of our soldiers, in the back country. These had stolen from camp, or gone out under the pretext of "beef-hunting."

Hitherto, I had felt no apprehension, not believing that any small party would carry their foraging to so distant a point as the house of my friends. I knew that any detachment, commanded by an officer, would act in a proper manner; and, indeed, any respectable body of American soldiers, without an officer; but in all armies—in war time—there are robbers, who have thrown

---

* An instrument not unlike the guitar. It might be termed national in Mexico, as there is hardly a cottage that cannot boast of a *bandolon*. There is hardly a cottage, either, that cannot boast of half a dozen paintings, and many of them far from being either rude or new.

† A soldier—I regret to add—belonging to my own regiment, out upon the scout, fired upon a peasant out of sheer wantonness and cruelty. The bullet shivered the poor fellow's arm, and it required amputation at the elbow to save his life. The cruel act greatly exasperated the *paisanos*, and afterwards, whenever a soldier fell into their hands, he was murdered and mutilated in the manner described in the text.

themselves into the ranks, for no other purpose than to take advantage of the license of a stolen foray.

We were within less than a league of the ranche; and still the evidence of ruin and plunder continued. The evidence, too, of a retaliatory vengeance; for, on entering a glade, the mutilated body of a soldier lay across the path He was on his back, glaring with open eyes upon the moon. His tongue and heart were cut out; and his left arm had been struck off at the elbow-joint! Not ten steps beyond this, we passed another one, similarly disfigured. We were now on the neutral ground.

As we entered the forest, my forebodings became painfully oppressive. I imparted them to Clayley. My friend had been occupied with similar thoughts.

"It is just possible," said he, "that nobody has found the way. By heavens!" he added, with an earnestness unusual in his manner, "I have been far more uneasy about the other side—those half brigands, and that hellish villain, Dubrosc!"

"On! on!" I ejaculated, digging the spurs into my horse's flanks, who sprang forward at a gallop. I could say no more. Clayley had given utterance to my very thoughts; and a painful feeling shot through my heart.

My companions dashed after me, and we pressed through the trees at a reckless pace.

We entered an opening. Raoul, who was then riding in the advance, suddenly checked his horse, waving us to halt. We did so.

"What is it, Raoul?" I asked in a whisper

"Something entered the thicket, Captain

"At what point?"

"There, to the left;" and the Frenchman pointed in the direction. "I did not see it well; it might have been a stray animal."

"I seed it, Cap'n," said Lincoln, closing up; "it wur a mustang."

"Mounted, think you?"

"I aint confident; I only seed its hips. We were a gwine too fast to get a good sight on the critter; but it wur a mustang. I seed that, clar as daylight."

I sate for a moment, hesitating.

"I kin tell yer whether it wur mounted, Cap'n," continued the hunter, "if yer'll let me slide down, and take a squint at the critter's tracks."

"It is out of our way. Perhaps you had better," I added, after a little reflection. "Raoul, you and Chane dismount, and go with the sergeant Hold their horses, Jack!"

"If yer'll not object, Cap'n," said Lincoln, addressing me in a whisper, "I'd rayther go 'ithout kumpny. Thar aint two men I'd like, in a tight fix, better'n Rowl and Chane; but I hev done a smart chance o' trackin' in my time an' I allers gets along better when I'm by myself."

"Very well, sergeant; as you wish it, go alone—we will wait for you."

The hunter dismounted, and, having carefully examined his rifle, strode off n a direction nearly opposite to that where the object had been seen! I was about to call after him, impatient to continue our journey; but, reflecting a moment, I concluded it was better to leave him to his "instincts." In five minutes, he had disappeared, having entered the chapparal.

We sate in our saddles for half an hour—not without feelings of impatience. I was beginning to fear that some accident had happened to our comrade, when we heard the faint crack of a rifle, but in a direction nearly opposite to that which Lincoln had taken!

"It's the sergeant's rifle, Captain," said Chane.

"Forward!" I shouted; and we dashed into the thicket, in the direction whence the report came. We had ridden about a hundred yards through the chapparal, when we met Lincoln coming up with his rifle shouldered.

"Well?" I asked.

"'Twur mounted, Cap'n—'taint now."

"What do you mean, sergeant?"

"That the mustang hed a yeller-belly on his back; and that he haint got ne'er a one now, as I knows on. He got clar away from me—that is the mustang. The yeller-belly didn't."

"What! you haven't—?"

"But I hev, Captain. I had good soun reason."

"What reason?" I demanded.

"In the first place, the feller wur a gurillye; and, in the next, he wur an outpost picket."

"How know you this?"

"Wal, Cap'n, I struck his trail on the edge of the thicket. I knowed he hedn't kum fur, as I looked out for feet whar we crossed the crik bottom, an seed none. I tuk the back track, an soon come up with his dam under a big buttonwood. He had been thar some time, for the ground wur stomped like a bullock-penn."

"Well?" said I, impatient to hear the result.

"I follered him up 'till I seed him leaning forard on his horse, clost to th track we oughter take. From this I suspicioned him, but gettin a leetle closter, I seed his gun and fixins strapped to the saddle. So I tuk a sight and whummelled him. The darned mustang got away with his traps. This yeer's the only thing worth takin from his carcage,—it wudn't do much harm to a grizzly bar."

"Good Heaven!" I exclaimed, grasping the glittering object which the hunter held towards me. What have you done?"

It was a silver-handled stiletto. I recognised the weapon. I had given it to the boy Narcisso!

"No harm, I reckin, Cap'n?"

"The man,—the Mexican? How did he look,—what like?" I demanded anxiously.

"Like?" repeated the hunter. "Why, Cap'n, I ud call him as ugly a skunk as yer kin skeer up anywhar,—'ceptin it mout be among the Flatheads, but yer kin see for yerself,—he's clost by."

I leaped from my horse, and followed Lincoln through the bushes. Twenty paces brought us to the object of our search, upon the border of a small glade. The body lay upon its back, where it had been flung by the rearing mustang. The moon was shining full upon the face. I stooped down to examine it. A single glance was sufficient. I had never seen the features before. They were coarse and swarth, and the long black locks were matted and woolly. He was a Zambo, and, from the half-military equipments that clung around his body, I saw that he had been a guerillero. Lincoln was right.

"Wal, Cap'n," said he, after I had concluded my examination of the corpse; "ain't he a picter?"

"You think he was waiting for us?"

"For us, or some other game,—that's sartin."

'There's a road branches off here to Medellin," said Raoul coming up.

"It could not have been for us,—they had no knowledge of our intention to come out."

"Possible enough, Captain," remarked Clayley, in a whisper to me. 'That villain would naturally expect us to return here. He will have learned all that has passed—Narcisso's escape—our visits. You know he would watch night and day to trap either of us."

"Oh, heavens!" I exclaimed, as the memory of this man came over me 'Why did I not bring more men? Clayley, we must go on now. Slowly Raoul,—slowly, and with caution,—do you hear?"

The Frenchman struck into the path that led to the ranche, and rode silently forward. We followed in single file, Lincoln keeping a look-out some paces in the rear.

CHAPTER XXXII.

CAPTURED BY GUERILLEROS.

We emerged from the forest, and entered the fields. All silent. No sign, or sound, of a suspicious nature. The house still standing and safe.

"The guerillero must have been waiting for some one, whom he expected by the Medellin road. Ride on, Raoul!"

"Captain," said the man in a whisper, and halting at the end of the guarda-raya.

"Well?"

"Some one passed out at the other end."

"Some of the domestics, no doubt—you may ride on, and—never mind, I will take the advance myself."

I brushed past, and kept up the guarda-raya. In a few minutes, we had reached the lower end of the pond, where we halted. Here we dismounted; and, leaving the men, Clayley and I stole cautiously forward. We could see no one; though everything about the house looked as usual.

"Are they a-bed, think you?" asked Clayley.

"No, it is too early—perhaps below, at supper."

"Heaven send! we shall be most happy to join them. I am as hungry as a wolf."

We approached the house. Still all silent.

"Where are the dogs?"

We entered.

"Strange—no one stirring. Ha! the furniture gone!"

We passed into the porch in the rear; and approached the stairway.

"Let us go below—can you see any light?"

I stooped and looked down. I could neither hear nor see any signs of life. I turned, and was gazing up at my friend in wonderment, when my eye was attracted by a strange movement upon the low branches of the olive trees. The next moment, a dozen forms dropped to the ground; and, before we could draw sword or pistol, myself and comrade were bound hand and foot, and flung upon our backs!

At the same instant, we heard a scuffle down by the pond. Two or three shots were fired; and a few minutes after, a crowd of men came up, bringing with them Chane, Lincoln and Raoul, as prisoners.

We were all dragged out into the open ground in front of the ranche, where our horses were also brought and picketed.

Here we lay upon our backs—a dozen guerilleros remaining to guard us. The others had gone back among the olives, where we could hear them laughing, talking and yelling. We could see nothing of their movements, as we were tightly bound, and as helpless as if under the influence of the nightmare.

Lincoln was a little in front of me. I could perceive that they had doubly bound him, in consequence of the fierce resistance he had made. He had killed one of the guerilleros. He was banded and strapped all over like a mummy, and he lay gnashing his teeth, and foaming with fury. Raoul and the Irishman appeared to take things more easily, or rather more recklessly.

"I wonder if they are going to hang us to night, or keep us till morning. What do you think, Chane?" asked the Frenchman, laughing as he spoke.

"Be the Crass! they'll lose no time—yez may depind on that same. There's not an ounce ov tinder mercy in their black hearts; yez may sware till that, from the way this eelskin cuts."

"I wonder, Murt," said Raoul, speaking from sheer recklessness, "if Saint Patrick couldn't help us a bit. You have him around your neck, haven't you?"

"Be the powers! Rowl, though yez be only jokin, I've a good mind to thry his holiness upon thim. I've got both him and the mother undher me jacket, av I could only rache thim."

"Good!" cried the other. "Do!"

"It's aisy for yez to say 'Do!' when I can't budge my little finger."

"Never mind. I'll arrange that," answered Raoul. "*Hola! señor!*" shouted he to one of the guerilleros.

"*Quien?*" said the man approaching.

"*Usted su mismo,*" (Yourself.) replied Raoul

"*Que cosa?*" (What is it?)

"This gentleman," said Raoul—still speaking in Spanish, and nodding towards Chane—"has a pocket full of money."

A hint upon that head was sufficient; and the guerilleros, who seemed to have overlooked this part of their duty, immediately commenced rifling our pockets, ripping them open with their long knives. They were not a great deal the richer for their pains; our joint purse yielding about twenty dollars. Upon Chane there was no money found; and the man, whom Raoul had deceived, repaid the latter, by a curse, and a couple of kicks.

The Saint, however, turned up, attached to the Irishman's neck by a leathern string; and along with him a small crucifix, and a pewter image of the Virgin Mary.

This appeared to please the guerilleros; and one of them, bending over the Irishman, slackened his fastening—still, however, leaving him bound.

"Thank yer honor,' said Chane; "that's dacent of ye. That's what Misther O'Connell wud call *amaylioration.* I'm a hape asier now."

"*Mucho bueno?*" said the man, nodding and laughing.

[The expression *muy bueno* (very good) was corrupted by the soldiers to *mucho bueno*, which is, of course, ungrammatical. As it was one of the earliest phrases caught up by the Americans, it was frequently used, with many smiles and nods, to express a good feeling between them and the peasants of the country. It would correspond to a Frenchman's "ver good."]

"Oh, be my sowl! yes—mucho bueno. But I'd have no objecshun if yer honner wud make it *mucho bettero.* Could'nt yez just take a little turn aff me wrist here—it cuts like a rayzyer?"

I could not restrain myself from laughing, in which Clayley and Raoul joined me; and we formed a chorus that seemed to astonish our captors. Lincoln alone preserved his sullenness.

He had not spoken a word.

Little Jack had been placed upon the ground near the hunter. He was but loosely tied, our captors not thinking it worth while to trouble themselves about so diminutive a subject. I had noticed him wriggling about, and using all his Indian craft to undo his fastenings; but he appeared not to have succeeded, as he lay perfectly still again.

While the guerilleros were occupied with Chane and his saints, I observed, the boy roll himself over and over, until he lay close up against the hunter. One of the guerilleros noticing this, picked Jack up by the waist-belt, and, holding him at arm's length, shouted out:

Mira, camarados! que briboncito!" (Look, comrades what a little rascal!)

Amidst the laughing of the guerilleros, Jack was swung out, and fell in a bed of aloes, where we saw no more of him. As he was bound, we concluded that he could not help himself, and was lying where he had been thrown.

My attention was called from this incident, by an exclamation from Chane

"Och! blood, turf, and murther! If there isn't that Frinch schoundrel Durbrosc!"

I looked up. The man was standing over us.

"Ah, *Monsieur le Capitaine!*" cried he, in a sneering voice, "*comment vous portez-vous?* You came out dove-hunting, eh? The birds, you see, are not in the cot."

Had there been not a thread around my body, I could not have moved at that moment. I felt cold and rigid as marble. A thousand agonizing thoughts crowded upon me at once—my doubts, my fears on *her* account drowning all ideas of personal danger. I could have died at that moment, and, without a groan, to have ensured her safety.

There was something so fiendish, so utterly hellish, in the character of this man—a polished brutality, too—that caused me to fear the worst.

"Oh, Heaven!" I muttered; "in the power of such a man!"

"Ho!" cried Dubrosc, advancing a pace or two, and seizing my horse by the lariat, "a splendid mount! An Arab, as I live! Look here, Yañez!" he continued, addressing a guerillero who accompanied him, "I claim this, if you have no objection."

"Take him!" said the other, who was evidently the leader of the party.

"Thank you. And you, Monsieur le Capitaine," he added, ironically turning to me, "thank you for this handsome present. He will just replace my brave Moro, for whose loss I expect I am indebted to you, you great brute!—*sacré!*"

The last words were addressed to Lincoln, and, as though maddened by the memory of La Virgen, he approached the latter, and kicked him fiercely in the side.

The wanton foot had scarcely touched his ribs, when the hunter sprang up as if by galvanic action—the thongs flying from his body in fifty spiral fragments! With a bound he leaped to his rifle; and, clutching it—he knew i was empty—struck the astonished Frenchman a blow upon the head. The latter fell heavily to the earth. In an instant, a dozen knives and swords were aimed at the hunter's throat. Sweeping his rifle around him, he cleared an opening, and dashing past his foes with a wild yell, bounded off through the shrubbery! The guerilleros followed, screaming with rage; and we could hear an occasional shot, as they continued the pursuit into the distant woods. Dubrosc was carried back into the ranche, apparently lifeless!

We were still wondering how our comrade had untied himself, when one of the guerilleros, lifting a piece of the thong, exclaimed:

"*Carajo! ha cortado el briboncito!*" (the little rascal has cut it); and the man darted into the aloes, in search of Little Jack. It was with us a moment of fearful suspense. We expected to see poor Jack sacrificed instantly. We watched the man with intense emotion, as he ran to and fro.

At length, he threw up his arms with a gesture of surprise, calling out, at the same time:

"*Por todos santos—se fue!*" (by all the saints! he's gone.)

"Hurrah!" cried Chane, "holies—such a gossin as that boy!"

Several of the guerilleros dived into the bed of aloes; but their search was in vain.

We were now separated, so that we could no longer converse, and were more strictly watched—two sentries standing over each of us. We spent about an hour in this way. Straggling parties, at intervals, came back from the pursuit; and we could gather, from what we overheard, that neither Lincoln nor Jack had yet been retaken.

We could hear talking in the rear of the ranche; and we felt that our fate was being determined. It was plain Dubrosc was not in command of the party. Had he been so, we should never have been carried beyond the olive grove. It appeared we were to be hung elsewhere. A movement was visible that betokened departure. Our horses were taken away, and saddled mules were led out in front of the ranche. Upon these we were set, and strapped tightly to the saddles. A *serapé* was passed over each of us, and we were blinded by *tápojos*, A bugle then sounded the "forward!" We could hear a confusion of noises—the prancing of many hoofs—and the next moment we felt ourselves moving along at a hurried pace through the woods.

The *serapé*, above referred to, is a species of motley-colored blanket, nearly square, with a slit in the centre to admit the head. Any one who has seen a Mexican of the lower classes without his serapé, has seen something which has escaped my observation. These serapés cost from two to two hundred dollars, and it would be difficult for a person not acquainted with the article to see any great difference, either in size or beauty, between the one at two dollars and that costing two hundred!

CHAPTER XXXIII.

A BLIND RIDE.

We rode all night. The mule-blinds, although preventing us from seeing a single object, proved to be an advantage. They saved our eyes and faces from the thorny claws of the acacia and mezquite. Without hands to fend them off, these would have torn us badly, as we could feel them, from time to time, penetrating even the hard leather of the *tapojos*. Our thongs chafed us, and we suffered great pain from the monotonous motion. Our road lay through thick woods. This we could perceive from the constant rustle of the leaves, and the crackling of branches, as the cavalcade passed on.

We travelled over many hills—steep and difficult, we could tell from the attitudes of our animals. There was no passing or re-passing. From this I concluded we were journeying along a narrow road, and in single file.

Raoul was directly in front of me, and we could converse at times.

"Where do you think they are taking us, Raoul?" I inquired, speaking in French.

"To Cenobio's Hacienda. I hope so at least."

"Why do you hope so?"

"Because we shall stand some chance for our lives. Cenobia is a noble fellow."

You know him then?"

"Yes, Captain; I have helped him a little in the contraband trade."

"A smuggler, is he?"

"Why, in this country, it is hardly fair to call it by so harsh a name, as the government itself dips out of the same dish. Smuggling here, as in most other countries, should be looked upon rather as the offspring of necessity and mal-administration, than a vice in itself. Cenobio is a *contrabandista*, and upon a large scale."

"And you are a political philosopher, Raoul."

"*Bah!* Captain, it would be bad if I could not defend my own calling," replied my comrade, with a laugh.

"You think, then, that we are in the hands of Cenobio's men."

"I am sure of it, Captain. Sacré! had it been Jarauta's band, we would have been in heaven—that is our souls—and our bodies would now be embellishing some of the trees upon Don Cosme's plantation. Heaven protect us from Jarauta! The priest gives but short shrift to any of his enemies; but if he could lay his hands on your humble servant, you would see hanging done in double quick time."

"Why think you we are with Cenobio's guerilla?"

"I know Yañez, whom we saw at the ranche. He is one of Cenobio's officers, and the leader of this party, which is only a detachment. I am rather surprised that *he* has brought us away, considering that Dubrosc is with him; there must have been some influence in our favor, which I cannot understand."

I was struck by the remark, and began to reflect upon it in silence. The voice of the Frenchman again fell upon my ear.

"I cannot be mistaken. No—this hill—it runs down to the San Juan."

Again, after a short interval:—

"Yes, the San Juan—I know the stony bottom—just the depth, too, at this season."

Our mules plunged through the swift current, flinging the spray over our heads. We could feel the water up to the saddle-flaps, cold as ice; and yet we were journeying it the hot tropic! But we were fording a stream fed by the snows of Orizava.

"Now I am certain of the road," continued Raoul, after we had crossed. I know this bank well—the mule slides! Look out, Captain!"

"For what?" I asked with some anxiety.

The Frenchman laughed as he replied:

"I believe I am taking leave of my senses. I called to you to look out, as if you had the power to help yourself in case the accident should occur."

"What accident?" I inquired with a nervous sense of some impending danger.

"Falling over—we are on a precipice that is reckoned dangerous on account of the clay ; if your mule should stumble here, the first thing you would strike would be the branches of some trees five hundred feet below."

" Good heaven !" I ejaculated. "Is it so ?"

"Never fear, Captain; there is not much danger. These mules appear to be sure-footed, and certainly," added he, with a laugh, "their loads are well packed and tied !"

I was in no condition just then to relish a joke, and my companion's humor was completely thrown away upon me. The thought of my mule missing his foot, and tumbling over a precipice, while I was stuck to him like a Centaur, was anything else than pleasant. I had heard of such accidents, and the knowledge did not make it any easier. I could not help muttering to myself:

" Why, in the name of mischief, did the fellow tell me till we had passed it ?"

I crouched closer to the saddle, allowing my limbs to follow every motion of the animal, lest some counteracting shock might disturb our joint equilibrium. I could hear the torrent, as it roared and hissed far below, and lirectly under us; and the "sough" grew fainter and fainter as we ascended.

On we went, climbing up—up—up, our strong mules straining against the precipitous path. It was daybreak. There was a faint glimmer of light under our *tapojos*. At length, we could perceive a brighter beam. We felt a sudden glow of heat over our bodies,—the air seemed lighter —our mules walked on a horizontal path. We were on the ridge, and warmed by the beams of the rising sun.

" Thank heaven we have passed it !"

I could not help feeling thus ; and yet we were riding perhaps to death !

CHAPTER XXXIV.

A STAMPEDE.

The guerilleros now halted, dismounting. We were left in our saddles. Our mules were picketed upon long lariats, and commenced browsing. They carried us under the thorny branches of the wild locust. The maguey, with its bill-shaped claws, had torn our uniform overalls to shreds. Our limbs were lacerated, and the cactus had lodged its poisoned prickles in our knees. But these were nothing to the pain of being compelled to keep our saddles,—or rather saddle-trees, for we were upon the naked wood. Our hips ached intensely, and our limbs smarted under the chafing thong.

There was a crackling of fires around us. Our captors were cooking their breakfasts, and chatting gaily over their chocolate. Neither food nor drink was offered to us, although we were both thirsty and hungry. We were kept in this place for about an hour.

"They have joined another party here," said Raoul, "with pack mules."

"How know you?" I inquired.

"I can tell by the shouts of the *arrieros*—listen!—they are making ready to start."

There was a mingling of voices. Exclamations addressed to their animals by the arrieros, such as:—

"*Mula! anda! vaya! levantate! carrai! mula — mulita — anda! — st —st!*"

In the midst of this din I fancied that I heard the voice of a woman!

"Can it be——?"

The thought was too painful.

A bugle at length sounded, and we felt ourselves moved onward.

Our road appeared to run along the naked ridge. There were no trees, and the heat became intense. Our *serapés*, that had served us during the night, should have been dispensed with now, had we been consulted in relation to the matter. I did not know, until some time after, why these blankets had been given to us; as they had been hitherto very useful in the cold. It was not from any anxiety in regard to our comfort, as I learned afterwards.

We began to suffer from thirst, and Raoul asked one of the guerilleros for water.

"*Carajo!*" answered the man, "it's no use; you'll be choked by and bye with something else than thirst."

The brutal jest called forth a peal of laughter from his comrades.

About noon, we commenced descending a long hill. I could hear the sound of water ahead.

"Where are we, Raoul, I inquired faintly.

"Going down to a stream—a branch of the Antigua."

"We are coming on another precipice?" I asked, with some uneasiness, as the roar of the torrent began to be heard more under our feet, and I snuffed the cold air rising from below.

"There is one, Captain. There is a good road, though, and well paved."

"Paved! why the country around is wild—is it not?"

"True; but the road was paved by the priests."

"By the priests!" I exclaimed with some astonishment.

"Yes, Captain; there's a convent in the valley—near the crossing; that is, there *was* one. It is now a ruin."

We crept slowly down—our mules, at times, seeming to walk on their heads. The hissing of the torrent gradually grew louder, until our ears were filled.

I heard Raoul below me shouting some words in a warning voice, when suddenly he seemed borne away, as if he had been tumbled over the precipice!

"I expected to feel myself next moment launched after him into empty space, when my mule, uttering a loud yell, sprang forward and downward!

Down—down! the next leap into eternity! No! she keeps her feet! She gallops along a level path—I am safe!

I was swung about until the thongs seemed to cut through my limbs, and, with a heavy plunge, I felt myself carried thigh-deep into water!

Here the animal suddenly halted.

As soon as I could gain breath, I shouted at the top of my voice for the Frenchman.

"Here, Captain!" he answered, close by my side; but, as I fancied, with a strange, gurgling voice.

"Are you hurt, Raoul?" I inquired.

"Hurt! No, Captain."

"What was it, then?"

"Oh! I wished to warn you. But I was too late. I might have known they would stampede, as the poor brutes have been no better treated than ourselves. Hear how they draw it up!"

CHAPTER XXXV.

A DRINK A LA CHEVAL.

"Good God, I am choking!" I exclaimed, listening to the water as it filtered through the teeth of my mule.

"Do as I do, Captain," said Raoul, speaking as if from the bottom of a well.

"How?" I asked.

"Bend down; and let the water run into your mouth."

This accounted for Raoul's strange voice.

"They may not give us a drop," continued he, "It is our only chance."

"I have not even that," I replied, after having vainly endeavored to touch the surface.

"Why?" asked my comrade.

"I cannot reach it."

"How deep are you?"

"To the saddle-flaps."

"Ride this way, Captain. It's deeper here."

"How can I? My mule is her own master, as far as I am concerned."

"*Parbleu!*" said the Frenchman. "I did not think of that."

But whether to oblige me, or moved by a desire to cool her flanks, the animal plunged forward into a deeper part of the stream.

After straining myself to the utmost, I was enabled to "duck" my head In this painful position, I contrived to get a couple of swallows; but, I should think, I took in quite as much at my nose and ears.

Clayley and Chane followed our example, the Irishman swearing loudly that it was "a burnin' shame to make a dacent Chrystyin dhrink like a horse in winkers."

Our guards now commenced driving our mules out of the water. As we were climbing the bank, some one touched me lightly upon the arm; and, at the same instant, a voice whispered in my ear, "Courage, Captain!" I started —it was the voice of a female. I was about to reply, when a soft small hand was thrust under the tapojo, and pushed something between my lips. The hand was immediately withdrawn; and I heard the voice urging a horse onward.

The clatter of hoofs convinced me, that this mysterious agent was gone; and I remained silent.

"Who can it be? Jack? No. Jack has a soft voice—a small hand. But how could he be here? and with his hands free? No—no—no. Who, then? It was certainly the voice of a woman—the hand, too. What other should have made this demonstration. I know no other—it must—it must have been —— !"

I continued my analysis of probabilities, always arriving at this result. It was both pleasant and painful. Pleasant, to believe she was thus, like an angel, watching over me—painful to think, that she might be in the power of my fiendish enemy!

But is she so? Lincoln's blow may have ended him. We have heard nothing of him since. Would to heaven——!

It was an impious wish, but I could not control it.

"What have I got between my lips? A slip of paper! Why was it placed there, and not in my bosom, or my button-hole? Ha! there is more providence than at first thought appears. How could I have taken it from either the one or the other, bound as I am? Moreover, it may contain what would destroy the writer, if known to—cunning thought—for one so young and innocent, too—but love——!"

I pressed the paper against the tapojo, concealing it.

"Halted, again?"

"It is the ruin, Captain—the old convent of Santa Bernardina."

"But why do they halt here?"

"Likely, to noon and breakfast—that on the ridge was only their *desayuna* The Mexicans of the *tierra caliente* never travel during mid-day. They will doubtless rest here until the cool of the evening."

"I trust they will extend the same favor to us." said Clayley; "God knows we stand in need of rest. I'd give them three months' pay for an hour upon the treadmill, only to stretch my limbs."

"They will take us down, I think. Not on our account, but to ease the mules. Poor brutes! they are no party to this transaction."

Raoul's conjecture proved correct. We were taken out of our saddles; and, being carefully bound as before, we were hauled into a damp room, and flung down upon the floor. Our captors went out. A heavy door closed after them, and we could hear the regular footfall of a sentry on the stone pavement without. For the first time since our capture, we were left alone. This my comrades tested, by rolling themselves all over the floor of our prison! It was but, a scant addition to our liberty; but we could converse freely, and that was something.

CHAPTER XXXVI.

AN ODD WAY OF OPENING A LETTER.

"Has any of you heard of Dubrosc on the route?" I inquired of my comrades.

No; nothing had been heard of him since the escape of Lincoln.

"Faix, Captain," said the Irishman, "it's meself that thinks Mister Dubrosc won't throuble any ov us any more—it was a purty lick that same, ayquil to ould Donnybrook itself."

"It is not easy to kill a man with a single blow of a clubbed rifle." observed Clayley, " unless, indeed, the lock may strike the scull But we are still living; and I think that is some evidence that the deserter is dead. By the way, how has the fellow obtained such influence as he appeared to have among them; and so soon too?"

"I think, lieutenant, replied Raoul, "Monsieur Dubrosc has been here before."

"Ha! say you so?" I inquired with a feeling of anxiety.

"I remember, Captain, some story current at Vera Cruz, about a Creo' having married, or run away with a girl of good family there. I am almo certain that was the name; but it was before my time, and I am unacquaint with the circumstances. I remember, however, that the fellow was a gam 'er, or something of the sort; and the occurrence made much noise in the ountry."

I listened with a sickening anxiety to every word of these details. There w is a painful correspondence between them, and what I already knew. The i ought that this monster could be in any was connected with *her* was a disagreeable one. I questioned Raoul no farther. Even could he have detailed every circumstance, I should have dreaded the relation!

Our conversation was interrupted by the creaking of a rusty hinge The door opened, and several men entered. Our blinds were taken off, and oh! how pleasant to look upon the light. The door had been closed again, and there was only one small grating, yet the slender beam through this was like the bright noon-day sun! Two of the men carried earthen platters filled with *frijoles*, a single *tortilla* in each platter. They were placed near our heads, one for each of us.

Frijoles are a species of bean, much used—I might say universally—by the lower classes in Mexico. The *tortilla* is a thin cake made of maize, and, like the frijoles, in universal use. It has been often described by travellers; but the most essential point in which it differs from other maize bread seems to have escaped their observation. It is this: Corn bread is made from corn meal; but the tortilla is manufactured from the corn itself, which, instead of being ground, is boiled soft with lye or potash, and then bruised between a pair of tortilla stones—clapped out with the hands into thin round cakes and thrown upon a hot stone, or griddle. A moment on the griddle suffices, and they are brought to the table, or rather to the mouth (in most instances no table being near), while warm. Cold tortillas that have lain over, are moistened and replaced upon the griddle before being eaten. As spoons, knives, and forks are hardly known among the peasants of Mexico, the tortilla is twisted into the form of a scoop, or spoon, and by this the thin peppery stews are raked out of the earthen platter, spoon and all going down the throat together! The potash used in softening the maize gives to the tortilla a flavor which is entirely different from our corn bread. It is somewhat unpleasant to the palate of a stranger.

"It's blissid kind of yez, gentlemen," said Chane; "but how are we goin to ate it, if ye plaze?"

"The plague!" exclaimed Clayley, "do they expect us to lick this up without either hands, spoon, or knives?"

"Won't you allow us the use of our fingers?" asked Raoul, speaking to one of the guerilleros.

"No," replied the man, gruffly.

"How do you expect us to eat, then?"

"With your mouths. What else?"

"Thank you, Sir; you are very polite."

"If you don't choose that, you can leave it alone," added the Mexican, going out with his companions, and closing the door behind them.

"Thank you, gentlemen!" shouted the Frenchman, after them, in a tone of subdued anger. "I won't please you so much as to leave it alone. By my word!" he continued, "we may be thankful—it's more than I expected from Yañez—that they've given us any. Something's in the wind." So saying, the speaker rolled himself on his breast, bringing his head to the dish.

"Och! the mane haythins," cried Chane, following the example set by his comrade; "to make dacent men ate like brute bastes. Och! murther an ouns!"

"Come, Captain; shall we feed?" asked Clayley.

"Go on. Do not wait for me," I replied.

Now was my time to read the note. I rolled myself under the grating and, after several efforts, succeeded in gaining my feet. The window, which was not much larger than a pigeon-hole, widened inwards like the embrazure of a gun-battery. The lower slab was just the height of my chin; and upon this, after a good deal of dodging and lip jugglery, I succeeded in spreading out the paper to its full extent.

"What on earth are you at, Captain?" inquired Clayley, who had watched my manœuvres, with some astonishment.

Raoul and the Irishman stopped their plate-licking, and looked up.

"Hush! go on with your dinners—not a word. I read as follows:

"To-night your cords will be cut, and you must escape as you best can afterwards. Do not take the road back, as you will be certain to be pursued in that direction; moreover, you run the risk of meeting other parties of the guerilla. Make for the National road, at San Juan, or Manga di Clavo. Your posts are already advanced beyond these points. The Frenchman can easily guide you. Courage, Captain! Adieu!

P. S. They waited for you. I had sent one to warn you; but he has either proved traitor, or missed the road. Adieu! Adieu!"

"Good heavens!" I involuntarily exclaimed: "the man that Lincoln——!"

I caught the paper into my lips again, and, chewed it into a pulp, to avoid the danger of its falling into the hands of the guerilla.

I stood turning over its contents in my mind. I was struck with the masterly style—the worldly cunning exhibited by the writer. There was something almost unfeminine about it. I could not help being surprised, that one so young, and hitherto so secluded from the world, should possess such a knowledge of men and things. I was already aware of the presence of a pow 'rful intellect, but one, as I thought, altogether unacquainted with practical life and action. Then there was the peculiarity of her situation.

"Is she a prisoner, like myself? or, is she disguised, and perilling her life to save mine? or, can she be —? Patience! To-night will unravel the mystery."

CHAPTER XXXVII.

THE COBRA DI CAPELLO.

Up to this moment my attention had been engrossed with the contents of the note, and I had no thought of looking outward. I raised myself on tiptoe, stretching my neck as far as I could into the embrazure.

A golden sunlight was pouring down upon broad green leaves, where the palms grew wildly. Red vines hung in festoons, like curtains of scarlet satin. There were bands of purple and violet—the maroon-colored morus, and the snowy magnolia—a glittering opal! Orange trees, with white, wax-like flowers, were bending under their golden globes. The broad plumes of the corozo palm curved gracefully over—their points trailing downwards, and without motion.

A clump of these grew near, their naked stems laced by a huge parasite of the liana species, which rose from the earth, and traversing diagonally, was lost in the feathery frondage above. These formed a canopy, underneath which, from tree to tree, three hammocks were extended! One was empty. The other two were occupied. The elliptical outlines, traceable through the gauzy network of Indian grass, proved that the occupants were females.

Their faces were turned from me. They lay motionless. They were asleep!

As I stood gazing upon this picture, the occupant of the nearest hammock awoke, and turning, with a low murmur upon her lips, again fell asleep. Her face was now towards me. My heart leaped, and my whole frame quivered with emotion. I recognised the features of Guadalupe Rosales!

One limb, cased in silk, had fallen over the selvidge of her pendant couch and hung negligently down. The small satin slipper had dropped off, and was lying on the ground. Her head rested upon a silken pillow, and a band of hair, that had escaped from its turquoise clasp, struggling over the cords of the hammock, trailed along the grass. Her bosom heaved above the network as she breathed and slept!

My heart was full of mixed emotions—surprise, pleasure, love, pain! Yes, pain—for she could thus sleep—sleep sweetly, tranquilly; while I, within a few paces of her couch, was bound—racked—brutally treated!

"Yes, she can sleep!" I muttered to myself, as my chagrin predominated in the tumult of emotions. "Ha! heavens!"

My attention was attracted from the sleeper to a fearful object. I had noticed a spiral-like appearance upon the liana. It had caught my eye once or twice, while looking at the sleeper; but I had not dwelt upon it, taking it for a smaller vine wrapped upon the larger, a peculiarity often met with in the forests of Mexico.

A bright sparkle now attracted my eye; and, on looking at the object attentively, I discovered, to my horror, that the spiral protuberance upon the vine was nothing else than the folds of a huge snake! Squeezing himself silently down the parasite—for he had come from above—the reptile slowly uncoiled two or three of the lowermost rings, and stretched his glistening neck horizontally over the hammock. Now, for the first time, I perceived his hood, and recognised the dreaded monster—the *Cobra di Capello!*

In this position he remained for some moments perfectly motionless, his neck proudly curved like that of a swan, while his head was not twelve inches from the face of the sleeper. I fancied that I could see the soft down upon her lip, playing under his breath!

He now commenced slowly vibrating from side to side, while a low hissing sound proceeded from his open jaws. His hood swelled out, adding to the hideousness of his appearance, and, at intervals, his fangs shot forth, glancing in the sun like diamonds!

He appeared to be gloating over his victim, in the act of charming her to death. I even fancied that her lips moved, and her head began to stir backward, and forward, following the oscillations of the reptile!

All this I witnessed, without the power to move. My soul, as well as my body, was chained; but even had I been free, I could have offered no help. I knew that the only hope of her safety lay in silence. Unless disturbed and angered, the snake might not bite; but was he not, at that moment, distilling some secret venom upon her lips?

"Oh, Heaven!" I gasped out, in the intensity of my fears, "is this the fiend himself?" She moves—now he will strike! Not yet—she is still again. Now—now—mercy! she trembles—the hammock shakes—she is quivering under the fascin— Ha!"

A shot rang from the walls—the snake suddenly jerked back his head—his rings flew out, and he fell to the earth, writhing as in pain!

The girls started with a scream, and sprang simultaneously from their hammocks.

Grasping each other by the hand, with terrified looks they rushed from the spot, and disappeared.

Several men ran up, ending the snake with their sabres. One of them stooped, and, examining the carcase of the dead reptile, exclaimed—

"*Carai!* the friar* is shot through the head!"

A moment after, half-a-dozen of the guerilleros burst open the door, and rushed in, crying out as they entered—

"*Quien tira?*" (Who fired?)

"What do you mean?" angrily asked Raoul, who had been in ill-humour ever since the guerillero had refused him a draught of water.

"I ask you who fired the shot?" repeated the man.

"Fired the shot!" echoed Raoul, knowing nothing of what had occurred outside. "We look like firing a shot, don't we? If I possessed that power, my gay friend, the first use I should make of it would be to send a bullet through that clumsy skull of yours."

"Santissima!" ejaculated the Mexican, with a look of astonishment. "It could not be these—they are all tied!"

And the Mexicans passed out again, leaving us to our reflections.

* Alluding to the snake. It, in fact, takes its name from the supposed resemblance of the singular formation over its head and neck to the hood of a capellan.

CHAPTER XXXVIII.

THE HACIENDA.

Mine were anything but agreeable. I was pained and puzzled. I was pained to think that *she*—dearer to me than life—was thus exposed to the dangers that surrounded us. It was her sister that had occupied the other hammock.

"Are they alone? Are they prisoners in the hands of these half robbers? May not their hospitality to us have brought them under proscription? And are they not being carried, father, mother, and all, before some tribunal? Or, are they travelling for protection with his band—protection against the less scrupulous robbers that infest the country?

"It was not uncommon upon the Rio Grande, when rich families journeyed from point to point, to pay for an escort of this sort. This may elucidate—"

"But I tell yez I did hear a crack; and, be me sowl! it was the sargint's rifle, or I've lost me hayrin intirely."

"What is it?" I asked, attracted to the conversation of my comrades.

"Chane says he heard a shot, and thinks it was Lincoln," answered Clayley.

"His gun has a quare sound, Captain," said the Irishman, appealing to me. "It's diffirint intirely from a Mexican piece—and not like our own naither. It's a way he has in loadin it."

"Well—what of that?"

"Why, Raowl says one of thim axed him who fired. Now, I heerd a shot, for my ear was close till the door here. It was beyant like; but I cud swear upon the blissed crass, it was aither the sargint's rifle, or another as like it as two pays."

"It is very strange!" I muttered, half in soliloquy, for the same thought had occurred to myself.

"I saw the boy, Captain," said Raoul, I saw him crossing when they opened the door."

"The boy!—what boy?" I asked.

"The same we brought out of the town."

"Ha! Narcisso—you saw him?"

"Yes; and, if I'm not mistaken, the white mule that the old gentleman rode to camp. I think it accounts for our being still alive."

A new light flashed upon me. In the incidents of the last twenty hours, I had never once thought of Narcisso. Now all was clear—clear as daylight. The Zambo whom Lincoln had killed—poor victim—was our friend—sent to warn us of danger. The dagger—Narcisso's—a token for us to trust him. The soft voice—the small hand thrust under the tapojo—yes—all were Narcisso's!

A web of mystery was torn to shreds in a single moment. The truth did n yield gratification. No—but the contrary. I was chagrined at the indi ference exhibited in another quarter.

"She must know that I am here, since her brother is master of the fact— here, bleeding and bound. Yet, where is her sympathy? She sleeps! She journeys within a few paces of me, where I am tied painfully—yet not a word of consolation. No! She is riding upon her soft cushion, or carried upon a *litera*,* escorted, perhaps, by this accomplished villain, who plays the gallant cavalier upon my own barb! They converse together—perhaps of the poor captives in their train—and with jest and ridicule—he at least—and *she* can hear it, and then fling herself into her soft hammock and sleep—sleep sweetly —calmly!"

These bitter reflections were interrupted. The door creaked once more upon its hinges. Half-a-dozen of our captors entered. Our blinds were pu on, and we were carried out and mounted as before.

In a few minutes, a bugle rang out, and the route was resumed.

We were carried up the stream bottom, a kind of glen, or *cañaca*. We

---

* The litera is frequently met with in Mexico, especially where the roads will not admit of any species of carriage. It is sometimes carried by peons; oftener by mules attached to the long shafts that stretch out both before and behind the body of the vehicle.

could feel, by the cool shade and the echoes, that we were travelling under heavy timber. The torrent roared in our ears, and the sound was not unpleasant. Twice or thrice we forded the stream, and sometimes left it, returning, after having travelled a mile or so. This was to avoid the *cañons* where there is no path by the water. We then ascended a long hill, and after reaching its summit, commenced going downwards.

The words cañada and cañons require explanation:—Cañada, a glen with a running stream; a word adopted into our language by the usage of the hunters on the frontier. The cañon is a great cleft between two mountains, or rather two parts of the same mountain, that seem to have been split asunder by the torrent rushing between. There is rarely any path along the stream—the sides of the chasm rising perpendicularly up from the water—and persons following the route of a river that cañons, frequently require to make a circuit of ten or fifteen miles before being able to get back to the stream. The word is both a noun and verb. A stream is said to cañon when passing through one of these chasms.

Having thus explained, we will resume our story.

I know this road well," said Raoul. "We are going down to the house of Cenobio."

"Par Dieu! I ought to know this hill!"

"For what reason?"

"First, Captain, because I have carried many a *bulto* of cochineal, and many a bale of smuggled tobacco over it; aye, and upon nights when my eyes were of as little service to me as they are at present."

"I thought that you *contrabandistas* hardly needed the precaution of dark nights?"

"True, at times; but there were other times when the government became lynx-eyed, and then smuggling was no joke. We had some sharp skirmishing. Sacre! I have good cause to remember this very hill. I came near being rubbed out on the other side of it.

"Ha! how was that?"

"Cenobio had got a large lot of cochineal from a crafty trader at Oaxaca. It was *cachéd* about two leagues from the *hacienda* in the hills, and a vessel was to drop into the mouth of the Medellin to take it on board."

Having expressed my ignorance of the true signification of the word *haci enda*, Raoul gave it to me as follows:—"*Hacienda* means an estate, though often, by the Mexicans themselves (and always by foreigners), the name is used to designate the principal dwelling-place, or head-quarters, of an estate where the proprietor, or his representative, lives. There are different kinds of estates, or haciendas, as sugar haciendas, haciendas where tobacco is cultivated, haciendas de ganados (cattle farms), but in one thing they all agree that is in the general appearance of the "great house," which we may term the hacienda. It bears no more resemblance to an English country-house, than the latter does to a burning mountain.

A distant front view of a hacienda gives you a long, low wall (usually white), with a great black gateway, and three or four grated apertures—passing for windows—placed at irregular intervals on either side of the gate. As you approach nearer, you do not find that this wall gets much higher, and, when you have arrived on the spot, you perceive that it is not above ten or fifteen feet high at the most (for the hacienda is almost universally a single story house).

You now discover that what appeared only a simple massive wall is the front of a house, which, in its turn, is the front of a large square yard (the patio). The other three sides of this yard are enclosed by houses, though generally somewhat lower than the front range, in which are the principal dwelling apartments.

The other houses are the stables, granaries, &c., and are usually numbered over the door-head, and dignified with titles, as *caballariza* (stable), *pajeria* (fodder crib), *cocina* (kitchen), &c. A long piazza, or *portale*, usually traverses the front range looking into the patio, in the centre of which there is a fountain.

In this piazza members of the family may be seen, and on this side objects wear a less guarded aspect. It is, in fact, the real front of the hacienda, and, if such a house may be said to wear a smile, this is the side of its face upon which to look for it.

The unsettled state of Spanish society in all ages and climes, has rendered it necessary that that part of their dwellings looking outward, should bear a stern and frowning aspect. Indeed, the hacienda, with its ponderous gates, and ironed windows, resembles a prison, or a fort, more than a peaceful dwelling-house.

In some haciendas belonging to the more wealthy proprietors, an attempt is made at ornament, by raising a serrated parapet along the front, and over the gateway. Often, too, the little family chapel, with its quaint steeple, or cupola, adds much to the picturesque effect of the hacienda and the surrounding scenery.

Usually at the distance of fifty rods from the hacienda may be observed a cluster of black huts. These are constructed of cane or wattles in the *tierra caliente*, of adobes (sun-dried bricks), in the *tierva templada*. These are the homes of the *peons*—the serfs and laborers belonging to the estate. They are miserable cabins, and, if the peon wishes to vote for his rulers, he must advocate the principles of universal suffrage, as his house, and all it contains, would be a bad bargain at five dollars. In it, however, he sleeps, with no other bed than his *petaté*, and no blanket excepting the everlasting *serapé* Even in this temperate clime, he is frequently chilled by sudden cold winds from the north.

Strolling one evening through a cluster of wattle-built peon-huts, at the hacienda of San Antonio (twenty miles from Peroté, on the National Road) I was struck with several low, clay structures, half buried in the ground, and looking more like dog-kennels than anything I could think of. Knowing that the Mexicans were not so nice about housing their dogs, I was induced from curiosity to inquire the uses of these singular huts.

"Para dormir, Señor," said a peon, taking off his sombrero, and bowing, para dormir, cuando es fria." (To sleep in, Sir, when it is cold.)

The doors were certainly not higher than those of a dog-kennel; yet into this dark hut, or rather hole, the poor serf, with his wife and wild-looking progeny was glad to crawl during the season of chill winds. No fire-wood. I looked around. I could see the country for twenty miles in every direction —its bleak barren plains without a tree—its mountain cones shooting up dry and naked, and nurturing nought but the never-ending and useless cactus! The owner of a hacienda is styled *haciendado*.

But to return to Cenobio and Raoul's adventure:

"A party of us were engaged to carry it across to the coast, and, as the cargo was very valuable, we were all of us armed to the teeth, with orders from the *patrone* to defend it at all hazards. His men were just the fellows who would obey that order, coming from Cenobio.

"The Government somehow or other got wind of the affair, and slipped a strong detachment out of Vera Craz in time to intercept us. We met them on the other side of this very hill, where a road strikes off towards Medellin.'

"Well! and what followed?'

"Why, the battle lasted nearly an hour; and, after having lost half-a-core of their best men, the valiant Lancers rode back to Vera Cruz quicker than they came out of it"

"And the smugglers?"

"Carried the goods safe on board. Three of them, poor fellows! are lying not far off, and I came near sharing their luck. I have a lance-hole through my thigh, here, that pains me at this very moment. *Sacre!*"

My ear at this moment caught the sound of dogs barking hoarsely below Horses of the cavalcade commenced neighing, answered by others from the adjacent fields, who recognised their old companions.

"It must be near night." I remarked to Raoul,

"I think about sunset, Captain," rejoined he. "It *feels* about that time."

I could not help smiling. There was something ludicrous in my comrade' remark about "feeling" the sunset.

The barking of the dogs now ceased, and we could hear voices ahead, wel coming the guerilleros.

The hoofs of our mules struck upon a hard pavement, and the sounds echoed as if under an arched way.

Our animals were presently halted, and we were unpacked and flung rudely down upon rough stones like so many bundles of merchandize.

CHAPTER XXXIX.

THE HEAD-QUARTERS OF THE GUERILLA.

WE lay for some minutes, listening to the strange voices around us. The neighing of horses—the barking and growling of dogs—the lowing of cattle—the shouts of the arrieros unpacking their mules—the clanking of sabres along the stone pavements—the tinkling of spurs—the laughter of men, and the voices of women—all were in our ears at once.

Two men approached us conversing.

"They are of the party that escaped us at La Virgen. Two of them are officers."

"*Chingaro!* I got this at La Virgen; and a full half mile off. 'Twas some black jugglery in their bullets. I hope the *patrone* will hang the Yankee savages."

"*Quien sabe?*" replied the first speaker. "Pinzon has been taken this morning at Puenta Moreno, with several others. They had a *fandango* with the Yankee dragoons. You know what the old man thinks of Pinzon. He'd sooner part with his wife."

"You think he will exchange them, then?"

"It is not unlikely."

"And yet he wouldn't trouble much if we had been taken. No—no; he let us be hanged like dogs."

"Well; that's always the way, you know."

"I begin to get tired of him. By the Virgin! José, I've half a mind to slip off, and join the Padré."

"Jarauta?"

"Yes; he's by the Bridge, with a brave set of Jaroches—some of our old comrades upon the Rio Grande among them. They're living at free quarters along the road, and having gay times of it, I hear. If Jarauta had taken these Yankees yesterday, the zopiloté would have made his dinner upon them to-day.

"That's true," rejoined the other; "but come—let us unblind the devils, and give them their beans. It may be the last they'll ever eat."

With this consoling remark, José commenced unbuckling our tapojos, and we once more looked upon the light. The brilliance at first dazzled us painfully; and it was some minutes before we could look steadily at the objects around us.

We had been thrown upon the pavement in the corner of the *patio*—a large court, surrounded by massive walls and flat-roofed houses.

These buildings were low, single storied, except the range in front, which contained the principal dwellings. The remaining three sides were occupied by stables, granaries, and quarters for the guerilleros and servants. A *portale* extended along the front range, and large vases, with shrubs and flowers ornamented the balustrade. The *portale* was screened from the sun by curtains of bright-colored cloth. These were partially drawn, and objects of elegant furniture appeared within.

Near the centre of the patio, was a large fountain, boiling up into a reservoir of hewn mason-work; and around this fountain were clumps of orange-trees —their leaves, in some places, dropping down into the water. Various arms hung or leaned against the walls—guns, pistols, and sabres—and two small pieces of cannon with their caissons and carriages stood in a prominent position. In these we recognized our old acquaintances of La Virgen.

A long trough stretched across the patio, and out of this a double row of mules and mustangs were greedily eating maize. The saddle-tracks, upon their steaming sides, showed them to be the companions of our late wearisome journey.

Huge dogs lay basking upon the hot stones; growling at intervals, as some one galloped in through the great doorway. Their broad jaws and tawny hides bespoke the Spanish blood-hound—the descendants of that race, with which Cortez had harried the conquered Aztec!

The guerilleros were seated or standing in groups around the fires—broiling jerked beef upon the points of their sabres. Some mended their saddles, or were wiping out an old carbine, or a clumsy escopette. Some strutted around the yard, swinging their bright mangas, or trailing after them the picturesque *scrapé*. Women in *rebosos* and colored skirts walked to and fro among the men.

The rebozo is a long cotton scarf, of a bluish grey color. The pattern varies, but the general character is a bluish grey. I can state of the rebozo something similar to what I have already said respecting the serapé. If any traveller has seen a Mexican peasant woman without the rebozo, his observation has been more extensive than mine—they wear it on all occasions.

The mode is thus. It is first hung over the head, the selvidge touching the brow. One end is then seized in the right hand, and, with a dexterous whisk, flung over the left shoulder, where it hangs down the back. The face, by this operation becomes partially concealed, and it may be further hidden by drawing the edge of the rebozo down over the forehead. Frequently only one eye—and that always a dark one—gleams out from the peep-hole thus constructed.

The arms, otherwise nude, are gathered up under the folds of the rebozo. The right is buried in that end that traverses across the breast, and " over the left," while the sinister arm is free, beneath the hanging end of the scarf, and carries—concealed likewise—many curious articles that form the solicitude of a Mexican *manola's* life.

I think the rebozo is three yards long, including fringe, by half a yard in width. It is neither a graceful nor a useful garment, never rich looking, though I have seen several that cost thirty dollars each. They are bought at prices from a dollar up to that mentioned, though (as in the case of the *serapé*) an unpractised eye would hardly see any difference between the dollar rebozo, and that at thirty times the cost!

The rebozo is rarely worn by ladies of the *haut ton*. They have adopted the shawl, which, however, they manage in their own way, drawing it over the (unbonnetted) head, and clutching it in their tiny little claws under the chin. The face is thus partially concealed, and can be so wholly, whenever they choose, by a single jerk of their nimble fingers.

The women carried jars filled with water. They knelt before smooth stones, and kneaded *tortillas*. They stirred *chilé* and chocolate in earthern *ollas*. They cooked *frijoles* in flat pans; and, amidst all these occupations, they joked and laughed and chatted with the men.

Several men—officers, from their style of dress, came out of the portale and, after delivering orders to the guerilleros on guard, returned to the house.

Packages of what appeared to be merchandize, lay in one corner of the court. Around this were groups of *arrieros*, in their red-leathern garments, securing their charge for the night; and laying out their mule-packs in long rows by the wall. The *arrieros* of Mexico are generally men of the pure Spanish race—that is the head arrieros; and, from all I saw of them, they are decidedly the best specimens of the *genus homo* to be met with in the country. They are celebrated for the virtue of honesty, which, in Mexico, *is* a virtue. An arriero, with his high conical hat, his swarthy complexion, and his pointed beard, his leathern spenser, and brown calzoneros, his brilliant serapé and big spurs, is a most picturesque object. Bands of these, with their *atajos*, are constantly meeting the traveller, reminding him of many a scene he may have read of or witnessed on the roads of old Spain.

Over the opposite roofs—for our position was elevated—we could see the bright fields and forest, and far beyond the Cofre di Peroté, and the undulating outlines of the Andes. Above all, the white-robed peak of Orizava rose up against the heavens like a pyramid of spotless snow.

The sun had gone down behind the mountains, but his rays still rested upon Orizava, bathing its cone with a yellow light, like a mantle of burnished gold. Clouds of red, and white, and purple, hung like a glory upon his track, and descending, rested upon the lower summits of the Cordillera. The peak of the "star" alone appeared above the clouds, towering in sublime and solitary grandeur!

There was a picturesque loveliness about the scene—an idea of sublimity—that caused me for the moment to forget where I was, or that I was a captive. My dream was dispelled by the harsh voice of José, who, at that moment, came up with a couple of peons, carrying a large earthen dish that contained our supper.

This consisted of black beans, with half a dozen tortillas; but as we were all half famished, we did not offer any criticism on the quality of the viands. The dish was placed in our midst, and our arms were untied for the first time since our capture. There were neither knives, forks, nor spoons; but Raoul showed us the Mexican fashion of "eating our spoons," and, twisting up the tortillas, we scooped and swallowed "right ahead."

CHAPTER XL.

CHANE'S COURTSHIP.

THE dish was emptied in a "squirrel's jump."

"Be my soul! it ates purty well, black as it is," said Chane, looking ruefully into the empty vessel. "It's got a worse complaint than the colur Cudn't yez fetch us a thrifle more ov it, my darlint boy?" he added, squinting up at José.

"*No entiende*,"* said the Mexican, shaking his head.

"Och! git out wid your tin days, bad luck to yer pitcher; in tin days it's Murtagh Chane that'll ayther be takin his tay in purghathory, or atin betther than black banes in some other part of the world."

"*No entiende*," repeated the Mexican as before.

"Tin days, indade! Sure we ud be did wid hunger in half the time. We want the banes now."

"*No entiende, Señor*," again replied the man.

"Go to owld Nick!" cried Chane, whose patience was now exhausted.

"*Que quiere?*" asked the Mexican, speaking to Raoul, who was by this time convulsed with laughter.

"Phwat's that he sez, Raowl?" inquired Chane, sharply.

"He says he don't understand you."

"Thin spake to him yerself, Raoul. Till him we want more banes, and a few more ov thim pancakes, if he plazes."

Raoul translated the Irishman's request.

"*No hay*," answered the Mexican, shaking his forefinger in front o his nose.

This is pronounced *no-i*, "there is none;" a phrase that every reader, who may have travelled in Mexico, will recognise with a painful distinctness

* Pronounced *no-in-ten-day*

Many a scene, such as that of the Georgia hotel, described by Lieut. Sibley has occurred to the traveller in the land of Anahuac.

"Well, iv yez won't go yerself, sind somebody else; it's all the same thing so yez bring us the ateables."

"*No entiende*," said the man, with the same shake of the head.

"Oh! there agin, but it's no use; yez understand me well enough, but ye don't want to bring the banes."

"He tells you there is no more," said Raoul.

"Oh! the desaving Judas; and five hundred ov thim grazers atin over beyant there. No more banes; oh, the lie!"

"*Frijoles**—*no hay*," said the Mexican, guessing at the purport of Chane's remarks.

"Oh! git out wid yer fray holeys! there isn't the size of a flay of holiness about the place. Git out!"

Raoul, and indeed all of us, except the Irishman himself, were bursting with laughter.

"I'm chokin," said the latter, after a pause; "ask him for wather, Raowl—sure he can't deny that—with that purty little sthrame boilin up undher our noses, as clear as the potyeen of Innishowen."

Raoul asked for water, which we all needed. Our throats were as dry as charcoal. The Mexican made a sign to one of the women, who shortly after came up with an earthen jar filled with water.

"Give it first to the Captin, Misthress," said Chane, pointing to me, "sarve all ayqually, but respict rank."

The woman understood the sign, and handed me the jar. I drank copiously, passing it to my comrades, Clayley and Raoul. Chane at length took the jar, but, instead of drinking immediately, as might have been expected, he set it between his knees, and looked quizzically up at the woman.

"I say, my little darlint," said he, winking and poking her lightly under the ribs, "my little Moochacha,† that's what they call thim—isnt it, Raoul?"

"Muchacha? oh yes."

"Well, thin, my pretty little moochacha cudn't yez? ye know what I mane? Cudn't yes—? Oh! ye know well enough?—only a little—just mouthful to take the cowld taste aff the wather."

* Pronounced *fray-holys*.
† Muchacha—girl; pronounced as by Chane. It means a young girl, bu, has a more specfis sense at times. "*Visitar las muchachas*," to visit the young ladies.

"*No entiende*," said the woman, smiling good-naturedly at Chane's comical gestures.

"Och! the plague! there's that tin days agin—talk to her Rawol. Tell her what I mane."

Raoul translated his comrade's wishes.

"Tell her, Raowl, I've got no money, bekase I have been robb'd, de ye see but I'll give her ayther of these saints for the smallest thrifle of agwardent," and he pulled the images out of his jacket, as he spoke.

The woman, seeing these, bent forward with an exclamation, and recognising the crucifix with the images of the saint and virgin, dropped upon her knees, and kissed them fervently, uttering some words in a language half Spanish—half Aztec!

Rising up, she looked kindly at Chane, exclaiming, "Bueno Catolico?" She then tossed the rebozo over her left shoulder, and hurried off across the yard.

"De yez think, Raowl, she's gone after the licker?"

"I am sure of it," answered the Frenchman.

In a few minutes the woman returned, and, drawing a small flask out of the folds of her *rebozo*, handed it to Chane.

The Irishman commenced undoing the string that carried his "relics."

"Which ov thim de yez want, Misthress—the saint, or the bowly u other, or both?—it's all the same to Murtagh."

The woman observing what he was after, rushed forward, and, placing her hands upon his, said in a kind tone:

"*No, Señor! Su proteccion necessita V.*"

"Phwat dez she say, Raoul?"

"She says, keep them; you will need their protection yourself."

"Oh, be me sowl! she's not far asthray then. I need it bad enough now, an a hape ov good they're likely to do me. They've hung there for tin years—both of thim; an this nate little flask's the first binifit I iver resaved from aither of them. Thry it, Captin. It'll do yez good."

I took the bottle and drank. It was the *chingarito*—a bad species of *aguardiente** from the wild aloe—and hot as fire. A mouthful sufficed. I handed the flask to Clayley, who drank more freely. Raoul followed suit and the bottle came back to the Irishman.

* Literally, burning water; and the name is by no means inappropriate.

"Your hilth, darlint," said he, nodding to the Mexican woman. "May yez live till I wish ye did!"

The woman smiled, and repeated: "*No entiende.*"

"Oh! nivir mind the tin days—we won't quarrel about that. Yer a swate crayteur," continued he, winking at the woman; "but sure yer petticoats is mighty short; an yez want a pair of stockings† bad too—but niver mind—yez stand well upon thim illigant ankles—dade ye do; and yez have a purty little futt into the bargain."

"*Que dice?*" (what did he say?) asked the Mexican, speaking to Raoul.

"He is complimenting you on the smallness of your feet," answered the Frenchman.

The woman was evidently pleased, and commenced cramping up—what was in fact—a very small foot, into its faded satin slipper. In regard to feet, all nations, I think, must yield the palm to Mexico. The females of that country have the smallest feet and best formed ankles I ever saw. They usually wear slippers—rarely the bootee—and these, even upon the feet of the leperas —the poorest peasant girls—must be silk or satin. The heel is generally down; the front part very low, scarcely covering the toes, and how they manage to "hold on" to the tiny little thing—walking gracefully all the while—is a theorem that has puzzled a good many. But they do it, and we must set it down as a "sleight-of-foot" trick.

"Till me, me dear," continued Chane, "are yez married?"

"*Que dice?*" again asked the woman.

"He wants to know if you are married?"

She smiled, waving her forefinger in front of her nose.

Raoul informed the Irishman that this was a negative answer to his question.

"By my sowl, thin," said Chane, "I wudn't mind marryin ye meself, and joinin the thribe—that is if they'll let me off from the hangin. Tell her that, Raowl."

As desired, Raoul explained his comrade's last speech, at which the woman laughed, but said nothing.

"Silence gives consint. But tell her, Raowl, that I won't buy a pig in a poke; they must first let me off from the hangin, de ye hear—tell her that."

"*El señor esta muy allegre,*" (the gentleman is very merry) said the woman; and, picking up her jar, with a smile, she left us.

---

† It is rare to see the ankles of a Mexican paisana cased in anything but their own natural (and not very white) skins.

"I say, Raowl, does she consint?"

"She hasn't made up her mind, yet."

"By the holy vistment, thin it's all up wid Murt! The saints won't save him. Take anther dhrap, Raowl!"

CHAPTER XLI.

THE DANCE OF THE TAGAROTA.

Night fell, and the blazing fagots threw their glare over the patio, striking upon objects picturesque at all times, but doubly so under the red light of the pine fires. The grouping of guerilleros—their broad, heavy hats, many of them plumed—their long, black hair, and pointed beards—their dark, flashing eyes—their teeth, fierce and white—the half-savage expression of their features—their costumes, high-colored and wild-like—all combined in impressing us with strange feelings.

The mules—the mustangs—the dogs—the peons—the slippered wenches with their coarse, trailing tresses—the low roofs—the iron-barred windows—the orange-trees by the fountain—the palms hanging over the wall—the glistening cocuyos—were all strange sights to us.

The sounds that rang in our ears were not more familiar. Even the voices of the men, unlike the Saxon, sounded wild and sharp. It was the Spanish language spoken in the *patois* of the Aztec Indian. In this the guerilleros chatted, and sang, and swore. There was a medley of other sounds, not less strange to our ears—as the dogs howled and barked their bloodhound-notes—as the mustangs neighed, or the mules hinnied—as the heavy sabre clanked or the huge spur tinkled its tiny bells—as the *majas*, sitting by some group touched the strings of their bandolons, and chanted their half-Indian songs.

By a blazing pile, close to where we sate, a party of guerilleros, with their women, were dancing the Tagarota—a species of fandango.

The men had thrown aside their heavy hats and accoutrements. Some of them had unbuttoned the legs of their calsoneros, and tucked them up to the waist, *à la Bedouin*. The women had cast off their rebozos, leaving a light sleeveless chemise, as the only covering between their bosoms and the light, while their flaming petticoats were short enough to have suited a Parisian coryphée.

Two men, seated upon raw-hide stools, strummed away upon a pair of bandolons, while a third pinched and pulled at the strings of an old guitar—all three aiding the music with their shrill, disagreeable voices.

The dancers formed the figure of a parallelogram, each standing opposite his partner, or rather moving, for they were never at rest, but kept constantly beating time with feet, head, and hands. The last they struck against their cheeks and thighs; and, at intervals, clapped them together.

One would suddenly appear as a hunchback, and, dancing out into the centre of the figure, perform various antics to attract his partner. After a while she would dance up—deformed also—and the two bringing their bodies in contact, and performing various disgusting contortions, would give place to another pair. These would appear without arms or legs, walking on their knees, or sliding along on their hips!

One danced with his head under his arm, and another with one leg around his neck; all eliciting more or less laughter, as the feat was more or less comical. During the dance, every species of deformity was imitated and caricatured—for this is the Tagarota. It was a series of grotesque and repulsive pictures. Some of the dancers flinging themselves flat, would roll across the open space without moving hand or foot. This always elicited applause, and we could not help remarking its resemblance to the gymnastics we had lately been practising ourselves. I have seen the Tagarota but once, and I wish never to see it again. I believe that it is a species of dance, the stranger in Mexico will have but few opportunities of witnessing. It is not every one who may have the good or ill fortune to be in the company where it is danced. I am not certain of the orthography of the word. I never saw it written, and I have followed the orthoepy as closely as I could.

"Oh! be me sowl! We can bate yez at that!" cried Chane, who appeared to be highly amused at the Tagarota, making his comments as the dance went on.

I was sick of the scene, and watched it no longer. My eyes turned to the *portale*, and I looked anxiously through the half drawn curtains.

"It is strange I have seen nothing of them! Could they have turned off on some other route? No—they must be here. Narcisso's promise for to-night. He, at least, is here. And she?—perhaps occupied within—gay, happy, indifferent—oh!"

The pain shot afresh through my heart

Suddenly the curtain was drawn aside, and a brilliant picture appeared within—brilliant but to me—like the glimpse which some condemned spirit might catch over the walls of Paradise. Officers in bright uniforms, and amongst these I recognised the elegant person of Dubrosc. Ladies in rich dresses, and amongst these ——. Her sister, too, was there, and the Doña Joaquina, and half-a-dozen other ladies rustling in silks, and blazing w jewels!

Several of the gentlemen—young officers of the band—wore the pictures costume of the guerilleros.

They were forming for the **dance.**

"Look, Captain!" cried Clayley, "Don Cosme and his people, by the livir earthquake!"

"Hush! do not touch me—do not speak to me!"

I felt as though my heart would stop respiration. It rose in my bosom, and seemed to hang, for minutes, without beating. My throat felt dry and husky, and a cold perspiration broke out upon me.

"He approaches her—he asks her to dance, she consents! No! she refuses. Brave girl! She has strayed away from the dancers, and looks over the balustrade. She is sad. Was it a sigh that caused her bosom to rise? Ha' he comes again. She is smiling!—he touches her hand!

"Fiend! false woman!" I shouted at the top of my voice. I sprang up impelled by passion. I attempted to rush toward them. My feet wer bound, and I fell heavily upon my face!

The guards seized me, tying my hands. My comrades, too, were re bund. We were dragged over the stones into a small room in one corner c the patio.

The door was bolted and locked, and we were left alone.

CHAPTER XLII.

A KISS IN THE DARK.

It would be impossible to describe my feelings, as I was flung upon the floor of our prison. This was cold, damp, and filthy; but I heeded not these grievances. Greater sorrows absorbed the less. There is no torture so racking—no pain so painful, as the throbbings of a jealous heart; but how much harder to bear under circumstances like mine! She could sleep—smile—dance—dance by my prison, and with my jailor!

I felt spiteful—vengeful. I was stung to a desire for retaliation; and along with this, came an eagerness to live for the opportunity of indulging in this passion.

I began to look around our prison, and see what chances it offered for escape.

"Good Heavens! if our being transferred to the cell should destroy the plans of Narcisso. How is he to reach us? The door is double-locked, and a sentry is pacing without!"

After several painful efforts, I raised myself upon my feet, propping my body against the side of the prison. There was an aperture—a window about as large as a loop-hole for musketry. I spun myself along the wall, until I stood directly under it. It was just the height of my chin. Cautioning my companions to silence, I placed my ear to the aperture and listened. A low sound came wailing from the fields without. I did not heed this. I knew it was the wolf. It rose again louder than before. A peculiarity in the howl struck me, and I turned, calling to Raoul.

"What is it, Captain?" inquired he.

"Do you know if the prairie wolf is found here?"

"I do not know if it be the true prairie wolf, Captain. There is one something like—the *coyoté*."

I returned to the aperture, and listened.

"Again the howl of the prairie wolf—the bark! By Heavens! it is Lincoln!"

Now it ceased for several minutes, and then came again; but from another direction.

"What is to be done? If I answer him, it will alarm the sentry. I will wait until he comes closer to the wall." I could tell that he was creeping nearer and nearer.

Finding he had not been answered, the howling ceased. I stood listening eagerly to every sound from without. My comrades, who had been apprised of Lincoln's proximity, had risen to their feet, and were leaning against the walls.

We were about half an hour in this situation, without exchanging a word when a light tap was heard from without, and a soft voice whispered—

"*Hola Capitan!*"

I placed my ear to the aperture. The whisper was repeated—it was not Lincoln. That was clear.

It must be Narcisso.

"*Quien?*" I asked.

"*Yo, Capitan.*"

I recognised the voice that had addressed me in the morning.

"It is Narcisso."

"Can you place your hands in the aperture?" said he.

"No; they are tied behind my back."

"Can you bring them opposite, then?"

"No; I am standing on my toes, and my wrists are still far below the sill."

"Are your comrades all similarly bound?"

"All."

"Let one get on each side, and raise you up on their shoulders."

Wondering at the astuteness of the young Spaniard, I ordered Chane and Raoul to lift me as he directed.

When my wrists came opposite the window, I cautioned them to hold on. Presently a soft hand touched mine, passing all over them. Then I felt the blade of a knife pressed against the thong, and in an instant it leaped from my wrists. I ordered the men to set me down, and I listened as before.

"Here is the knife; you can release your own ankles, and those of your comrades. This paper will direct you further. You will find the lamp inside."

A knife, with a folded and strangely shining note, were passed through by the speaker!

"And now, Capitan—one favor," continued the voice, in a trembling tone

"Ask it—ask it!"

"I would kiss your hand, before we part."

"Dear—noble boy!" cried I, thrusting my hand into the aperture.

"Boy! ah—true—you think me a boy. I am no boy, Captain, but a woman—one who loves you with all her blighted, broken heart!"

"Oh, heavens! it is then! dearest Guadalupe!"

"Ha! I thought as much—now I will not—but no—what good would it be to me? No—no—no! I will keep my word."

This appeared to be uttered in soliloquy and the tumult of my thoughts prevented me from noticing the strangeness of these expressions. I thought of them afterwards.

"Your hand—your hand!" I ejaculated.

"You would kiss my hand? do so!" The little hand was thrust through, flashing with brilliants. I caught it in mine, covering it with kisses. It seemed to yield to the fervid pressure of my lips.

"Oh!" I exclaimed, in the transport of my feelings, "let us not part—let us fly together! I was wronging you, loveliest, dearest Guadalupe——"

A slight exclamation, as if from some painful emotion, and the hand was plucked away, leaving one of the diamonds in my fingers. The next moment, the voice whispered, with a strange sadness of tone as I thought:

"Adieu, Capitan, adieu! *In this world of life we never know who best loves us!*"

I was puzzled—bewildered. I called out, but there was no answer. I listened until the patience of my comrades was well nigh exhausted, but still there was no voice from without; and, with a strange feeling of uneasiness and wonderment. I commenced cutting the thongs from my ankles.

Having set Raoul at liberty, I handed him the knife. and proceeded to open the note. Inside I found the cocuyo, and, using it as I had been already instructed, I read:

"The walls are adobé. You have a knife. The side with the loop-hole fronts outward. There is a field of magueys; and, beyond this, you will find the forest. You may then trust to yourselves. I can help you no farther Carissimo caballero. Adieu!"

I had no time to reflect upon the peculiarities of the note, though the boldness of the style struck me as corresponding with the other. I flung down the fire-fly, crushing the paper into my bosom; and, seizing the knife, was about to attack the adobe wall, when voices reached me from without. I sprang forward, and placed my ear to listen. It was an altercation—a woman—a man—" By heaven, it is Lincoln's voice!"

"Yer cussed whelp, ye'd see the Cap'n hung, would yer? a man that's good vally for the full of a pararer of green-gutted greasers; but I aint a gwine to let *you* look at his hangin; if yer dont show me, which of these yere pigeon holes is his'n, an' help me to get him outer it, I'll skin yer like a mink!"

"I tell you, Mister Lincoln," replied a voice which I recognised as the one whose owner had just left me, "I have this minute given the Captain the means of escape, through that loop-hole."

"Whar?"

This one," answered the female voice.

"Wal—that's easy to circumstantiate; kum along yeer! I aint agwine to 'et yer go, till it's all fixed, de ye hear!"

I heard the heavy foot of the hunter, as he approached; and presently his voice, calling through the loop-hole, in a guarded whisper:

"Cap'n."

Hush! Bob, it's all right," I replied, speaking in a low tone, for the sentries were moving suspiciously around the door.

"Good!" ejaculated he, "yer kin go now," he added to the other, whose attention I endeavored to attract, but dared not call loud enough, lest the guards should hear me. "Dash my buttons! I don't want yer to go—yer a good un arter all—why can't yer kum along; the "Cap'n 'll make it all straight agin."

"Mr. Lincoln, I cannot go with you; please suffer me to depart!"

"Wal! yer own likes; but if I kin do yer a good turn, you can depend on Bob Linkin, mind that."

Thank you, thank you!"

And, before I could interfere to prevent it, she was gone. I could hear the voice, sad and sweet, in the distance, calling back "*Adios!*"

I had no time for reflection, else the mystery that surrounded me would have occupied my thoughts for hours. It was time to act. Again I heard Lincoln's voice at the loophole.

"What is it?" I inquired.

"How are yer ter get out, Cap'n?"

"We are cutting a hole through the wall."

"If yer can give me the spot, I'll meet yer half-ways."

I measured the distance from the loop-hole, and handed the string to Lincoln. We heard no more from the hunter, until the moonlight glanced through the wall upon the blade of his knife. Then he uttered a short ejaculation, such as may be heard from the "mountain men" at peculiar crises; and fter that we could hear him exclaiming:

"Look out, Raoul! Hang it, man, yer a cuttin my claws!"

In a few minutes, the hole was large enough to pass our bodies; and one, by one, we crawled out, and were once more at liberty.

CHAPTER XLIII.

MARIA DE MERCED.

THERE was a deep ditch under the wall, filled with cactus plants and dry grass. We lay in the bottom of this for some moments, panting with fatigue Our limbs were stiff and swollen, and we could hardly stand upright. A little delay then was necessary, to bring back the blood, and determine our future course.

"We had best ter keep the gully," whispered Lincoln, "I kum across the fields myself, but them pulkies* is thin, and they may sight us."

"The best route is the ditch," assented Raoul; "there are some windows but they are high, and we can crawl under them."

"Forward, then!" I whispered to Raoul.

We crept down the ditch on all fours, passing several windows that were dark and shut. We reached one, the last in the row, where the light streamed through. Notwithstanding our perilous situation, I resolved to look in. There was an impulse upon me which I could not resist. I was yearning for some clue to the mystery that hung around me.

The window was high up, but it was grated with heavy bars; and, grasping two of these, I swung myself to its level. Meanwhile, my comrades had crept into the maguey to wait for me.

I raised my head cautiously and looked in. It was a room—somewhat elegantly furnished—but my eye did not dwell long on that. A man sitting by the table engrossed my attention. This man was Dubrosc. The light was full upon his face, and I gazed upon its hated lines until I felt my frame trembling with passion.

I can give no idea of the hate this man had inspired me with. Had I pos-

* Maguey plants, called by the soldiers pulque plants.

sessed fire-arms, I could not have restrained myself from shooting him; and but for the iron grating, I should have sprung through the sash and grappled him with my hands. I have thought since, that some providence held me back from making a demonstration, that would have baffled our escape. I am sure at that moment I possessed no restraint within myself.

As I gazed at Dubrosc, the door of the apartment opened, and a young man entered. He was strangely-attired, in a costume half military, half ranchero. There was a fineness—a silky richness—about the dress and manner of this youth that struck me. His features were dark and beautiful.

He advanced and sate down by the table, placing his hand upon it. Several rings sparkled upon his fingers. I observed that he was pale, and that his hand trembled.

After looking at him for a moment, I began to fancy I had seen the features before. It was not Narcisso. Him I should have known; and yet there was a resemblance! Yes, he even resembled *her!* I started as this thought crossed me. I strained my eyes; the resemblance grew stronger!

Oh, heaven! could it be?—dressed thus; no, no, those eyes—ha! I remember—the boy at the rendezvous—on board the transport—the island—the picture! It is she—the cousin—*Maria de Merced!*"

These recollections came with the suddenness of a single thought, and passed as quickly. Later memories crowded upon me. The adventure of the morning—the strange words uttered at the window of my prison—the small hand—this, then, was the author of our deliverance!

A hundred mysteries were explained in a single moment. The unexpected elucidation came like a shock—like a sudden light. I staggered back, giving way to new and singular emotions!

"*She* knows nothing of my presence then. *She* is innocent!"

This thought alone restored me to happiness. A thousand others rushed through my brain in quick succession. Some pleasant—others painful.

There was an altercation of voices over my head. I caught the iron rods, and, resting my toes upon a high bank, swung my body up, and again looked into the room. Dubrosc was now pacing angrily over the floor.

"Bah!" he ejaculated, with a look of cold brutality, "you think to make me jealous, I believe. That isn't possible. I was never so, and *you* can't do it. I know you love the cursed Yankee. I watched you on the ship—on the island, to. You had better keep him company where he is going; ha ha

Jealous, indeed! Your pretty cousins have grown up since I saw them last."

The insinuation sent the blood through my veins like lava.

It appeared to produce a similar effect upon the woman, for, starting from her seat, she looked towards Dubrosc, her eye flashing like globes of fire.

"Yes!" she exclaimed; "and, if you dare whisper your polluting thoughts either of them—lawless as is this land—you know that I still possess the power to punish *you*. You are villain enough, heaven knows, for anything, but *they* shall not fall; one victim is enough and such a one!"

"Victim, indeed!" replied the man, evidently cowed by the other's threat; "you call yourself victim, Marie? The *wife* of the handsomest man in Mexico? ha! ha!"

There was something of irony in the latter part of the speech, and the emphasis placed on the word "wife."

"Yes; you may well taunt me with your false priest, you unfeeling wretch! Oh! *Santissima Madre!*" continued she, dropping back into her chair, and pressing her head between her hands; "Beguiled—beggared—almost unsexed! and yet I never loved the man. It was not love, but madness—madness and fascination!"

The last words were uttered in soliloquy, as though she regarded not the presence of her companion.

"I don't care a claco!" cried he, fiercely, and evidently piqued at her declaration, "not one claco whether you ever loved me or not. That's not the question, now, but *this is*. You must make yourself known to your Crœsus of an uncle here, and demand that part of your fortune that he still clutches within his avaricious old fingers. You must do this to-morrow."

"I will not!"

"But you shall, or —"

The woman rose suddenly, and walked towards the door.

"No, not to-night, dearest," said Dubrosc, grasping her rudely by the arm. "I have my reasons for keeping you here. I noted you to-day speaking with that cursed Yankee; and you're just traitor enough to help him to escape I'll look to him myself; so you may stay where you are. If you should choose to rise early enough to-morrow morning, you will have the felicity of seeing him dance upon the tight rope. Ha! ha! ha!"

And, with a savage laugh, the Creole walked out of the room, locking the door behind him.

A strange expression played over the features of the woman. A blending of triumph with anxiety. She ran forward to the window, and pressing her small lips close to the glass, strained her eyes outward.

I held the diamond in my fingers, and stretching up until my hand was opposite her face, I wrote the word " Maria." At first seeing me, she had started back. There was no time to be lost. My comrades were already chafing at my delay; and, joining them, we crept through the magueys, parting the broad, stiff leaves with our fingers. We were soon upon the edge of the chapparal wood. I looked back towards the window. The woman stood holding the lamp, and its light was full upon her face. She had read the scrawl, and was gazing out with an expression I shall never forget. Another bound, and we were " in the woods."

CHAPTER XLIV.

THE PURSUIT.

For a time there was a strange irresolution in my flight. The idea of leaving *her* in such company; that, after all, they might be prisoners, or even if not, the thought that they were in his power, to any extent, was enough to render me wretched and irresolute. But what could we do? Five men, almost unarmed?

"It would be madness to remain—madness and death. The woman—she possesses some mysterious power over this brute, her paramour—she will guard them."

This thought decided me, and I yielded myself freely to flight. We had but little fear of being caught again. We had too much confidence—particularly Lincoln and myself—in our forest craft. Raoul knew all the counrtry, the thickets and the passes. We stopped a moment to deliberate on the track we would take. A bugle rang out, and the next instant the report of a cannon thundered in a thousand echoes along the glen.

"It is from the hacienda," said Raoul, "they have missed us already."

"Is that 'sign,' Raoul?" asked Lincoln.

"It is," replied the other; "it's to warn their scouts. They're all over these hills. We must look sharp."

"I don't like this yeer timber; it's too scant. Cudn't yer put us in the crik bottom, Rowl?"

"There's a heavy chapparal," said the Frenchman, musing; "it's ten miles off. If we could reach that we're safe—a wolf can hardly crawl through it. We must make it before day."

"Lead on then, Raoul!"

We stole along with cautious steps. The rustling of a leaf, or the cracking of a dead stick, might betray us, for we could hear signals upon all sides, and our pursuers passed us in small parties, within ear-shot.

We bore to the right, in order to reach the creek bottom, of which Lincoln had spoken. We soon came into this, and followed the stream down; but not on the bank. Lincoln would not hear of our taking the bank path, arguing that our pursuers would be "sartin ter foller the clar trail."

The hunter was right, for, shortly after, a party came down the stream. We could hear the clinking of their accoutrements, and even the conversation of some of the men.

"But, in the first place, how did they get loose within? and who cut the wall from the outside, unless some one helped them—*carajo!* in's not possible."

"That's true, José," said another voice. "Some one must; and I believe it was that giant, that got away from us at the ranche. The shot that killed the friar* came from the chapparal; and yet we searched and found nobody." Mark my words, it was he; and I believe he has hung upon our track all the way."

"*Vaya!*" exclaimed another. "I shouldn't like much to be under the range of his rifle; they say he can kill a mile off, and hit wherever he pleases. He shot the snake right through the eyes!"

"By the Virgin!" said one of the guerilleros, laughing. "he must have been a snake of good taste, to be caught toying around that dainty daughter of the old Spaniard! It reminds one of what the Book tells about mother Eva and the old Serpent. Now if the Yankee's bullet—"

We could hear no more, as the voices died away in the distance, and under the sound of the water.

"Ay," muttered Lincoln, finishing the sentence; "if the Yankee's bullet hadn't been needed for the varmint, some o' yer wudn't a been waggin yer clappers as ye ir."

"It *was* you, then?" I asked, turning to the hunter.

"'Twur, Cap'n, but for the cussed catawampus, I ud a gin Mister Dubrosc his ticket. I hed amost sighted him, whun I seed the flash o' the thing's ye, an I knowed it wur a gwine to strike the gal."

"And Jack?" I inquired, now for the first time thinking of the boy.

"I guess he's safe enuf, Cap'n. I sent the little feller back with word ter the kurnel."

* Alluding to the cobra.

"Ha! then we may expect them from camp?"

"No doubt on it, Cap'n; but yer see if they kum, they may not be able to foller us beyond the ranche. So it'll be best for us not to depend on them, but ter take Rowl's track."

"You are right. Lead on, Raoul!"

After a painful journey, we reached the thicket of which Raoul had spoken and, dragging ourselves into it, we came to a small opening, covered with long dry grass. Upon this luxurious couch we resolved to make a bivouac. We were all worn down by the fatigues of the day and night preceding, and, throwing ourselves upon the grass, in a few minutes were asleep.

CHAPTER XLV.

A NEW AND TERRIBLE ENEMY.

It was daylight when I awoke—broad daylight. My companions, all but Clayley, were already astir, and had kindled a fire, with a species of wood known to Raoul, that produced hardly any smoke. They were preparing breakfast! On a limb, close by, hung the hideous human-like carcass of an iguana, still writhing. Raoul was whetting a knife to skin it, while Lincoln was at some distance carefully re-loading his rifle. The Irishman lay upon the grass, peeling bananas, and roasting them over the fire.

The iguana was soon skinned and broiled; and we commenced eating all of us with good appetites.

"Be Saint Pathrick!" said Chane. "this bates frog-atin all hollow. It's little meself dhramed in the owld sod, hearin of thim niggers in furrin parts, that I'd be turning kannybawl meself some day!"

"Don't you like it, Murtagh?" asked Raoul jocosely.

"Oh! indade yes; it's betther than an empty brid-basket; but if yez could only taste a small thrifle ov a Wicklow ham this mornin, and a smilin pratie, instid of this brown soap, yez—"

"Hisht!" said Lincoln, starting suddenly, and holding the bite half way to his mouth.

"What is it?" I asked.

"I'll tell yer in a minit, Cap'n."

The hunter waved his hand to enjoin silence, and, striding to the edge of the glade, fell flat to the ground. We knew he was listening, and waited for the result. We had not long to wait, for he had scarce brought his ear in contact with the earth, when he sprang suddenly up again, exclaiming:

"*Houns trailin us by the Eternal God!*"

It was seldom that Lincoln uttered an oath, and when he did, there was something awful in his manner. He wore a despairing look too, unusual to the bold character of his features. This, with the appalling statement, acted on us like a galvanic shock; and by one impulse, we leaped from the fire; and threw ourselves flat upon the grass.

Not a word was spoken, as we strained our ears to listen.

"At first, we could distinguish a low moaning sound, like the hum of a wild bee; it seemed to come out of the earth! After a little, it grew louder and sharper; then it ended in a yelp, and ceased altogether. After a short interval it began afresh, this time still clearer; then came the yelp, loud sharp, and vengeful. There was no mistaking that sound. *It was the bark of the Spanish blood-hound!*

We sprang up simultaneously, looking around for weapons, and then staring at each other, with an expression of despair.

The rifle and two case-knives were all the weapons we had.

"What's to be done?" cried one; and all eyes were turned upon Lincoln.

The hunter stood motionless, clutching his rifle, and looking to the ground.

"How fur's the crik, Rowl?" he asked after a pause.

"Not two hundred yards; this way it lies."

"I kin see no other chance, Cap'n, than ter take the water; we may bamfoozle the houns a bit, if tho c's good wadin."

"Nor I." I had thought of the same plan.

"If we hed hed bowies, we mouter fit the dogs whar we ir; but yer see we aint; an I kin tell by thar yowl, thar aint less nor a dozen on em."

"It's no use to remain here lead us to the Creek, Raoul!" and, following the Frenchman, we dashed recklessly through the thicket.

On reaching the stream, we plunged in. It was one of those mountain torrents—common in Mexico—spots of still water alternating with cascades, that dash and foam over shapeless masses of amygdaloidal basalt. We waded through the first pool; and then clambering among the rocks, entered a second. This was a good stretch, a hundred yards or more of crystal water, in which we were waist-deep.

We took the bank at the lower and, on the same side; and, striking back into the timber, kept on parallel to the course of the stream. We did not go far away from the water, lest we might be pushed again to repeat the *ruse*.

All this time, the yelping of the blood-hounds had been ringing in our ears. Suddenly it ceased.

"They have reached the water," said Clayley.

'No," rejoined Lincoln, stopping a moment to listen, "they're a chawin them bones."

"There again!" cried one, as their deep voices rang down the glen, in a chorus of the whole pack. The next minute, the dogs were mute a second time, speaking, at intervals, in a fierce growl, that told us they were at fault.

Beyond an occasional bark, we heard nothing of the blood-hounds, until we had gained at least, two miles down the stream. We began to think we had baffled them in earnest, when Lincoln, who had kept in the rear, was seen to throw himself flat upon the grass. We all stopped, looking at him with breathless anxiety. It was but a minute. Rising up, with a reckless air, he struck his rifle fiercely upon the ground, exclaiming:

"Swamp them houns! they're arter us agin!"

By one impulse, we all rushed back to the creek; and scrambling over the rocks, plunged into the water, and commenced wading down.

A sudden exclamation burst from Raoul, in the advance. We soon learnt the cause, and, to our dismay—we had struck the water at a point where the stream *cañoned!*

On each side rose a frowning precipice, straight as a wall. Between these the black torrent rushed through a channel only a few feet in width, so swiftly that, had we attempted to descend by swimming, we should have been dashed to death against the rocks below.

To reach the stream farther down, it would be necessary to make a circuit of miles; and the hounds would be on our heels before we could gain three hundred yards.

We looked at each other and at Lincoln—all panting and pale.

"Stumped at last." cried the hunter, gritting his teeth with fury.

"No!" I shouted, a thought at that moment flashing upon me. "Follow me, comrades! We'll fight the blood-hounds upon the cliff."

I pointed upward. A yell from Lincoln announced his approval.

"Hooray!" he cried, leaping on the bank; that idee's jest like yer, Cap. Hooray! Now, boys, for the bluff!"

Next moment, we were straining up the gorge that led to the precipice and the next, we had reached the highest point, where the cliff, by a bold projection, butted over the stream. There was a level platform, covered with tufted grass, and upon this we took our stand.

CHAPTER XLVI.

A BATTLE WITH BLOODHOUNDS.

We stood for some moments gathering breath, and nerving ourselves for the desperate struggle. I could not help looking over the precipice. It was a fearful sight. Below, in a vertical line, two hundred feet below, the stream rushing through the *cañon* broke upon a bed of sharp, jagged rocks, and then glided on in seething, snow-white foam. There was no object between the eye and the water; no jutting ledge—not even a tree to break the fall,—nothing but the spiky boulders below, and the foaming torrent that washed them!

It was some minutes before our unnatural enemies made their appearance, but every howl sounded nearer and nearer. Our trail was warm, and we knew they were scenting it on a run. At length, the bushes crackled, and we could see their white breasts gleaming through the leaves. A few more springs, and the foremost bloodhound bounded out upon the bank, and throwing up his broad jaws, uttered a hideous "growl."

He was at fault where we had entered the water. His comrades now dashed out of the thicket, and, joining in a chorus of disappointment, scattered among the stones.

An old dog—scarred and cunning—kept along the bank until he had reached the top of the cañon. This was where we had made our crossing. Here the hound entered the channel, and springing from rock to rock, reached the point where we had dragged ourselves out of the water. A short yelp announced to his comrades that he had lifted the scent, and they all threw up their noses and came gallopping down.

There was a swift current between two boulders of basalt. We had leaped this. The old dog reached it, and stood straining upon the spring, when Lincoln fired, and the hound, with a short "wough," dropped in upon his head, and was carried off like a flash!

"Counts one less to pitch over," said the hunter, hastily reloading his rifle.

Without appearing to notice the strange conduct of their leader, the others crossed in a string, and, striking the warm trail, came yelling up the pass. It was a grassy slope—such as is often seen between two tables of a cliff—and, as the dogs strained upward, we could see their white fangs, and the red blood that had baited them clotted along their jaws. Another crack from Lincoln's rifle, and the foremost hound tumbled back down the gorge.

"Two rubbed out," cried the hunter, and at the same moment, I saw him fling his rifle to the ground.

The hounds kept the trail no longer. Their quarry was before them; their howling ended, and they sprang upon us with the silence of the assassin. The next moment we were mingled together—dogs and men—in the fearful struggle of life and death!

I know not how long this strange encounter lasted. I felt myself grappling with the tawny monsters, and hurling them over the cliff. They sprang at my throat, and I threw out my arms, thrusting them fearlessly between the shining rows of teeth. Then I was free again, and seizing a leg, or a tail, or the loose flaps of the neck, I dragged a savage brute towards the brink, and, summoning all my strength, dashed him against the brow, that he might tumble howling over.

Once I lost my balance, and nearly staggered over the precipice; and at length, panting, bleeding, and exhausted, I fell to the earth. I could struggle no longer. I looked around for my comrades. Clayley and Raoul had sunk upon the grass, and lay torn and bleeding. Lincoln and Chane holding a hound, were balancing him over the bluff.

"Now, Murter," cried the hunter; "giv him a good heist, and see if we kin pitch him clar on tother side; hee-woop—hoo!"

And with this ejaculation the kicking animal was launched into the air. I could not resist looking after. The yellow body bounded from the face of the opposite cliff, and fell with a heavy plash upon the water below.

He was the last of the pack!

CHAPTER XLVII.

AN INDIAN RUSE

A WILD shout now drew our attention, and, looking up the creek, we saw our pursuers just debouching from the woods. They were all mounted, and pressing their mustangs down to the bank, they halted, with a strange cry.

"What is that, Raoul? can you tell the meaning of that cry?"

"They are disappointed, Captain. They must dismount, and foot it, like ourselves; there is no crossing for horses."

"Good. Oh! if we had but a rifle each! This pass—" I looked down the gorge. We could have defended it against the whole party; but we were unarmed.

The guerilleros now dismounted, tying their horses to the trees, and preparing to cross over. One, who seemed to be their leader—judging from his brilliant dress and plumes—had already advanced into the stream, and stood upon a projecting rock, with his sword drawn. He was not more than three hundred yards from the position we occupied on the bluff.

"Do you think you can reach him?" I said to Lincoln, who had reloaded his rifle, and stood eyeing the Mexican, apparently calculating the distance.

"I'm feerd, Cap'n, he's too fur. I'd guv a half year's sodger-pay for a crock out o' the Major's Dutch gun. We kin loose nothin in tryin. Murter, will yer stan afore me? thar aint no kiver an the feller's watchin. He'll dodge like a duck, if he sees me takin sight on im."

Chane threw his large body in front; and Lincoln, cautiously slipping his rifle over his comrade's shoulder, sighted the Mexican.

The latter had noticed the manœuvre; and, perceiving the danger he had thrust himself into, was about turning to leap down from the rock, when the rifle cracked—his plumed hat flew off, and, throwing out his arms, he fell with a dea_ plunge upon the water! The next moment his body was sucked into the current; and followed by his hat and plumes, was borne down the cañon with the velocity of lightning!

Several of his comrades uttered a cry of terror; and those who had followed him out into the open channel, ran back towards the bank, holding themselves behind the rocks. A voice, louder than the rest, was heard exclaiming—

"*Carajo! guarda-s—esta el rifle del diablo!*" (Look out! it is the devil's rifle.)

It was doubtless the comrade of José, who had been in the skirmish of La Virgen, and had felt the bullet of the *spitz-nädel*.

The guerilleros, awed by the death of their leader—for it was Yañez who had fallen—crouched behind the rocks. Even those who had remained with the horses—six hundred yards off—sheltered themselves behind trees and projections of the bank! The party nearest us kept loading and firing their escopettes. Their bullets flattened upon the face of the cliff or whistled over our heads. Clayley, Chane, Raoul, and myself, being unarmed, had thrown ourselves behind the scarp, to avoid "catching a stray shot."

Not so Lincoln, who stood boldly out on the highest point of the bluff, as if disdaining to dodge their bullets. I never saw a man so completely soaring above the fear of death. There was a sublimity about him that I remember being struck with at the time; and I remember, too, feeling the inferiority of my own courage. It was a stupendous picture, as he stood like a colossus, clutching his deadly rifle, and looking over his long brown beard at the skulking and cowardly foe. He stood without a motion—without even winking—although the leaden hail hurtled past his head, and cut the grass at his feet, with that peculiar "zip-zip," so well remembered by the soldier, who has passed the ordeal of a battle!

There was something in it awfully grand—awful even to us—no wonder that it awed our enemies.

I was about to call upon Lincoln to fall back, and shelter himself, when I saw him throw up his rifle to the level. The next instant he dropped the butt to the ground, with a gesture of disappointment. A moment after, the manœuvre was repeated, with a similar result; and I could hear the hunter gritting his teeth.

"The cowardly skunks!" muttered he, "they keep a-gwine like a bull's tail in fly-time."

In fact, every time Lincoln brought his piece to a level, the guerilleros ducked, until not a head could be seen.

"They ain't as good as thar own dogs," continued the hunter, turning away from the cliff. "If we hed a wheen of loose rocks, Cap'n, we mout keep them down thar till doom-day."

A movement was now visible among the guerilleros. About one half of the party were seen to mount their horses, and gallop off up the creek.

"They're gone round by the ford," said Rac_al, "it's not over a mile and a half. They can cross with their horses there; and will be on us in half an hour!"

What was to be done? There was no timber to hide us now—no chaparal! The country behind the cliff was a sloping table, with here and there a stunted palm-tree, or a bunch of *Spanish bayonet*.* This would be no shelter. for, from the point we occupied—the most elevated on the ridge—we could have descried an object of human size five miles off. Here the woods began; but could we reach them before our pursuers would overtake us?

Had the guerilleros all gone off by the ford, we should have returned to the creek bottom; but a party remained below, and we were cut off from our former hiding-place. We must, therefore, strike for the woods.

But first decoy the party below, else they would be after us; and experience had taught us that these Mexicans could run like hares.

This was accomplished by an old Indian trick, that both Lincoln and myself had practiced before. It would not have "fooled" a Texan Ranger, but it succeeded handsomely with the guerilleros.

We first threw ourselves on the ground, in such a position that only our heads could be seen by the enemy, who still kept blazing away from their escopettes. After a short while, our faces gradually sunk behind the crest of the ridge, until nothing but our forage caps appeared above the sward. We lay thus for some moments, showing a face or two at intervals. Our time was precious; and we could not perform the pantomime to perfection; but we were not dealing with Comanches, and for "Don Diego" it was sufficiently artistical.

Presently we slipped our heads, one by one, out of their covers, leaving the five caps upon the grass, inclining to each other in the most natural positions. We then stole back, lizard-fashion, and after sprawling a hundred yards or so, sprang to our feet and ran like scared dogs. We could tell that we had duped the party below, as we heard them firing away at our empty caps, long after we had left the scene of our late adventure!

* The name of a peculiar and very beautiful palmetto found in both Mexico and the United States.

CHAPTER XLVIII.

A COUP D'ÉCLAIR.

Many an uneasy look was thrown over our shoulders, as we struggled down that slope. Our strength was urged to its utmost; and this was not much, for we had all lost blood in our encounter with the sleuth-hounds; and felt weak and faint.

We were baffled, too, by a storm—a fierce tropical storm. The rain, thick and heavy, plashed in our faces, and made the ground slippery under our feet. The lightning flashed in our eyes, and the electric sulphur shortened our breathing. Still we coughed, and panted, and staggered onward; nerved by the knowledge that death was behind us.

I shall never forget that fearful race. I thought it would never end. I can only liken it to one of those dreams, in which we are always making endeavors to escape from some horrible monster, and are as often hindered by a strange and mysterious helplessness. I remember it now as then. I have often repeated that flight in my sleep, and always awoke with a feeling of shuddering horror.

We had got within five hundred yards of the timber. Five hundred yards is not much to a fresh runner; but to us toiling along at a trot, that much more resembled a walk, it seemed an infinity. A small prairie, with a stream beyond, separated us from the edge of the woods—a smooth sward without a single tree. We had entered upon it—Raoul, who was light of foot, being in the advance, while Lincoln, from choice, hung in the rear.

An exclamation from the hunter caused us to look back. We were too much fatigued and worn out to be frightened at the sight. Along the crest of the hill an hundred horsemen were dashing after us, in full gallop; and the next moment, their vengeful screams were ringing in our ears!

"Now, do yer best, boys," cried Lincoln, "an I'll stop the cavortin of that ere foremost feller, afore he gits much furrer."

We trailed our bodies on, but we could hear the guerilleros fast closing upon us. The bullets from their escoppettes whistled in our ears, and cut the grass among our feet. I saw Raoul, who had reached the timber, turn suddenly round, and walk back. He had resolved to share our fate.

"Save yourself, Raoul!" I called with my weak voice; but he could not have heard me, above the din. I saw him still walking toward us. I heard the screams behind; I heard the shots, and the whizzing of bullets, and the fierce shouts.

I heard the clatter of hoofs, and the rasping of sabres, as they leaped out of their iron sheaths; and among these, I heard the crack of Lincoln's rifle, and the wild yell of the hunter! Then a peal of thunder drowned all other sounds—the heavens, one moment, seemed on fire, then black, black. I felt the stifling smell of sulphur—a hot flash—a quick stroke from some invisible hand, and I sank senseless to the earth!

* * * * * * * * *

Something cool in my throat, and over my face, brought back the consciousness that I lived. It was water. I opened my eyes, but it was some moments before I could see that Raoul was bending over me, and laving my temples with water from his boot!

I muttered some half-coherent inquiries.

"It was a *coup d'éclair*, Captain," said Raoul.

Good heavens! *We had been struck by lightning!*

Raoul, being in the advance, had escaped.

The Frenchman left me and went to Clayley, who, with Chane and the hunter, lay close by—all three, as I thought, dead. They were pale as corpses, with here and there a spot of purple, or a livid line traced over their skins, while their lips presented the whitish bloodless hue of death!

"Are they dead?" I asked feebly.

"I think not—we shall see;" and the Frenchman poured some water into Clayley's mouth.

The latter sighed heavily, and appeared to revive. Raoul passed on to the hunter, who, as soon as he felt the water, started to his feet, and clutching his comrade fiercely by the throat, exclaimed:

"Yer cussed catamount! yer wud hang me, wud yer?"

Seeing who it was, he stopped suddenly, and looked round with an air of extreme bewilderment. His eye now fell upon the rifle; and all at once seeming to recollect himself, he staggered toward it, and picked it up. Then, as if by instinct, he passed his hand into his pouch, and coolly commenced loading!

While Raoul was busy with Clayley and the Irishman, I had risen to my feet, and looked back over the prairie. The rain was falling in torrents, and the lightning still flashed at intervals. At the distance of fifty paces a black mass was lying upon the ground, motionless—a mass of men and horses, mingled together as they had fallen in their tracks! Here and there a single horse and his rider lay prostrate together. Beyond these, twenty or thirty horsemen were gallopping in circles over the plain, and vainly endeavoring to head their frightened steeds towards the point where we were. These, like Raoul, had escaped the stroke.

"Come," cried the Frenchman, who had now resuscitated Clayley and Chane, "we have not a moment to lose. The mustangs will get over their fright, and these fellows will be down upon us."

His advice was instantly followed, and, before the guerilleros could manage their scared horses, we had entered the thicket, and were crawling along under the wet leaves.

CHAPTER XLIX.

A BRIDGE OF MONKEYS.

Raoul thought that their superstition might prevent the enemy from pursuing us further. They would consider the lightning as an interference from above. But we had little confidence in this; and, notwithstanding our exhaustion, toiled on through the chapparal. Wearied with over-exertion, half famished—for we had only commenced eating when roused from our repast—wet to the skin, cut by the bushes, and bitten by the poisoned teeth of the blood-hounds, blinded, and bruised, and bleeding, we were in but poor travelling condition.

Even Lincoln, whose buoyancy had hitherto borne up, appeared cowed and broken. For the first mile or two he seemed vexed at something, and "out of sorts," stopping every now and again, and examining his rifle in a kind o' bewilderment.

Feeling that he was once more "in the timber" he began to come to himself.

"Thet sort o' an enemy's new ter me," he said, speaking to Raoul. "Done the thing! it makes the airth look yeller!"

"You'll see better by and bye," replied his comrade.

"I had need ter, Rowl, or I'll butt my brainpan agin one of these yeer saplins. Whooh! I cudn't sight a bar, if we were to scare him up jest now.

About five miles farther on, we reached a small stream. The storm had abated, but the stream was swollen with the rain, and we could not cross it. We were now a safe distance from our pursuers—at least we thought so—and we resolved to "pitch our camp" upon the bank.

This was a simple operation, and consisted in pitching ourselves to the ground, under the shade of a spreading tree. Raoul, who was a tireless spirit kindled a fire, and commenced knocking down the nuts of the corozo palm, that hung in clusters over our heads. We dried our wet garments, and Lincoln set about dressing our numerous wounds. In this surgical process, our shirts suffered severely; but the skill of the hunter soothed our swelling limbs, and, after a frugal dinner upon palm-nuts and *pitahayas*, we stretched ourselves along the green sward, and were soon asleep.

I was in that dreamy state—half sleeping, half waking—when I was aroused by a strange noise, that sounded like a multitude of voices—the voices of children. Raising my head, I perceived the hunter in the attitude of listening.

" What is it, Bob ?" I inquired

"Dod rot me if I kin tell, Cap'n! Yeer, Rowl! what's all this yeer hannerin ?"

" It's the *comadreja*," muttered the Frenchman, half asleep.

" The comb o' Nick! Talk sense, Rowl—what is it ?"

" Monkeys, then," replied the latter, waking up, and laughing at his companion.

" Thar's a good grist on em, then, I reckin," said Lincoln, throwing himself back unconcernedly.

" They are coming towards the stream; they will most likely cross by the rocks yonder," observed Raoul.

" How—swim it ?" I asked. " It is a torrent there!"

" Oh, no," answered the Frenchman; " monkeys would rather go into fire than water. If they cannot leap the stream, they will bridge it."

' Bridge it! and how ?"

" Stop a moment, Captain—you shall see."

The half-human voices now sounded nearer, and we could perceive that the animals were approaching the spot where we lay. Presently they appeared upon the opposite bank, headed by an old grey chieftain, and officered like so many soldiers. They were, as Raoul had stated, of the *comadreja*, or ring-tailed tribe.

One—an aide-camp, or chief pioneer, perhaps—ran out upon a projecting rock, and, after looking carefully across the stream, as if calculating the distance, scampered back, and appeared to communicate with the leader. This produced a movement in the troop. Commands were issued, and fatigue parties were detailed, and marched to the front. Meanwhile, several of the comadrejas—engineers, no doubt—ran along the bank, examining the trees in both sides of the *arroyo*.

At length, they all collected around a tall cottonwood, that grew over the narrowest part of the stream, and twenty or thirty of them scampered up its trunk. On reaching a high point, the foremost—a strong fellow—ran out upon a limb, and, taking several turns of his tail around it, slipped off, and hung head downwards. The next on the limb—also a stout one—climbed down the body of the first, and whipping his tail tightly around the neck and fore arm of the latter, dropped off in his turn, and hung head down. The third repeated this manœuvre upon the second, and the fourth upon the third, and so on, until the last one upon the string rested his fore paws upon the ground!

The living chain now commenced swinging backwards and forwards, like the pendulum of a clock. The motion was slight at first, but gradually increased, the lowermost monkey striking his hands violently on the earth as he passed the tangent of the oscillating curve. Several others upon the limbs above aided the movement.

This continued until the monkey at the end of the chain was thrown among the branches of a tree on the opposite bank. Here, after two or three vibrations, he clutched a limb, and held fast. This movement was executed adroitly, just at the culminating point of the oscillation, in order to save the intermediate links from the violence of a too sudden jerk!

The chain was now fast at both ends, forming a complete suspension bridge, over which the whole troop, to the number of four or five hundred, passed with the rapidity of thought!

It was one of the most comical sights I ever beheld, to witness the quizzical expression of countenances along that living chain!

The troop was now on the other side, but how were the animals, forming the bridge, to get themselves over? This was the question that suggested itself. Manifestly, by number one letting go his tail. But then the *point d'appui* on the other side was much lower down, and number one, with half-a-dozen of his neighbors, would be dashed against the opposite bank, or soused into the water.

Here, then, was a problemn, and we waited with some curiosity for its solution. It was soon solved. A monkey was now seen attaching his tail to the lowest on the bridge; another girdled him in a similar manner, and another, and so on, until a dozen more were added to the string. These last were all powerful fellows; and, running up to a high limb, they lifted the bridge into a position almost horizontal.

Then a scream from the last monkey of the new formation warned the tail end that all was ready; and the next moment the whole chain was swung over, and landed safely on the opposite bank. The lowermost links now dropped off like a melting candle, while the higher ones leaped to the branches, and came down by the trunk. The whole troop then scampered off into the chapparal, and disappeared!

"Aw, be the powers of Moll Kelly! av thim little crayteurs hasn't more sinse than the humans av these parts. It's a quare counthry, any how. Be ne sowl! it bates Bannagher intirely!"

A general laugh followed the Irishman's remarks; and we all sprang to our feet, refreshed by our sleep, and lighter in spirits.

The storm had disappeared, and the sun, now setting, gleamed in upon us through the broad leaves of the palms. The birds were abroad once more— brilliant creatures—uttering their sweet songs. Parrots and *troupiales* flashed around our heads, and chattered in the branches above. The stream had become fordable, and, leaving our "lair," we crossed over, and struck into the woods on the opposite side.

CHAPTER L.

THE JAROCHOS.

We headed toward the National Bridge. Raoul had a friend—half way on the route, an old comrade upon whom he could depend. We should find refreshment there; and, if not a bed a roof and a *petaté*. His ranche was in a secluded spot, near the road that leads to the rinconada of San Martin. We should not be likely to meet any one, as it was ten miles off; and it would be late when we reached it.

It *was* late, near midnight, when we dropped in upon the *contrabandista*—for such was the friend of Raoul—but he and his family were still astir, under the light of a very dull wax candle.

José Antonio, that was his name, was a little "sprung" at the five bare headed apparitions that -- so suddenly upon him; but recognising Raoul, we were cordially w   . Our host was a spare, bony, old fellow, in leathern jacket and calsoneros, with a keen shrewd eye, that took in our situation at a single glance, and saved the Frenchman a great deal of explanation. Notwithstanding the cordiality with which his friend received him, I noticed that Raoul seemed uneasy about something, as he glanced around the room; for the ranche—a small cane structure—had only one.

There were two women stirring about—the wife of the contrabandista, and his daughter, a plump good-looking girl of eighteen or thereabout.

"*No han ceñado, caballeros?*" (You have not supped, gentlemen) inquired, or rather affirmed, José Antonio, for our looks had answered the question before it was asked.

"*Ni comido—ni almorzado.*" (Nor dined; Nor breakfasted); replied Raoul with a grin.

"*Carrambo!*—*Rafaela*—*Jesusita!*" shouted our host, with a sign; such as, among the Mexicans, often conveys a whole chapter of intelligence. The effect was magical. It sent Jesusita (Little Jesus) to her knees before the tortilla stones; and Rafaela, José's wife, seized a string of tassajo, and plunged it into the *olla*. Then the little palm-leaf fan was handled; and the charcoal blazed and crackled; and the beef boiled; and the black beans simmered; and the chocolate frothed up, and we all felt happy under the prospect of a savory supper.

It may appear strange to some Christians, when they learn that the name of the Saviour is much used as a surname among the Mexicans. Such, however, is the fact; and what is equally strange to a Saxon foreigner, it is used indifferently as far as regards sex. Men as well as women carry this appellation.

Tasajo, or jerk beef is much used in all Spanish countries where salt is scarce. It is beef cured by being cut into long strings and dried in the sun. It is generally eaten in hashes, stews, &c., and cooked by the Mexicans with *chilé colorado*, is not bad eating. It frequently, however, by its smell, suggests unpleasant ideas of decomposition.

I think that any one who has spent a week among the Mexican peasantry will recognise these little incidents. Cooking is accomplished almost everywhere by charcoal. This proceeds from the scarcity of fuel in nearly all parts of the country. There are no chimneys therefore, as there is no smoke. There are no grates nor stoves, and no great fires for people to warm themselves at. The climate does away with the necessity of these things. There are not a dozen houses in Mexico where you might sit by a fire—except in their kitchens—and the few fire-places I have seen were luxuries of the wealthy, kept for some peculiar visit from the northern winds. In the cottage you find a bank of painted mason-work as high as a table. It is frequently in the centre of the cottage in the cane huts of the *tierra caliente* but oftener built against the side. Several square holes, nine inches square are sunk on the top and near the edge; and from the bottoms of these, small apertures run out horizontally to the sides of the bank. The charcoal is placed in these little wells and ignited. It is fanned by means of the horizontal apertures below. This structure then is a *brazero*, found in almost every Mexican house; of course larger and containing a greater number of charcoal wells, in the kitchens of the wealthy.

I had noticed that, notwithstanding all the bright prospects of a good supper, Raoul seemed uneasy. In the corner I discovered the cause of his solicitude, in the shape of a small spare man. wearing the shovel hat, and black *capoté* of a priest. I knew that my comrade was not partial to priests, and that he would sooner have trusted Satan himself than one of the tribe; and I attributed his uneasiness to this natural dislike.

"Who is he, Antone?" I heard him whisper to the contrabandista.

"The curé of San Martin," was the reply.

"He is new, then" said Raoul.

"*Hombre de bien*," (a good man) answered the Mexican, nodding as he spoke.

Raoul seemed satisfied, and remained silent.

I could not help noticing the "hombre de bien" myself; and no more could I help fancying, after a short observation, that the ranche was indebted for the honor of his presence, more to the black eyes of Jesusita, that to any zeal on his part, regarding the spiritual welfare of the contrabandista.

There was a villanous expression upon his lip, as he watched the girl moving over the floor; and, once or twice, I caught him scowling upon Chane, who, in his usual Irish way, was "blarneying" with her, and helping her to fan the charcoal.

"Where's the Padre?" whispered Raoul, to our host.

"He was in the Rinconada this morning."

"In the Rinconada!" exclaimed the Frenchman, starting.

"They're gone down to the bridge. The band has had a *fandango* (as our battles were jocularly termed by the Mexicans), with your people, and lost some men. They say they have killed a good many stragglers along the road."

"So he was in the Rinconada, you say? and this morning too?" inquired Raoul, in a half soliloquy, and without heeding the last remarks of the contrabandista.

"We've got to look sharp then," he added.

"There's no danger," replied the other, "if you keep from the road. Your people have already reached El Plan, and are preparing to attack the Pass of the Cerro. *El Cojo*,* they say, has twenty thousand men to defend it."

During this dialogue, which was carried on whispers, I had noticed the little Padre shifting about uneasily on his seat. At its conclusion he rose up and bidding our host "*buenas noches!*" was about to withdraw, when Lin

---

† "The lame one," a name given in derision to Santa Anna, and given by his own countrymen, in whose cause he lost the very leg which has rendered him eligible to the appellation.

coln, who had been quietly eyeing him for some time, with that sharp searching look peculiar to men of his kidney, jumped up, and placing himself before the door, exclaimed in a drawling emphatic tone,

"*No, yer don't!*"

"*Que cosa?*" (what's the matter?) asked the Padre indignantly.

"Kay or no Kay—Cosser or no Cosser—yer don't go out o' here, afore w do. Rowl, axe yer friend for a piece o' twine, will yer?"

The Padre appealed to our host, and he, in turn, appealed to Raoul. The Mexican was in a dilemma. He dared not offend the Curé, and, on the other hand, he did not wish to dictate to his old comrade Raoul. Moreover, the fierce hunter, who stood like a huge giant in the door, had a voice in the matter; and therefore José Antonio had three minds to consult at one time.

"It aint Bob Linkin id infringe the rules of hospertality," said the hunter "but this yeer's a peculiar case—an I don't like the look of that ar priest, ne how yer kin fix it."

Raoul, however, sided with the contrabándista, and explained to Lincoln that the Padre was the peaceable *curé* of the neighboring village, and the friend of Don Antonio; and the hunter, seeing that I did not interpose—for at the moment I was in one of those moods of abstraction, and scarcely noticed what was going on—permitted the priest to pass out. I was recalled to myself, more by some peculiar expressions, which I heard Lincoln muttering, after it was over, than by the incidents of the scene itself.

The occurrence had rendered us all somewhat uneasy; and we resolved upon swallowing our suppers hastily, and, after pushing forward some distance, to sleep in the woods.

The tortillas were now ready, and the pretty Jesusita was pouring out the chocolate; so we set to work like men who had appetites.

The supper was soon dispatched, but our host had some *puros* in the house —a luxury we had not enjoyed lately; and hating to hurry away from such comfortable quarters, we determined to stay, and take a smoke.

We had hardly lit our cigars, when Jesusita, who had gone to the door came hastily back, exclaiming:—

"*Papa—papa! hay gente fuera!*" (Papa, there are people outside).

As we sprang to our feet, several shadows appeared through the open walls. Lincoln seized his rifle, and ran to the door. The next moment he rushed back, shouting out·

"Hell! I told yer so."

And, dashing his huge body against the back of the ranche, he broke through the cane pickets with a crash!

We were hastening to follow him, when the frail structure gave way; and we found ourselves buried, along with our host and his women, under a heavy thatch of *tulé* (a species of gigantic rushes) and palm leaves.

We heard the crack of our comrade's rifle without—the scream of a victim—the reports of pistols and escopettes—the yelling of savage men—and then the roof was raised again; and we were pulled out and dragged down among the trees and tied to eir trunks and taunted and goaded, and kicked and cuffed, by the most villanous looking set of desperadoes, it has ever been my misfortune to fall among. They seemed to take a delight in abusing us—yelling all the while, like so many demons let loose.

Our late acquaintance—the curé—was among them; and it was plain that he had brought the party on us. His "reverence" looked high and low to Lincoln; but, to his great mortification, the hunter had escaped.

CHAPTER LI.

PADRE JARAUTA.

We were not long in learning into whose hands we had fallen; for the name, "Jarauta,"* was on every tongue. They were the dreaded Jarochos of the bandit priest.

"We'rr in for it now," said Raoul, deeply mortified at the part he had taken in the affair with the curé. "It's a wonder they have kept us so long. Perhaps *he's* not here himself, and they're waiting for him."

As Raoul said this, the clatter of hoofs sounded along the narrow road; and a horseman came galloping up to the ranche, riding over everything and everybody, with a perfect recklessness.

"That's Jarauta," whispered Raoul. "If he sees *me*—but it don't matter much," he added, in a lower tone, "we'll have a quick shrift all the same: he can't more than hang—and that he'll be sure to do."

"Where are these Yankees?" cried Jarauta, leaping out of his saddle.

"Here, Captain," answered one of the Jarochos, a hideous looking griffe, dressed in a scarlet uniform, and apparently the lieutenant of the band.

"How many?"

"Four, Captain."

"Very well—what are you waiting for?"

"To know whether I shall hang or shoot them."

"Shoot them, by all means! Carrambo! we have no time for neck-stretching!"

"There are some nice trees here, Captain," suggested another of the band, with as much coolness as if he had been conversing about the hanging of so

Pronounced *Harowta*

many dogs. He wished—a curiosity not uncommon—to witness the spectacle of hanging.

"*Madre de Dios!* stupid. I tell you we havn't time for such silly sport. Out with you there. Sanchez! Gabriel! Carlos! send your bullets through their Saxon skulls. Quick!"

Several of the Jarochos commenced unslinging their carbines, while those who guarded us fell back, to be out of range of the lead.

"Come," exclaimed Raoul, "it can't be worse than this—we can only die; and I'll let the Padre know whom he has got, before I take leave of him—a souvenir that won't make him sleep any sounder to-night. *Oyez! Padre Jarauta,*" continued he, calling out in a tone of irony; "have you found, Marguerita yet?"

We could see between us and the dim rushlight that the Jarocho started, as if a shot had passed through his heart!

"Hold!" he shouted to the men, who were about taking aim, "trail those scoundrels hither! A light there—fire the thatch! Vaya!"

In a moment, the hut of the contrabandista was in flames, the dry palm leaves blazing up like flax.

"Merciful Heaven! *they are going to roast us!*"

With this horrible apprehension, we were dragged up toward the burning pile, close to which stood our fierce judge and executioner.

The bamboos blazed and crackled, and, under their red glare, we could now see our captors with a terrible distinctness. A more demon-like set, I think, could not have been found anywhere out of the infernal regions.

Most of them were Zamboes* and Mestizoes,† and not a few pure Africans of the blackest hue, maroons from Cuba, and the Antilles, many of them with their fronts and cheeks tatooed, adding to the natural ferocity of their features. Their coarse woolly hair sticking out in matted tufts, their white teeth, set in savage grins, their strange armor and grotesque attitudes, their wild and picturesque attire, formed a *coup d'œil* that might have pleased a painter in his studio, but which, at the time, had no charm for us.

There were Pintos among them, too—spotted men from the tangled forests of Acapulco—pied and speckled with blotches of red, and black and white, like hounds and horses. They were the first of this race I had ever seen, and their unnatural complexions, even at this fearful moment, impressed me with feelings of disgust and loathing. There exists a vast tribe of these strange men in a district of the *tierra caliente*, near Acapulco. They can scarcely be

---

* Zambo—half Indian, half negro   † Mestizoe, half Indian, half Spanish

said to belong to the Mexican government, as the only man, whose authority they care a claco for, is General Alvarez, an old Indian, who is himself quite as odd a character as any one of the Pintos. Alvarez obeyed the call of his government during the late war, and, collecting about three thousand Indians, among whom there was a sharp "sprinkling" of Pintos, turned the rear of our army at Puebla, and followed us up into the valley of Mexico, without striking a blow; and yet these Pintos and Indians of Alvarez are represented by the Mexicans as fierce and warlike! Alvarez frequently gets up a pronunciamento against the grovernment; and they have not been able hitherto to interfere either with him, or his spotted warriors.

A single glance at this motley crew would have convinced us, had we not been quite sure of it already, that we had no favors to expect. There was not a countenance among them that exhibited the slightest trait of grace, or mercy. No such expression could be seen around us, and we felt satisfied that our time was come

The appearance of their leader did not shake this conviction. Revenge and hatred were playing upon his sharp sallow features, and his thin lips quivered with an expression of malice, plainly habitual. His nose, like a parrot's beak, had been broken by a blow, which added to its sinister shape; and his small black eyes twinkled with metallic brightness.

He wore a purplish-colored *manga*, that covered his whole body and his feet were cased in the red leather boots of the country, with heavy silver spurs strapped over them. A black sombrero, with its band of gold bullion, and tags of the same material, completed the *tout ensemble* of his costume. He wore neither beard nor moustache, but his hair, black and snaky, hung down trailing over the velvet embroidery of his manga—which is a most beautiful and graceful garment, peculiar, I believe to Mexico.

This garment resembles the *serapé*, in one thing. Both have a vent, through which the head is thrust, leaving the garment to rest upon the shoulders. Around this, the manga is always embroidered and braided, over a circle of two feet in diameter. The serapé is only a blanket-shaped article, while the manga is fashioned something after the style of a circle cloak. It is uniform in color; in this again differing from the *serapé*, which is speckled like a carpet. The color of the manga is often very gay. Purple ones are frequently seen, and even red. Black and blue are common. The manga is rare, not being worn so commonly as the serapé. It is costly, and requires some art in the making up; still, you will meet with it now and then, and often covering the shoulders of a common ranchero. It is a picture to see a fine-looking specimen of the ranchero, dressed in one of these graceful robes.

Such was the Padre Jarauta.

Raoul's face was before him, upon which he looked for some moments without speaking. His features twitched, as if under galvanic action, and we could see that his fingers jerked in a similar manner.

They were painful memories that could produce this effect upon a heart of such iron deviltry; and Raoul alone knew them. The latter seemed to enjoy the interlude, for he lay upon the ground, looking up at the Jarocho with a smile of triumph upon his reckless features!

We were expecting the next speech of the Padre, to be an order for flinging us into the fire, which now burned fiercely. Fortunately, this fancy did not seem to strike him just then.

"Ha! Monsieur," exclaimed he at length, approaching Raoul. "I dreamt that you and I would meet again—I dreamt it—ha—ha—ha! it was a pleasant dream, but not half so pleasant as the reality; ha! ha! ha! Don't *you* think so?" he added, striking our comrade over the face with a mule quirt.*
"Don't *you* think so?" he repeated, lashing him as before, while his eyes sparkled with a fiendish malignity.

"Did you dream of meeting Marguerita again?" inquired Raoul with a satirical laugh, that sounded strange, even fearful, under the circumstances.

I shall never forget the expression of the Jarocho at that moment. His sallow face turned black, his lips white, his eyes burned like a demon's, and springing forward with a fierce oath, he planted his iron-shod heel upon the face of our comrade. The skin peeled off, and the blood followed.

There was something so cowardly—so redolent of a brutal ferocity in the act, that I could not remain quiet. With a desperate wrench, I freed my hands, skinning my wrists in the effort, and, flinging myself upon him, I clutched at the monster's throat.

He stepped back; my ankles were tied, and I fell upon my face at his feet.

"Ho! ho!" cried he, "what have we here? An officer, eh? Come!" he continued, "rise up from your prayers, and let me look at you; ha, a Captain! and this? a Lieutenant!* Gentlemen, you're too dainty to be shot like common dogs; we'll not let the wolves have you; we'll put you out of their

---

* A species of whip without any handle, except a band of leather that fastens it to the hand.

reach; ha!—ha!—ha! Out of reach of wolves do you hear? And what's this? continued he, turning to Chane, and examining his shoulders. "Bah, *soldado raso, Irlandes too, carajo!** What do you do fighting among these heretics against your own religion. There, renegade!" and he kicked th Irishman in the ribs.

"Thank yer honner," said Chano, with a grunt, "small fayvors thankfull resaved; much good may it do yer honner!"

"Here Lopez!" shouted the brigand.

"Now for the fire!" thought we.

"Lopez, I say!" continued he, calling louder.

"*Aca—aca!*" answered a voice, and the Lieutenant who had guarded us, came up, swinging his scarlet manga.

"Lopez, these I perceive are gentlemen of rank; and we must usher them into h— a little more gracefully, do you hear?"

"Yes, Captain," answered the griffe, with stoical composure.

"Over the cliffs, Lopez. *Facilis descensus averni*—but you don't under stand Latin, Lopez. Over the cliffs, do you hear? You understand that?"

"Yes, Captain," repeated the Jarocho, moving only his lips.

"You will have them at the Eagle's Cave, by six in the morning; by six, do you hear?"

"Yes, Captain," again replied the subordinate.

"And if any of them is missing—is missing, do you hear?"

"Yes, Captain."

"You will take his place in the dance — the dance, ha—ha—ha! You understand that, Lopez?"

"Yes, Captain."

"Enough then, good Lopez—handsome Lopez, beautiful Lopez; enough, and good night to you!"

So saying, the Jarocho drew his quirt several times across the red cheek of Raoul; and, with a curse upon his lips, he leaped upon his mustang and galloped off.

Whatever might be the nature of the punishment that awaited us at the Eagle's Cave, it was evident that Lopez had no intention of becoming proxy for any of us. This was plain from the manner in which he set about securing us. We were first gagged with bayonet shanks, and then dragged or into the bushes.

* He knew our rank from the designations upon our shoulder-straps.
† A private, an Irishman too.

Here we were thrown upon our backs, each of us in the centre of four trees that formed a parallelogram. Our arms and legs were stretched to their full extent, and tied severally to the trees; and thus we lay, spread out like raw hides to dry. Our savage captors drew the cords so taut, that our joints cracked under the cruel tension. In this painful position, with a Jaracho standing over each of us we passed the remainder of the night.

CHAPTER LII.

A HANG BY THE HEELS.

It was a long night—the longest I can remember: a night that fully illustrated the horror of monotony. I can compare our feelings to those of one under the influence of the nightmare. But no—worse than that. Our savage sentries, occasionally sate down upon our bodies, and, lighting their cigarettos, chatted gaily, while we groaned! We could not protest; we were gagged. But it would have made little difference; they would only have mocked us the more.

We lay glaring upon the moon, as she coursed through a cloudy heaven. The wind whistled through the leaves, and its melancholy moaning sounded like our death-dirge. Several times during the night I heard the howl of the prairie wolf, and I knew it was Lincoln; but the Jarochos had pickets all around; and the hunter dared not approach our position. He could not have helped us.

The morning broke at last; and we were taken up, and tied upon the backs of vicious mules, and hurried off through the woods. We travelled for some distance along a ridge, until we had reached its highest point, where the cliff beetled over. Here we were unpacked and thrown upon the grass. About thirty of the Jarochos guarded us, and we now saw them under the broad light of day, but they did not look a whit more beautiful than on the preceding night.

Lopez was at their head, and never relaxed his vigilance for a moment. It was plain that he considered the padre a man of his word.

An exclamation from one of the men drew our attention; and, looking around, we perceived a band of horsemen straggling up the hill at a slow gallop. It was Jarauta, with about fifty of his followers.

"*Buenas dias, caballeros!*"* cried he, in a mocking tone, leaping down

---

* "Good day, gentleman," the usual morning salutation. There is no "good morning" in Spanish, the words "buena mañan," which signify that, never passing the lips of a Spaniard.

and approaching us: "I hope you passed the night comfortably. Lopez, I am sure, provided you with good beds. Didn't you, Lopez?"

"Yes, Captain," answered the laconic Lopez.

"The gentlemen rested well, didn't they, Lopez?"

"Yes, Captain."

"No kicking, or tumbling about, eh?"

"No, Captain."

"Oh! then they rested well; it's a good thing; they have a long journey before them—haven't they, Lopez?"

"Yes, Captain."

"I hope, gentlemen, you are ready for the road. Do you think you are ready?"

As each of us had the shank of a bayonet between his teeth, besides being tied neck and heels, it is not likely that this interrogatory received a reply; nor did his reverence expect any, as he continued putting similar questions in quick succession, appealing occasionally to his Lieutenant for an answer.

The latter, who was of the taciturn school, contented himself, and his superior too, with a simple "yes," or "no." Up to this moment, we had no knowledge of the fate that awaited us. We knew we had to die—that we knew; but in what way, we were still ignorant. I, for one, had made up my mind that the Padre intended pitching us over the cliffs.

We were at length enlightened upon this important point. We were not to take that awful leap into eternity, which I had been picturing to myself. A fate more horrible still awaited us. *We were to be hanged over the precipice!*

As if to aid the monster in his inhuman design, several pine trees grew out horizontally from the edge of the cliff; and over the branches of these, the Jarochos commenced reeving their long lassos. Expert in the handling of ropes, as all Mexicans are, they were not long in completing their preparations, and we soon beheld our gallows. What they can accomplish with ropes and cords is almost incredible. I had a Mexican servant, a mere lad, who could lash my chests quicker and firmer, and more sure not to come undone, than could be accomplished by any two of our soldiers. I have seen them tie up the 'bois de vache' in ropes, and thus carry it upon the backs of donkeys; and I was almost tempted to believe them capable of that feat hitherto deemed impossible, of tying up sand in a rope.

"According to rank, Lopez," cried Jaurata, seeing that all was ready; the Captain first—do you hear?"

"Yes, Captain," answered the imperturbable brigand who superintended the operations.

"I shall keep you to the last, Monsieur," said the Priest, addressing Raoul; "you will have the pleasure of bringing up the rear in your passage through Purgatory. Ha—ha—ha! Won't he, Lopez?"

"Yes, Captain."

"Maybe some of you would like a priest, gentlemen,." This Jarauta uttered with an ironical grin that was revolting to behold. "If you would," he continued, "say so. I sometimes officiate in that capacity myself. Don't I, Lopez?"

"Yes, Captain."

A diabolical laugh burst from the Jarochos, who had dismounted, and were standing out upon the cliff, the better to witness the spectacle of our hanging.

"Well, Lopez, does any one of them say 'yes'?"

"No, Captain."

"Ask the Irishman there; ask him; he ought to be a good Catholic."

The question was put to Chane; in mockery, of course; for it was impossible for him to answer it; and yet he *did* answer it, for his look spoke a curse, as plainly as if it had been uttered through a trumpet. The Jarochos did not heed that, but only laughed the louder.

"Well, Lopez, what says St. Patrick? 'Yes' or 'no'?"

"'No,' Captain."

And a fresh peal of ruffian laughter rang out. The rope was placed around my neck in a running noose. The other end had been passed over the tree, and lay coiled near the edge of the cliff. Lopez held it in his hand a short distance above the coil, in order to direct its movements.

"All ready there, Lopez?" cried the leader.

"Yes, Captain."

"Swing off the Captain, then—no, not yet; let him look at the floor on which he is going to dance; that is but fair."

I had been drawn forward, until my feet projected over the edge of the precipice, and close to the root of the tree. I was now forced into a sitting posture, so that I might look below, my limbs hanging over. Strange to say, I could not resist doing exactly what my tormentor wished. Under other circumstances the sight would have been to me appalling; but my nerves were strung by the protracted agony I had been forced to endure.

The precipice, on whose verge I sate, formed a side of one of those yawning gulfs common in Spanish America, and known by the name *barrancas*. It seemed as if a mountain had been scooped out and carried away. Not two hundred yards, horizontally distant, was the twin jaw of the chasm, like a black-burnt wall; yet the torrent that roared and foamed between them was full six hundred feet below my position! I could have flung the stump of cigar upon the water; in fact an object dropping vertically from where I sate for it was a projecting point, must have fallen plumb into the stream!

It was not unlike the cañon, where we had tossed over the dogs; but it was higher, and altogether more dreadful and horrible.

As I looked down, several small birds, whose species I did not stay to distinguish, were screaming below, and an eagle on his broad bold wing came soaring over the abyss, and flapped up to my very face.

"Well, Captain," broke in the sharp voice of Jarauta, "what do you think of it; a nice soft floor to dance upon, isn't it? Isn't it, Lopez?"

"Yes, Captain."

"All ready there? Stop! some music; we must have music; how can h' dance without music? Hola! Sancho, where's your bugle?"

"Here, Captain."

"Strike up then; play Yankee Doodle. Ha! ha! ha! Yankee Doodle, do you hear?"

"Yes, Captain," answered the man; and the next moment the well-known strains of the American national air sounded upon my ear, producing a strange, sad feeling I shall never forget.

"Now, Lopez," cried the Padre. I was expecting to be swung out, when I heard him again shout, "stay!" at the same time stopping the music.

"By heavens! Lopez, I have a better plan," he cried; "why did I not think of it before? It's not too late, yet. Ha! ha! ha! *Carrambo!* They shall dance upon their heads! That's better, isn't it, Lopez?"

"Yes, Captain."

A cheer from the Jarochos announced their approval of this change in the ceremony.

The Padre made a sign to Lopez, who approached him, appearing to receive some directions.

I did not at first comprehend the novelty that was about to be introduced. I was not long in ignorance. One of the Jarochos, seizing me by the collar dragged me back from the ledge, and transferred the noose from my neck to my ankles. Horror heaped upon horror! I was to be *hung head downwards, and thus left to die by inches!*

"That will be much prettier, wont it, Lopez?"

"Yes, Captain."

"The gentleman will have time to make himself ready for Heaven before he dies; wont he, Lopez?"

"Yes, Captain."

"Take out the gag! let him have his tongue free; he'll need that to pray with; won't he Lopez?"

"Yes, Captain."

One of the Jarochos jerked the bayonet roughly from my mouth, almost dislocating my jaw. The power of speech was gone. I could not, if I had wished it, have uttered an intelligible word.

"Give him his hands, too; he'll need them to keep off the *Zopilotes;** won't he, Lopez?"

"Yes, Captain."

The thong that bound my wrists was cut, leaving my hands free. I was on my back, my feet towards the precipice. A little to my right stood Lopez holding the rope that was about to launch me into eternity.

"Now the music—take the music for your cue, Lopez; then jerk him up!" cried the sharp voice of the fiend.

I shut my eyes—waiting for the pull. It was but a moment, but it seemed a lifetime. There was a dead silence—a stillness like that which precedes the bursting of a rock, or the firing of a jubilee-gun. Then I heard the first note of the bugle, and along with it a crack—the crack of a rifle! A man staggered over me, besprinkling my face with blood; and, falling forwards, disappeared!

Then came the pluck upon my ankles, and I was jerked, head downwards, into the empty air. I felt my feet touching the branches above; and, throwing up my arms, I grasped one, and swung my body upwards. After two or three efforts, I lay along the main trunk, which I embraced with the hug of despair. I looked downward. A man was hanging below—far below—at the end of the lariat! It was Lopez. I knew his scarlet manga at a glance. He was hanging by the thigh in a snarl of the rope.

His hat had fallen off. I could see the red blood running over his face, and dripping from his long snaky locks. He hung head down. I could see that he was dead!

* The black vulture of Mexico.

The hard thong was cutting my ankles, and, oh, Heaven! under our united weight the roots were cracking!

Appalling thought! "*the tree will give way!*"

I held fast with one arm. I drew forth my knife—fortunately I still had one—with the other. I opened the blade with my teeth; and, stretching backward and downward, I drew it across the thong. It parted with a snig," and the red object left me like a flash of light. There was a plunge upon the black water below—a plunge and a few white bubbles, but the body of the Jarocho, with its scarlet trappings, never came up after that plunge.

CHAPTER LIII.

A VERY SHORT TRIAL.

During all this time, shots were ringing over me. I could hear the shouts and cheering of men, the trampling of heavy hoofs and the clashing of sabres. I knew that some strange deliverance had reached us. I knew that a skirmish was going on above me; but I could see nothing. I was below the level of the cliff.

I lay in a terrible suspense—listening. I dared not change my posture. I dared not move. The weight of the Jarocho's body had hitherto held my feet securely in the notch; but that was gone; and my ankles were still tied. A movement, and my legs might fall off the limb; and drag me downward. I was faint too, from the protracted struggle for life and death, and I hugged the tree, and held on like a wounded squirrel.*

The shots seemed less frequent; the shouts appeared to recede from the cliffs. Then I heard a cheer, an anglo-Saxon cheer, an American cheer—and the next moment, a well-known voice rang in my ears.

"By the livin catamount! he's yeer yit, whooray, whoop! Niver say die! Hole on, Cap'n, teeth an toe-nail! yeer, boys! clutch on a wheen o yer' quick, hook my claws, Nat! now—pull—all thegether! Hooray!"

I felt a strong hand grasping the collar of my coat, and I was raised from my perch, and landed upon the top of the cliff.

I looked around upon my deliverers. Lincoln was dancing like a lunatic uttering his wild half-Indian yells. A dozen men, in the dark-green uniform of the " mounted rifles," stood looking on, and laughing at this grotesqu

---

* These little animals, when wounded, will often hang suspended upon a branch til life is extinct.

exhibition. Close by, another party were guarding some prisoners; while a hundred others were seen, in scattered groups, along the ridge returning from the pursuit of the Jarochos whom they had completely routed.

I recognised Twing, and Hennessy, and Hillis, and several other officers whom I had met before. We were soon *en rapport*, and I could not have received a greater variety of congratulations, had it been the hour after my wedding.

Little Jack was the guide of the rescue.

After a moment spent in explanation with the Major, I turned to look for Lincoln. He was standing close by, holding in his hands a piece of a lariat, which he appeared to examine with a strange and puzzled expression. He had recovered from his burst of wild joy, and was "himself again."

"What's the matter, Bob?" I inquired, noticing his bewildered look.

"Why, Cap'n I'm a sorter bamfoozled yeer. I kin understan well enuf how the feller jirked yer inter the tree, afore he lot go. But how did this yeer whang kum cut? an whar's the other eend?"

I saw that he held in his hand, the noose of the lariat, which he had taken from my own ankles; and I explained the mystery of how it had "kum cut." This seemed to raise me still higher in the hunter's esteem. Turning to one of the rinemen, an old hunter like himself, he whispered—I overheard him:

"I'll tell yer what it is, Nat; he kin whip his weight in wild cats or grizzly bars any day in the year—*he kin*, or my name ain't Bob Linkin."

Saying this he stepped forward on the cliff and looked over; and then he examined the tree, and then the piece of lariat, and then the tree again, and then he commenced dropping pebbles down, as if he was determined to measure every object, and fix it in his memory with a proper distinctness!

Twing and the others had now dismounted. As I turned towards them, Clayley was taking a pull at the Major's pewter—and a good long pull too. I followed the Lieutenant's example, and felt the better for it.

"But how did you find us, Major?"

"This little soldier," said he, pointing to Jack, "brought us to the ranche where you were taken. From there we easily tracked you to a large hacienda."

"Ha! you routed the guerilla, then?"

"Routed the guerilla! We saw no guerilla."

"What! at the hacienda?"

"Peons and women; nothing more. Yes, there was too—what am I thinking about? There was a party there that routed *us;* Thornley and

Hillis, here, have both been wounded, and are not likely to recover—poor fellows!"

I looked towards these gentlemen for an explanation. They were both laughing, and I looked in vain.

"Hennessy, too," cried the Major, "has got a stab under the ribs.'

"Oh, by my sowl, have I, and no mistake!" cried the latter.

"Come, Major, an explanation, if you please."

I was in no humor to enjoy this joke. I half divined the cause of their mirth, and it produced in me an unaccountable feeling of annoyance, not to say pain.

"Be my faith, then, Captain!" said Hennessy, speaking for the Major, "if ye must know all about it, I'll tell ye myself. We overhauled a pair of the most elegant crayteurs you ever clapp'd eyes upon; and rich—rich as Craysus—wasn't they, boys?"

"Oh! plenty of tin," remarked Hillis.

"But, Captain," continued Hennessy, "how they took on to your tiger. I thought they would have eaten the little chap, body, bones, and all."

I was chafing with impatience to know more; but I saw that nothing worth knowing could be had in that quarter. I determined, therefore, to conceal my anxiety, and find an early opportunity to talk to Jack; so I shunned the subject.

"But beyond the hacienda?" I inquired.

"We trailed you down stream to the cañon, where we found blood upon the rocks. Here we were at fault, when a handsome, delicate-looking lad came up, and carried us to the crossing above, where he gave us the slip. We struck the hoofs once more, and followed them to a small prairie on the edge of the woods, where the ground was strangely broken and trampled. Here they had turned back, and we lost all trace."

"But how then did you come here?"

"By accident altogether. We were striking to the nearest point on the National Road, when that tall sergeant of yours dropped down upon us out of the branches of a tree."

"Whom did you see, Jack?" I whispered to the boy, having drawn him aside.

"I saw them all, Captain."

"Well?"

"They asked me where you were; and when I told them—"

"Well—well?"

"They appeared to wonder—"

"Well?"

"And the young ladies—"

"And the young ladies?"

"They ran round, and cried, and—"

Jack was the dove that brought the olive branch.

"Did they say where they were going?" I inquired, after one of those sweet waking dreams.

"Yes, Captain, they are going up the country to live."

"Where? Where?"

"I could not recollect the name; it was so strange."

"Jalapa? Orizava? Cordova? Puebla? Mexico?"

"I think it was one of them, but I cannot tell which. I have forgotten it, Captain."

"Captain Haller!" called the voice of the Major, "here a moment, if you please; these are some of the men who were going to hang you, are they not?"

Twing pointed to five of the Jarochos, who had been captured in the skirmish.

"Yes," replied I, "I think so, yet I could not swear to their identity."

"By the Crass, Major, I can sware to ivery mother's son av thim; there isnt a schoundrel among thim, but has given me rayzon to remimbir him, av a harty kick in the ribs might be called a rayzon. O—h! ye ugly spalpeens, kick me now, will yez; will yez jist be plazed to trid upon the tail av my jacket?"

"Stand out here, my man," said the Major.

Chane stepped forward, and swore away the lives of the five Jarochos in less than as many minutes.

"Enough," said the Major, after the Irishman had given his testimony. "Lieutenant Claiborne," continued he, addressing an officer, the youngest in rank, "what sentence?"

"Hang!" replied the latter in a solemn voice.

"Lieutenant Hills?"

"Hang!" was the reply.

"Lieutenant Clayley?"

"Hang!" said Clayley, in a quick and emphatic tone.

"Captain Hennessy?"

" Hang them !" answered the Irishman.
" Captain Haller ?"
" Have you determined, Major Twing— ?"
I asked intending, if possible, to mitigate this terrible sentence.
" We have no time, Captain Haller," replied my superior, interrupting me, ' nor opportunity to carry prisoners. Our army has reached Plan del Rio, and is preparing to attack the pass. An hour lost, and we may be too late for the battle. You know the result of that as well as I."

I knew Twing's determined character too well to offer further opposition; and the Jarochos were condemned to be hung.

The following extract from the Major's report of the affair, will show how the sentence was carried out :—

" We killed five of them, and captured as many more, but the leader escaped. The prisoners were tried, and sentenced to be hung. They had a gallows already rigged for Captain Haller and his companions; and, for want of a better, we hanged them upon that "

CHAPTER LIV.

A BIRD'S EYE VIEW OF A BATTLE.

It was still only an hour by sun as we rode off from the "Eagle's Cave." At some distance, I turned in my saddle, and looked back. It was a singular sight those five hanging corpses, and one not easily forgotten. What an appalling picture it must have been to their own comrades who, doubtless, watched the spectacle from some distant elevation!

Motionless they hung in all the picturesque drapery of their strange attire —draggling—dead. The pines bent slightly over, the osprey screamed as he swept past, and high in the blue air a thousand bald vultures wheeled and circled, descending at every curve.

Before we had ridden out of sight, the Eagle's cliff was black with zopilotes, hundreds clustering upon the pines, and whetting their fœtid beaks over their prey, still warm. I could not help being struck with this strange transportation of victims!

We forded the stream below, and travelled for some hours in a westerly course, over a half naked ridge. At mid-day we reached an *arroyo*—a clear cool stream—that gurgled along under a thick grove of the *palma redonda*. Here we "nooned," stretching our bodies along the green sward.

At sun-down we rode into the *pueblita** of Jacomulco, where we had determined to pass the night. Twing levied on the *alcalde*† for forage for

---

* Hamlet.
† In every village there is an alcalde, whose duties are somewhat similar to those of justice of the peace.

"man and beast." The horses were picketed in the plaza, while the men bivouacked by their fires—strong mounted pickets having been thrown out on the roads, or tracks, that led to the village.

By day-break we were again in our saddles, and, riding across another ridge, we struck the Plan river, five miles above the bridge, and commenced riding down the stream. We were still far from the water, that roared and "soughed" in the bottom of a *barranca*, hundreds of feet below our path.

On crossing an eminence, a sight suddenly burst upon us, that caused us to leap in our saddles. Directly before us, and not a mile distant, rose a high round hill, like a semi-globe; and, from a small tower upon its top, waved the standard of Mexico!

Long lines of uniformed men girdled the tower, formed in rank. Horsemen in bright dresses gallopped up and down the hill. We could see the glitter of brazen helmets, and the glancing of a thousand bayonets. The burnished howitzer flashed in the sunbeams, and we could discern the cannoniers standing by their posts. Bugles were braying, and drums rolling. So near were they, that we could distinguish the music. *They were sounding the "assembly!"*

"Halt! great Heaven!" cried Twing, jerking his horse upon his haunches "we are riding into the enemy's camp! Guide!" he added, turning fiercely to Raoul, and half-drawing his sword, "what's this?"

"The hill, Major," replied the soldier, coolly, "is 'El Telegrafo.' It is the Mexican head-quarters, I take it."

"And, Sir, what mean you? It is not a mile distant!"

"It is ten miles, Major,"

"Ten——! Why, Sir, I can trace the eagle upon that flag—it is not one mile, by Heaven!"

"By the eye, true; but by the road, Major, it is what I have said—ten miles. We have passed the crossing of the *barranca* some time ago; there is no other before we reach El Plan."

It was true. Although within range of the enemy's lightest metal, we were ten miles off!

A vast chasm yawned between us and them. The next moment we were upon its brink, and, wheeling sharply to the right, we trotted on as fast as the rocky road would allow us.

"Oh, Heavens! Haller, we shall be too late. Gallop!" shouted Twing, as we pressed our horses side by side. The troop, at the word, sprang into a gallop. El Plan, the bridge, the hamlet, the American camp, with its thousand white pyramids, all burst upon us like a flash—below—far below--lying like a map. We are still opposite El Telegrafo!

'By Heavens!' cried Twing, "the camp is empty!"

A few figures only were visible, straggling among the tents; the teamster the camp-guard, the invalid soldier!

"Look—look!"

I followed the direction indicated. Against the long ridge, that rose over the camp, a dark blue line could be traced. A line of uniformed men, glistening as they moved, with the sparkle of ten thousand bayonets. It wound along the hill, like a bristling snake; and, heading towards El Telegrafo, disappeared for a moment behind the ridge.

A gun from the globe-shaped hill—and then another! another! another! a roll of musketry! drums—bugles—shouts—cheering:

"The battle's begun!"

"We are too late!"

We were still eight miles from the scene of action. We checked up, and sat chafing in our saddles. And now the roll of musketry was incessant; and we could hear the crack-crack of the American rifles. And bombs hurtled, and rockets hissed through the air.

The round hill was shrouded in a cloud of sulphur; and through the smoke we could see small parties creeping up, from rock to rock, from bush to bush, firing as they went. We could see some tumbling back under the leaden hail, that was poured upon them from above. And then a strong band debouched from the woods below, and strained upward, daring all danger. Up, up! and bayonets were crossed, and sabres glistened, and grew red; and wild cries filled the air. And then came a cheer, long, loud and exulting, and under the thinning smoke, thousands were seen rushing down the steep, and flinging themselves into the woods!

We knew not as yet which party it was that were thus flying. We looked at the tower in breathless suspense. The cloud was around its base, where musketry was still rolling, sending its deadly missiles after the fugitives below.

The flag—it was gone!

"Look, look!" cried a voice; "*the star-spangled banner!*"

It was slowly unfolding itself over the blue smoke, and we could easily distinguish the stripes, and the dark square in the corner; and as if with one voice, our troops broke into a wild hurrah!

In less time than you have taken in reading this account of it, the battle of Cerro Gordo was lost and won.

CHAPTER LV.

AN ODD WAY OF ESCAPING FROM A BATTLE FIELD.

WE sate on our horses facing the globe-shaped summit of El Telegrafo, and watching our flag as it swung out from the tower.

"Look yonder! what is that?" cried an officer, pointing across the barranca.

All eyes were now turned in the direction indicated. A white line was slowly moving down the face of the opposite cliff.

"Rein back, men! rein back!" shouted Twing, as his eye rested upon the strange object. "Throw yourselves under cover of the hill!"

In a minute our whole party—dragoons, officers and all—had gallopped our horses into the bed of a dry arroyo, where we were completely screened from observation. Three or four of us dismounting, along with Twing, crept cautiously forward to the position we had just left; and raising our heads over the bunch-grass, looked across the chasm. We were close to its edge, and the opposite "check," a huge wall of traprock, rose about a mile horizontally distant, at least a thousand feet from the river bottom. Its face was almost vertical, with the exception of a few stairs or platforms in the basaltic strata, and from these hung out stunted palms, cedars, and dark shapeless masses of cacti and agave.

Down this front the living line was still moving—slowly, zigzag—along narrow ledges, and over jutting points, as though some white liquid, or a train of gigantic insects was crawling down the precipice. The occasional flash of a bright object would have told us, had we not guessed the nature of this strange phenomenon already. They were armed men—Mexicans—escaping from the field of battle; and in a wood upon the escarpment of the cliff, we could perceive several thousands of their comrades huddled up, and waiting for an opportunity to descend. They were evidently concealed, and out of all danger from their pursuers on the other side—indeed the main body of the American army had already passed their position and were moving along the Jalapa road, following up the clouds of dust that hung upon the retreating squadrons of Santa Anna.

We lay for some time observing the motions of these cunning fugitives, as they streamed downward. The head of their line had nearly reached the timbered bottom, through whose green fringes the stream swept onward curving from cliff to cliff.

Impatient looks were cast towards the Major, whose cold grey eye showed no signs of action.

"Well, Major—what's to be done?" asked one.

"Nothing," was the impressive reply.

"Nothing!" echoed every one.

"Why, what could we do?"

"Take them prisoners—every one of them."

"Whom prisoners?"

"These Mexicans—these before us."

"Ha! before you they are—a long way, too.. Bah! they are ten miles off, and, even if we could ride straight down the bluff with winged horses, what could our hundred men do in that jungle below! Look yonder; there are a thousand of them crawling over the rocks!"

"And what signify numbers?" asked I, now speaking for the first time. "They are already defeated and flying—half of them, I'll wager, without arms. Come, Major, let us go! We can capture the whole party without firing a shot."

"But, my dear Captain, we cannot reach them where they are."

"It is not necessary. If we ride up the cliffs, they will come to us."

"How?"

"You see this dark line. It is not three miles distant. You know that timber like that does not grow on the naked face of a cliff. It is a gorge, and I'll warrant a water-course, too. They will pass through it."

"Beautiful! We could meet them as they came up it," cried several at once.

"No, lads, no! You are all wrong. They will keep the bottom,—the heavy timber, I warrant you. It's no use losing time. We must round to the road, and forward. Who knows that we may not find work enough yet? Come!"

So saying, our commanding officer rose up, and, walking back to the arroyo leaped into his saddle. Of course we followed his example, but with no very amiable feelings. I, for one, felt satisfied that we might have made a dashing thing of it, and entered the camp with flying colors. I felt—and so did my friend Clayley—like a school-boy who had come too late for his lesson, and would gladly have been the bearer of a present to his master; moreover we had learned from our comrades, that it was the intention of the commander-in-chief to capture as many of the enemy as possible on this occasion. This determination arose from the fact—well authenticated—that hundreds who had marched out of Vera Cruz on parole, had gone direct to Cerro Gordo, with the intention of fighting us again, and no doubt some of these honorable soldiers were among the gentry now clambering down the barranca.

With these feelings, Clayley and I were anxious to do something that might cover our late folly, and win our way back to favor at head-quarters.

"Let me take fifty of your men and try this. You know, Major Twing, I have a score to rub out."

"I cannot, Captain,—I cannot. We must on. Forward!"

And the next moment we were moving at a trot in the direction of El Plan.

For the first time I felt angry at Twing; and, drawing my bridle tighter, I fell back to the rear. What would I not have given for the "Rifle Rangers" at that moment?

I was startled from a very sullen reverie, by a shot, the whistling of a rifle bullet, and the loud "Halt!" of the Major in front. Raising myself on the instant, I could see a greenish-looking object just disappearing over the spur of a ridge. It was a vidette who had fired, and ran in.

"Do you think they are any of our people?"

"That ar's one of our kumpny, Cap'n. I seed the green on his cap," said Lincoln.

I gallopped to the front. Twing was just detaching a small party to reconnoitre. I fell in along with this, and after riding a hundred yards, we looked over the ridge, and saw—not four hundred yards distant—a ten-inch howitzer, that had just been wheeled round, and now stood gaping at us! In rear of the gun stood a body of artillerists, and on their flanks a larger body of what appeared to be light infantry or rifles. It would have been anything but a pleasing sight, but that a small flag with red and white stripes was playing over the gun; and our party, heedless of their orders, leaped their horses on the ridge, and pulling off their caps, saluted it with a cheer!

The soldiers, by the battery, still stood undecided—not knowing what to make of our conduct, (as they were the advanced outpost in this quarter,) when a mounted rifleman gallopped up, and displayed the flag of his regiment.

A wild cheer echoed back from the battery, and the next moment both parties had met, and were shaking each other's hands with the hearty greetings of long-parted friends.

Not the least interesting to me was the fact, that my own corps. under the command of its lieutenant, formed the principal guard of the gun; and the welcome of our old comrades was such as we should have received had we come back from the grave. They had long since made up their minds that they had seen the last of us; and it was quite amusing to witness these brave tirailleurs, as they gathered around Lincoln and his comrades, to hear the story of our adventures.

CHAPTER LVI.

A WHOLESALE CAPTURE.

In a few minutes our greetings were over. Twing moved on, taking with him his squadron of mounted men. I had made up my mind to the *opposite road*. I was now in command of a force—my own—and I felt keennly the necessity of doing something to redeem my late folly. Clayley was as anxious as myself.

"You do not need them any longer?" said I to Ripley, a gallant young fellow, who commanded the howitzer.

"No, Captain; I have thirty artillerists here. It is strange if we can't keep the piece, and manage it against ten times that number of such heroes as we have seen over yonder."

"What say you to going with us?"

"I should like it devillish well—but duty, my dear H—, duty. I must stay by the gun."

"Good bye, then, comrade! We have no time to lose—fare well!"

"Good bye; and if you're whipped, fall back on me. I'll keep the piece here till you return, and there'll be a good load of grape ready for anybody that comes after you."

The company had by this time formed on the flank of the howitzer, and at the words "forward—quick time," started briskly across the hills.

In a few minutes, we had reached the point where the road trended for some distance, along the brow of the precipice. Here we halted a moment;

and taking Lincoln and Raoul, I crawled forward to our former point of observation.

Our time spent at the battery had been so short, that, with the difficulty which the enemy experienced in descending the cliff, the head of their line had only now reached the bottom of the barranca. They were running in twos and threes toward the stream, that, near this point, impinged upon the roof of the precipice. With a small glass, which I had obtained from Ripley, I could see their every movement. Some of them were without arms—they had doubtless thrown them away—while others still carried their muskets, and not a few were laden with knapsacks, and heavy burdens too—the household gods—perhaps stolen ones—of their own camp. As they reached the green sward, dropping down in a constant stream, they rushed forward to the water, scrambling into it in thirsty crowds, and falling upon their knees to drink. Some of them filled their canteens.

"They intend to take the hills," thought I. I knew there was no water for miles in that direction.

As I swept the glass around the bottom of the cliff, I was struck with an object that stood in a clump of palm-trees. It was a mule saddled, and guarded by several soldiers, more richly uniformed than the masses who were straggling past them.

"They are waiting for some officer of rank," thought I. I moved the glass slowly along the line of descending bodies, and upward against the rocks. On a small platform, nearly half-way up the cliff, several bright uniforms flashed upon the lens. The platform was shaded with palms; and I could see that this party had halted a moment for the purpose (as I then conjectured) of allowing the foremost fugitives to pioneer the wooded bottom. I was right. As soon as these had crossed the stream, and made some way in the jungle along its banks, the former continued their descent; and now I saw what caused my pulse to beat feverishly—that one of these carried a dark object on his back! An object?—a man—and that man could be no other than the lame tyrant of Mexico!

I can scarcely describe my feelings at this moment. The young hunter who sees noble game—a bear—a panther—a buffalo—within reach of his rifle for the first time, might feel as I did. I hated this man, as all honest men must and should hate a cowardly despot. During our short campaign, I had heard many a well-authenticated story of his base villany; and I believe at that moment I would have willingly parted with my hand to have brought him as near as he appeared under the field of the telescope. I thought I could even distinguish the lines—deep furrowed by guilt—on his dark malice-marked face; and as I became sure of the identity, I drew back my head cautioning my companions to do the same!

Now was the time for action, and putting up the glass, we crawled back to our comrades. I had learned from Raoul, that the dark line which I had noticed before, was as I had conjectured, the cañon of a small stream heavily timbered, and forming a gap or pass that led to the Plan river. It was five miles distant, instead of three. So much the better; and with a quick crouching gait, we were once more upon our way. I had told my comrades enough to make some of them as eager as I. Many of them would have given half a life for a shot at game like that. Not a few of them remembered they had lost a brother—on the plains of Goliad, or the fortress of the Alamo!

The Rangers, moreover, had been chafing "all day for a fight," and now so unexpectedly led at something like it, they were just in the humor. They moved as one man; and the five miles that lay between us and the gorge, were soon passed to the rear. We reached it, I think, in about half-an-hour. Considering the steep pass through which the enemy must come, we knew there was a breathing time, though not long, for us; and during this, I matured my plans, part of which I had arranged upon the route.

A short survey of the ground convinced us that it could not have been better fitted for an ambuscade had we chosen it at our leisure. The gorge, or cañon, did not run directly up the cliff, but in a zigzag line, so that a man at the top could only alarm another coming up after him, by shouting or firing his piece. This was exactly what we wanted, as although we might capture a few of the foremost, those in the rear being alarmed, could easily take to the river bottom and make their escape through the thickets. It was our design to make our prisoners without firing a single shot, and this under the circumstances, we did not deem an impossible matter.

The pass was a dry arroyo; its banks fringed with large pines and cottonwoods matted together by lianas and vines of almost every description. Where the gorge debouched into the uplands, its banks were high and naked—with here and there a few scattered palms that grew up from huge hassocks f bunch grass.

Behind each of these bunches a rifleman was stationed, forming a deployed line, with its concave arc facing the embouchure of the gorge, and gradually closing in, so that it ended in a clump of thick chapparal upon the very verge of the precipice. At this point, on each side of the path, were stationed half a-dozen men, in such a position as to be hidden from any party passing upward, until it had cleared the cañon, and its retreat was secured against. At the opposite end of the ellipse a stronger party was stationed with Clayley in command, and Raoul to act as interpreter. Oakes and I took our station commanding the separate detachments on the brow.

Our arrangements occupied us only a few minutes. I had to deal with men—many of whom had "surrounded" buffaloes in a somewhat similar manner; and it did not require much tact to teach them a few modifications in the sport. In five minutes we were in our places waiting anxiously, and in perfect silence.

As yet not a murmur had reached us from below, except the sighing of the wind through the tall trees, and the sough of the river as it tumbled away over its pebbly bed. Now and then we heard a stray shot, or the quick sharp notes of a cavalry bugle; but these were far off, and only told of the wild work that was still going on away along the road towards Encerro and Jalapa.

Not a word was spoken by us to each other. The men who were deployed along the hill lay hidden behind the hassocks of the palms; and, from our position, not one of them was to be seen. I must confess it was one of the most anxious moments of my life; and, although I felt no hate towards the enemy—no desire to injure one of them, excepting him of whom I have spoken, there was something so wild, so thrilling in the excitement of thus entrapping *man*—the highest of all animals—that I could not have foregone the inhuman sport. I had no intention that it should be inhuman. I well knew what would be their treatment as prisoners of war; and I had given orders that not a shot should be fired nor a blow struck, in case they threw down their arms and yielded without resistance. But for *him*—humanity had many a score to settle with him; and I must confess that, at the time, I did not feel a very strong inclination to resist, what would have been the Ranger's desire on that question.

"Is not all our fine ambuscade for nothing?"

I had begun to fancy as much, and to suspect that our enemy had kept along the river, when a humming sound, like that of bees, came creeping up the pass. Presently it grew louder until I could distinguish the voices of men. Our hearts as yet beat louder than their voices. Now the stones rattle as loosened from their sloping beds they rolled back and down wards:

"*Guardaos, hombre !*" (Look out, man), shouted one.

"*Carajo!*" cried another, "take care what you're about. I haven't the Yankee bullets to have my skull cloven in that fashion. *Arriba*, escaped *arriba!*"

"I say, Antonio, you're sure this leads out above?"

"Quite sure, camarado."

"And then on to Orizava?"

"On to Orizava—*derecho, derecho.*"

"But how far, hombre?"

"Oh! there are halting places—pueblitas."

"*Vaya!* I don't care how soon we reach them. I'm as hungry as a famished coyote."

"*Carrai!* the coyotes of these parts won't be hungry for some time. Vaya!"

"Who knows whether they've killed 'El Cojo?'"

"'Catch a fox, kill a fox.' No. He's found some hole to creep through, I warrant him."

"El que mata un ladron
Tiene cien años de perdon."

The meaning of which is, "he who kills a robber will receive a hundred years of pardon for the offence;" in other words, he will not be punished at all. A favorite saying among the Spaniards and Spanish-Americans.

This was hailed with a sally by the very men who, only one hour ago, were shouting themselves hoarse with the cries of "Viva el General! Viva Santa Anna!" And on they scrambled, talking as before, one of them informing his comrades with a laugh, that if "los Tejanos" could lay their hands on "El Cojo," they the Mexicans, would have to look out for a new President.

They had now passed us. We were looking at their backs! The first party contained a string of fifteen or twenty, mostly soldiers of the "raw battalions," conscripts who wore the white linen jackets and wide sailor-looking pantaloons of the volunteer. Raw as these fellows were, either from their position in the battle, or, more likely, from a better knowledge of the country they had been able thus far to make their escape, when thousands of their veteran companions had been captured. But few of them were armed. They had thrown their guns away in the hurry of flight. At this moment, we could distinguish the voice of Raoul—

"*Alto! abajo las armas!*" (Halt! ground arms!)

At this challenge we could see, for they were still in sight, that some of them leaped clear up from the ground. One or two looked up as if with the intention of re-entering the gorge, but a dozen muzzles met their gaze.

"*Adelante—adelante!—somos amigos!*" (Forward! we are friends) cried I. in a half whisper, fearing to alarm their comrades in the rear—at the same time waving them onward.

As on one side, Clayley presented a white flag, while, on the other, there was to be seen a bunch of dark yawning tubes, the Mexicans were not long in making their choice; in a minute they had disappeared from our sight, preferring the companionship of Clayley and Raoul, who would know how to dispose of them in a proper manner.

He had scarcely got rid of these, when another string debouched up the glen, unsuspicious as were their comrades of the fate that awaited them,

These were managed in a similar manner; and another, and another party, all of whom were obliged to give up their arms, and fling themselves to the earth, as soon as they had reached the open ground above.

This continued until I began to grow fearful that we were making more prisoners than we could safely hold; and, on the knowledge of this fact, they might try to overpower us. The tempting prize had not yet appeared. He could not be far distant, and, allured by this prospect, I determined to hold out a while longer. But an end was now put to our captures by an unexpected event. A party, consisting of some ten or fifteen men—many of them officers—suddenly appeared, and marched boldly out of the gorge.

As these struck the level ground we could hear the "Alto!" of Raoul; but, instead of halting, as their companions had done, several of them drew their swords and pistols, and rushed down the pass.

A volley from both sides stopped the retreat of some; others escaped along the sides of the cliff, and a few—not over half-a-dozen—succeeded in entering the gorge. It was, of course, beyond our power to follow them; and I ordered the deployed line to close in around the prisoners already taken, lest they should attempt to imitate their braver comrades.

We had no fear of being assailed from the ravine. Those who had gone down carried a panic along with them that would secure us from that danger, at the same time we knew that the tyrant would now be alarmed and escape.

Several of the Rangers—souvenirs of Santa Fé and San Jacinto—requested my permission to go upon his "trail," and pick him off.

This request, under the circumstances, I could not grant, and we set about securing our prisoners. Gun slings and waist belts were soon split into thongs, and with these our captives were tied—two and two, forming in all a battalion of a hundred and fifteen files—two hundred and thirty men!

With these, arranged in such a manner as we could most conveniently uard them, we marched into the camp at Plan del Rio.

CHAPTER LVII.

A DUEL, WITH AN ODD ENDING.

That night we slept on the field of battle, and next day were ordered on to Jalapa, where the army halted to bring up its wounded, and prepare for an advance upon the capital of Mexico.

The Jalapeños did not receive us inhospitably; nor the Jalapeñas neither. They expected, as a matter of course, that we would sack their beautiful city. This we did not do; and their gratitude enabled our officers to pass their time somewhat agreeably. The gay round, that always succeeds a battle—for dead comrades are soon forgotten, amidst congratulations and new titles—had no fascination for me.

The balls—the *tertulias*—the *dias de campo*,* were alike insipid and tiresome. *She* was not there, and where? I knew not. I might never see her again. All I knew was, that they had gone up the country—perhaps to Cordova, or Orizava?

I took occasion to make enquiry from a Jalapeño. He knew the family well—one of the highest in Mexico—the Doña Joaquina, a relation of the celebrated hero Guadalupe Victoria. Don Cosme had an estate near Jalapa, where he spent his summers. He was not there; and it was now summer. "He had gone to some distant point, to be out of the desolating track of war."

Clayley shared my feelings. The bright eyes in the balconies—the sweet voices in the orange-shaded *patios* of Jalapa—had neither brightness, nor music for us. We were both thoroughly miserable.

To add to this unhappy state of things, a bad feeling had sprung up among

* Pic-nics.

the officers of our army—a jealousy between the old and the new. Those of the old standing army, holding themselves as a species of military aristocracy looked upon their brethren of the new regiments as interlopers; and this feeling pervaded all ranks, from the commander-in-chief down to the 'owest subaltern.

It did not interest all individuals. There were many honorable men on both sides who took no part in a question so ridiculous, but on the contrary, endeavored to frown it down. It was the child of idleness, and a long spell of garrison duty. On the eve of a battle it always disappeared. I have adverted to this, not that it might interest the reader, but as explaining a result connected with ourselves.

One of the most prominent actors in this quarrel, on the side of the "old regulars," was a young officer named Ransom—a captain in an infantry regiment. He was a good fellow in other respects, and a brave soldier, I believe; but his chief weakness lay in a claim to be identified with the aristocracy.

It is strange that this miserable ambition is always strongest, where it should exist with the least propriety. I have observed, in travelling through life, and so has the reader, no doubt, that *parvenus* are the greatest sticklers for aristocratic privilege; and Captain Ransom was no exception to this rule. In tumbling over some old family papers, I had found a receipt from the gallant Captain's grandfather to my own progenitor, acknowledging the payment of a bill for leather breeches!

It so happened that this very receipt was in my portmanteau at the time and nettled at the "carryings on" of the tailor's grandson, I drew it forth, and spread it out upon the mess table. My bretheren of the mess were highly tickled at the document; several of them copying it off for future use!

It soon reached Ransom, who, in his hour of indignation, made use of certain expressions, that, in their turn, soon reached me. The result was a challenge, borne by my friend Clayley; and the affair was arranged for the following morning.

The spot chosen for our morning's diversion was a sequestered one, upon the banks of the river Zedena, and along the solitary road that leads out towards the Cofre di Perote.

At sunrise we rode out in two carriages, six of us, including our seconds and surgeons. About a mile from town we halted; and leaving the carriages upon the road, crossed over into a small glade, in the midst of the chapparal.

It was as pretty a spot for our purpose as the heart could wish for; and had often, we were informed, been used for similar morning exercises—that was, before chivalry had died out among the descendants of Cortez.

The ground was soon lined off—ten paces—and we took our stands, back to back. We were to wheel at the word "Ready!" and fire at "One, two three!"

We were waiting for the word, with that death-like silence which always precedes a similar signal, when Little Jack, who had been left with the carriages, rushed into the glade, calling with all his might:

"Captain! Captain!"

Every face was turned upon him with scowling inquiry, when the boy, gasping for breath, shouted out:

"The Mexicans—are—on the road!"

The word had scarcely passed his lips, when the trampling of hoofs sounded upon our ears, and the next moment, a band of horsemen came driving pell-mell into the opening. At a single glance we recognised the guerilla!

Ransom, who was nearest, blazed away at the foremost of the band, missing his aim. With a spring the guerillero was over him, his sabre raised for the blow. I fired, and the Mexican leaped from his saddle with a groan.

"Thank you, Haller," cried my antagonist, as we rushed side by side towards the pistols. There were four pairs in all, and the surgeons and seconds had already armed themselves, and were pointing their weapons at the enemy. We seized the remaining two, cocking them as we turned.

At this moment my eye fell upon a black horse; and looking, I recognised the rider. He saw and recognised me at the same moment, and driving the spurs into his horse's flanks, sprang forward with a yell. With one bound he was over me, his white teeth gleaming like a tiger's. His sabre flashed in my eyes—I fired—a heavy body dashed against me—I was struck senseless to the earth!

I was only stunned, and in a few moments I came to my senses. Shots and shouts rang around me. I heard the trampling of hoofs, and the groans of wounded men.

I looked up. Horsemen in dark uniforms were galloping across the glade, and into the woods beyond. I recognised the yellow facings of the American dragoons.

I drew my hand over my face; it was wet with blood. A heavy body lay across mine, which Little Jack, with all his strength, was endeavoring to drag off. I crawled from under it, and bending over, looked at his features. I knew them at a glance. I muttered to my servant:

' Dubrosc! he is dead!"

His body lay spread out in its picturesque attire. A fair form it was. A bullet—my own—had passed through his heart, killing him instantly. I placed my hand upon his forehead. It was cold already, and his beautiful features were white and ashy. His eyes glared with the ghastly expressio of death.

"Close them," I said to the boy, and turned away from the spot.

Wounded men lay around—dragoons and Mexicans—and some were dead.

A party of officers was returning from the pursuit, and I recognised my late adversary, with our seconds and surgeons. One of the latter had found use for his skill, as I observed that he carried his arm in a sling. A dragoon officer gallopped up.

It was Colonel Harding.

"These fellows, gentlemen," cried he, reining up his horse, "just came in time to relieve me from a disagreeable duty. I have orders from the commander-in-chief to arrest Captains Haller and Ransom.

" Now, gentlemen," he continued, with a smile, "I think you have had fighting enough, for one morning, and if you will promise me to be quiet young men, and keep the peace, I will, for once in my life, take the liberty of disobeying a general's orders. What say you, gentlemen?"

It needed not this appeal. There had been no serious cause of quarrel between my adversary and myself, and, moved by a similar impulse, we both stepped forward, and grasped one another by the hand.

" Forgive me, my dear Haller." said the officer; "I retract all. I assure you my remarks were only made upon the spur of the moment, when I was angry about those cursed leather breeches."

" And I regret to have given you cause," I replied. "Come with me to my quarters. Let us have a glass of wine together, and we will light our cigars with the villanous document."

A burst of laughter followed, in which Ransom good-naturedly joined and we were soon on our way to town, seated in the same carriage, and the best friends in creation.

* * * * * * * * *

Some of the soldiers who had ' rifled " the body of Dubrosc, found a paper upon him, which proved that the Frenchman was a spy in the service of Santa Anna. He had thrown himself into the company at New Orleans with the intention of gaining information, and then deserting on his arrival in Mexico. This he succeeded in doing in the manner detailed. Had he commanded the company, he would doubtless have found an opportunity to have delivered them over to the enemy, at La Virgen, or elsewhere

CHAPTER LVIII.

AN ADIOS.

We were enjoying ourselves in the Fonda de Diligencias—the principal hotel of Jalapa—when Jack touched me on the shoulder, and whispered in my ear:

"Captain, there's a Mexican wants to see ye."

"Who is it?" I demanded, somewhat annoyed at the interruption.

"It's the brother," replied Jack, still speaking in a whisper.

"The brother! What brother?"

"Of the young ladies, Captain."

I started from my chair, overturning a decanter and several glasses.

"Hilloa! what's the matter?" shouted several voices in a breath.

"Gentlemen, will you excuse me?—one moment only—I—I—will—"

"Certainly, certainly!" cried my companions all at once, wondering what was the matter.

The next moment I was in the *antesala*, embracing Narcisso.

"And so you are all here; when did you arrive?"

"Yesterday, Captain. I came to town for you, but could not find you.'

"And they are well? all well?"

"Yes, Captain. Papa expects you will come out this evening, with the lieutenant and the other officer."

"The other officer! who, Narcisso?"

"I think he was with you on your first visit to La Virgen—*un señor gordo.*"

"Oh! the Major! Yes, yes, we will come; but where have you been since we met Narcissito?"

"To Orizava. Papa has a tobacco farm near Orizava; he always goes to it when he comes here. But, Captain, we were so astonished to hear from your people that you had been a prisoner, and travelling along with us. We knew the guerilleros had some American prisoners, but we never dreamt of its being you. *Carrambo!* if I had known that!"

"But how came you, Narcisso, to be with the guerilla?"

"Oh? papa had many things to carry up the country; and he, with som other families, paid Colonel Cenobio for an escort. The country is so full of robbers."

"Ah! sure. Tell me, Narcisso, how came I by this?"

I held out the dagger.

"I know not, Captain. I am ashamed to tell you that I lost it the day after you gave it me."

"Oh! never mind. Take it again, and say to your papa I will come, and bring 'El señor gordo' along with me."

"You will know the way, Captain? Yonder is our house." And the lad pointed to the white turrets of an aristocratic-looking mansion that appeared over the tree-tops about a mile distant.

"I shall easily find it."

"Adieu, then, Captain; we shall be impatient until you arrive. *Hasta la tarde!*"

So saying, the youth departed.

I communicated to Clayley the cause of my temporary withdrawal; and seizing the earliest opportunity, we left our companions over their cups.

It was now near sundown, and we were about to jump into our saddles, when I recollected my promise to bring the Major. Clayley proposed leaving him behind, and planning an apology; but a hint from me that he might be useful in "keeping off," Don Cosme and the Señora caused the Lieutenant suddenly to change his tactics, and we set out for Blossom's quarters.

We had no difficulty in persuading "El señor gordo" to accompany us, as soon as he ascertained where we were going. He had never ceased to remember *that* dinner. Hercules was brought out, and saddled in a jiffey; and we all three gallopped off for the mansion of our friends.

After passing under the shadows of green trees, and through copses filled with flowers and bright singing-birds, we arrived at the house, one of the fairest mansions it had ever been our fortune to enter. We were just in time to enjoy the soft twilight of an eternal spring—of a landscape *siempre verde;* and, what was more to the Major's mind, in time for a supper that rivalled the well-remembered dinner.

As I had anticipated, the Major proved exceedingly useful during the visit. In his capacity of quarter-master, he had already picked up a little Spanish— enough to hold Don Cosme in check over the wine; while Clayley and myself, with "Lupé" and "Luz," walked out into the veranda to take a peep at the moon. Her light was alluring, and we could not resist the temptation of a stroll through the gardens. It was a celestial night; and we dallied along, *dos y dos*, under the pictured shadows of the orange-trees, and sat upon curiously-formed benches, and gazed upon the moon, and listened to the soft notes of the tropic night-birds.

The perils of the past were all forgotten, and the perils of the future—we thought not of them.

It was late when we said "*buenas noches*" to our friends, and we parted with a mutual "*hasta la mañana.*" It is needless to say, that we kept our promises in the morning, and made another for the following morning, and kept that too; and so on, till the awful bugle summoned us once more to the "Route."

The detail of our actions during these days would have no interest for the reader, though to us the most interesting of our lives. There was a sameness —a monotony—it is true; but a monotony that both my friend and myself could have endured for ever.

I do not even remember the details. All I can remember is that, on the eve of our march, I found myself "cornering" Don Cosme, and telling him plainly to his teeth, that I meant to marry one of his daughters; and that my friend, (who had not yet learnt the "lingo," and had duly commissioned me as his "go-between,") would be most happy to take the other off his hands!

I remember very well, too, Don Cosme's reply; which was given with a half smile, half grin, somewhat cold, though not disagreeable in its expression. It was thus:

"Captain——*when the war is over.*"

Don Cosme had no intention that his daughters should become widows before they had fairly been wives; and we bade adieu, once more, to the light of love, and walked in the shadow of war; and we toiled up to the high tables of the Andes, and crossed the burning plains of Peroté; and we forded the cold streams of the Rio Frio, and climbed the snowy spurs of Popocatepec; and after many a toilsome march, our bayonets bristled along the borders of the Lake Tezcoco. And here we fought—a death struggle, too—for we knew there was no retreat. But our struggle was crowned with victory; and the starry flag waved over the ancient city of the Aztecs!

Neither my friend nor myself escaped unhurt. We were shot "all over," but fortunately no bones were broken, and neither of us converted into a ripple.

And then came the "piping times of peace;" and Clayley and I spent our days in riding out upon the Jalapa Road, watching for that great old family carriage, which, it had been promised, should come.

And it came rumbling along at length, drawn by twelve mules, and deposited its precious load in a palace in the Calle Capuchinas.

And shortly after, two officers in shining uniforms entered the portals of that same palace, and sent up their cards, and were admitted on the instant. Ah! these were rare times. But rarer still—for it should only occur once in a man's lifetime—was an hour spent in the little chapel of San Barnardo—

* * * * * * *

There is a Convent—Santa Catarina—the richest in Mexico—the richest, perhaps, in the world. There are some nuns there—beautiful creatures—who possess property (each one of them worth a million of dollars,) and yet these children of heaven never look upon the face of man!

About a week after my visit to San Barnardo, I was summoned to the Convent, and permitted—a rare privilege for one of my sex—to enter its sacred precincts. It was a painful scene. Poor "Mary of Mercy!" How lovely she looked in her vestments of snow-white lawn!—lovelier in her sorrow than I had ever seen her before! May God pour the balm of oblivion into the heart of this erring but repentant angel!

* * * * * * *

I returned to New Orleans in the latter part of 1848. I was walking one morning along the Levee, with a fair companion on my arm, when a well-known voice struck on my ear, exclaiming—

"I'll be dog-goned, Rowl, if it aint the Cap'n!"

I turned, and beheld Raoul and the hunter. They had doffed the regimentals, and were preparing to "start" on a trapping expedition to the Rocky Mountains.

I need not describe our mutual pleasure at meeting, which was more than shared by my wife, who had often made me detail to her the exploits of my comrades. I inquired for Chane. The Irishman, at the breaking up of the "war troops," had entered one of the old regiments, and was at this time, as

Lincoln expressed it, "the first sargin of a kumpny." I could not permit my old ranging companions to depart without a souvenir. My wife drew off a pair of rings, and presented one to each upon the spot. The Frenchman, with the gallantry of a Frenchman, drew his upon his finger; but Lincoln, after trying to do the same, declared, with a comical grin, that he couldn't "git the eend of his wipin-stick inter it." He wrapped it up carefully, however, and deposited it in his bullet-pouch.

My friends accompanied us to our hotel, where I found them more appropriate presents than the rings. To Raoul I gave my revolving pistols, not expecting to have any farther use for them myself; and to the hunter, that which he valued more than any other earthly object, the Major's Dutch gun." Doubtless, ere this, the *Spitz-nadel* has slain many a "grizzly bar" among the wild ravines of the Wind-River mountains.

A few days after, I had a visit from Major Twing, who, with Hollis, and others of my old comrades, was on his way to the frontier garrisons of Texas. From him I learnt that Blossom, on account of his gallant behavior in the affair at La Virgen, had received the brevet of a colonel, and was now employed in the department at Washington

Courteous reader, I was about to write the word "adieu," when "Little Jack" handed me a letter, bearing the Vera Cruz postmark. It was dated "*La Virgen, November* 1, 1849. It concluded as follows:—

"You were a fool for leaving Mexico, and you'll never be half as happy anywhere else as I am here. You would hardly know the 'rancho.'—I mean the fields. I have cleared off the weeds; and expect next year to take a couple of hundred bales off the ground. I believe I can raise as good cotton here as in Louisiana; besides, I have a little corner for vanilla. It would do your heart good to see the improvements, and little "Spousie," too, takes such an interest in all I do. Haller, I'm the happiest man in creation.

"I dined yesterday with our old friend Cenobio, and you should have seen him, when I told him the man he had in his company. I thought he would have split his sides. He's a perfect old trump, this Cenobio, notwithstanding his smuggling propensities.

"By the way, you have heard, I suppose, that our "other old friend,' the Padre, has been shot. He took part with Paredes against the government. They caught him at Queretaro, and shot him, with a dozen or so of his 'beauties,' in less than a squirrel's jump.

"And now, my dear Haller a last word. We all want you to come back

The house at Jalapa is ready for you; and Doña Joaquina says it is yours and SHE wants you to come back.

" Don Cosmé, too—with whom it appears Lupé was the favorite—HE wants you to come back. Old Cenobio, who is still puzzled about how you got the knife to cut through the adobes, HE wants you come back. Luz is fretting after Lupé, and SHE wants you to come back. And, last of all, I want you to come back. So stand not on the order of your coming, but come at once

Yours, for ever,

"EDWARD CLAYLEY."

Reader, do you want me to come back?

THE END

www.ingramcontent.com/pod-product-compliance
Lightning Source LLC
Chambersburg PA
CBHW031928230426
43672CB00010B/1857